Amnesiac

Amnesiac Hide

Mike Nelson

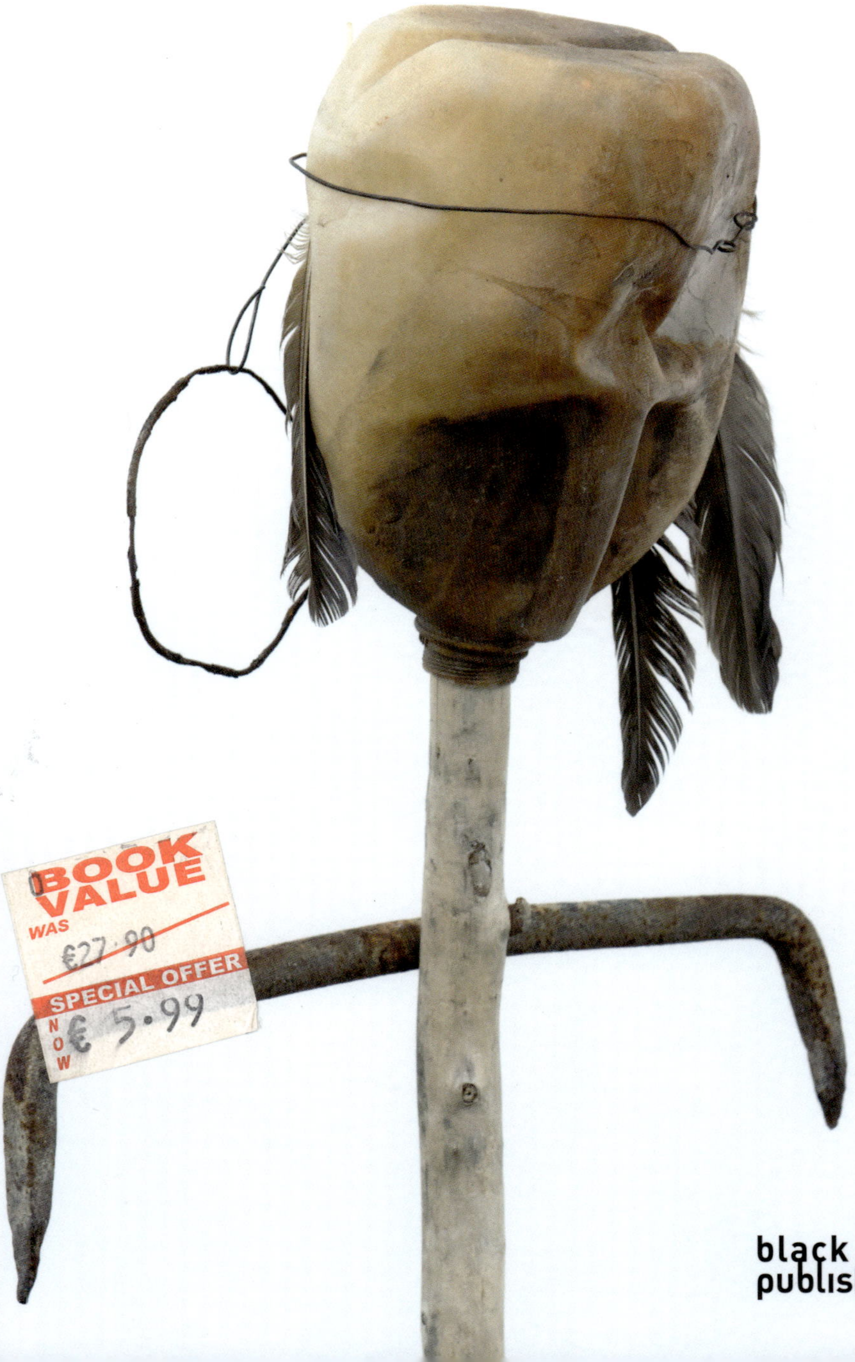

black dog publishing

Amnesiac Hide

Mike Nelson

black dog
publishing
london uk

Contents

(to the memory of Erlend Williamson)

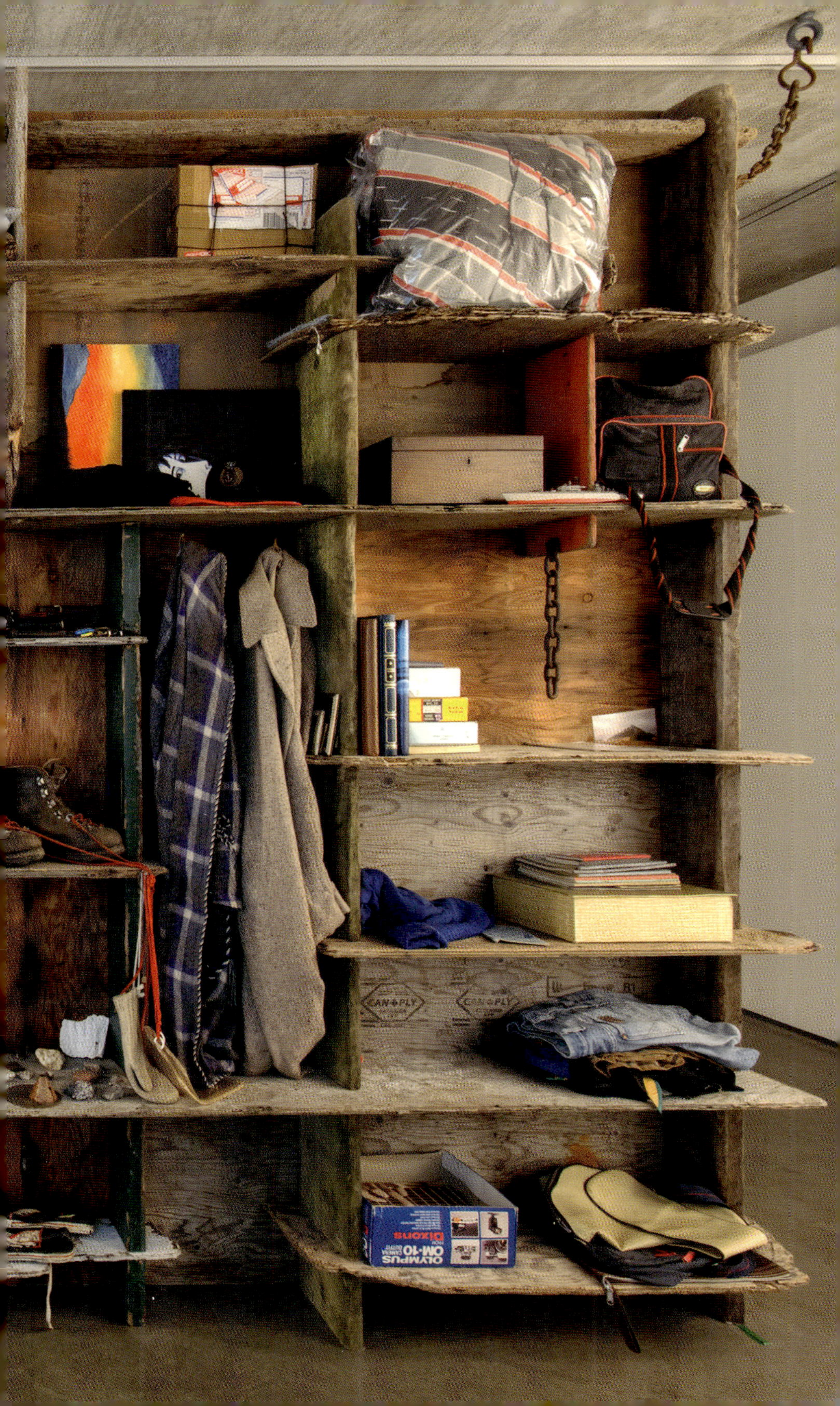
CANPLY
CANPLY
OLYMPUS
OM-10
CAMERA OUTFIT
FROM
Dixons

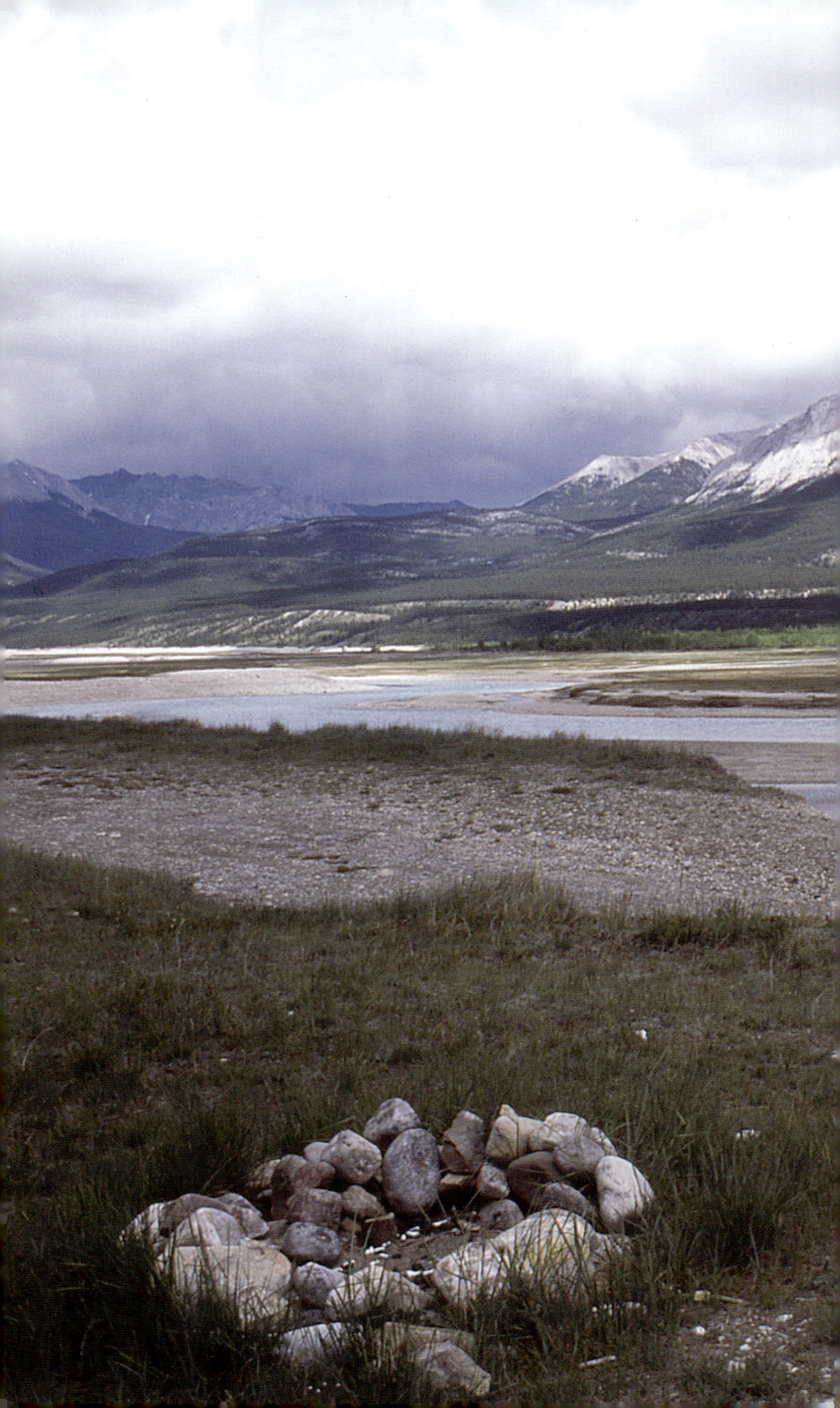

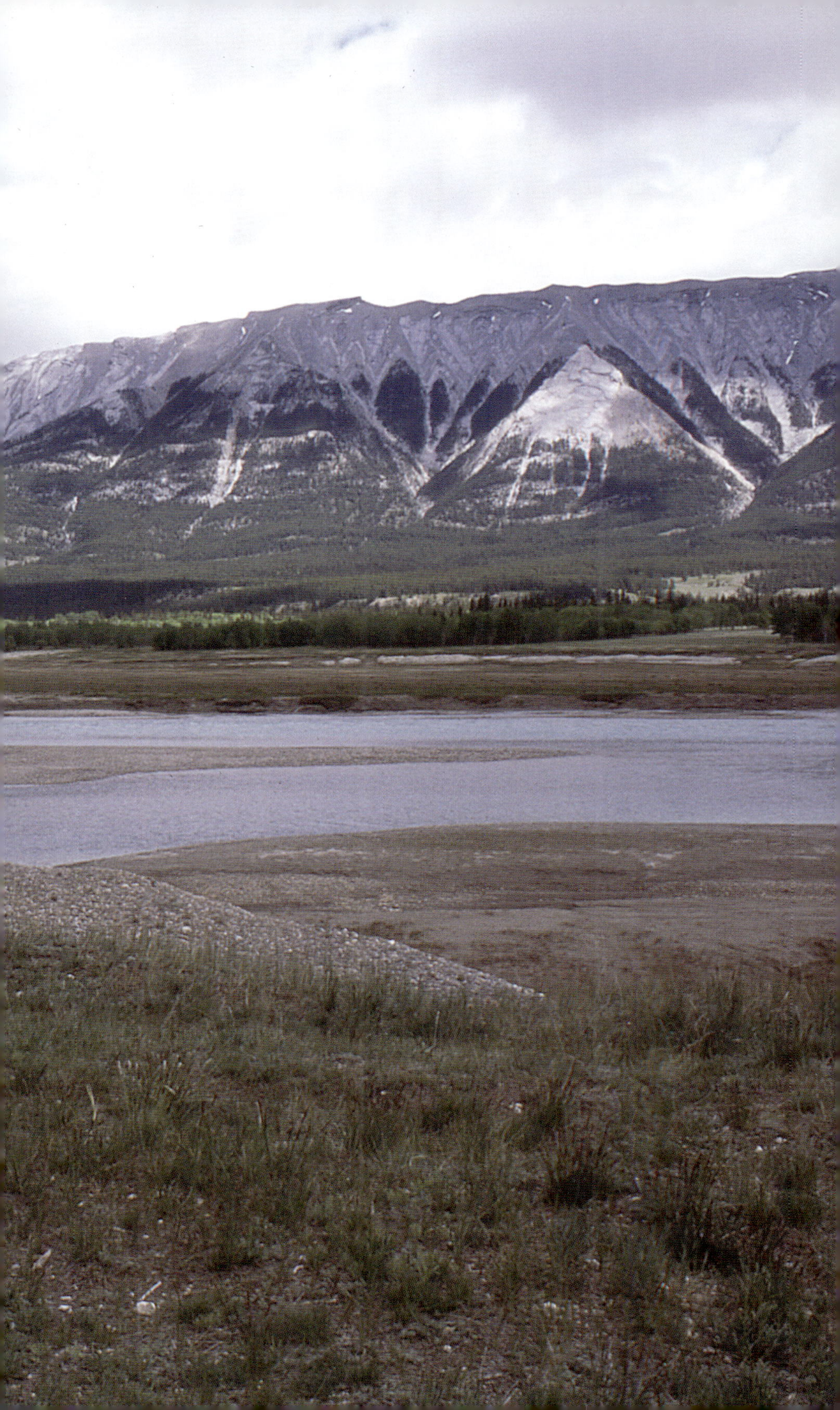

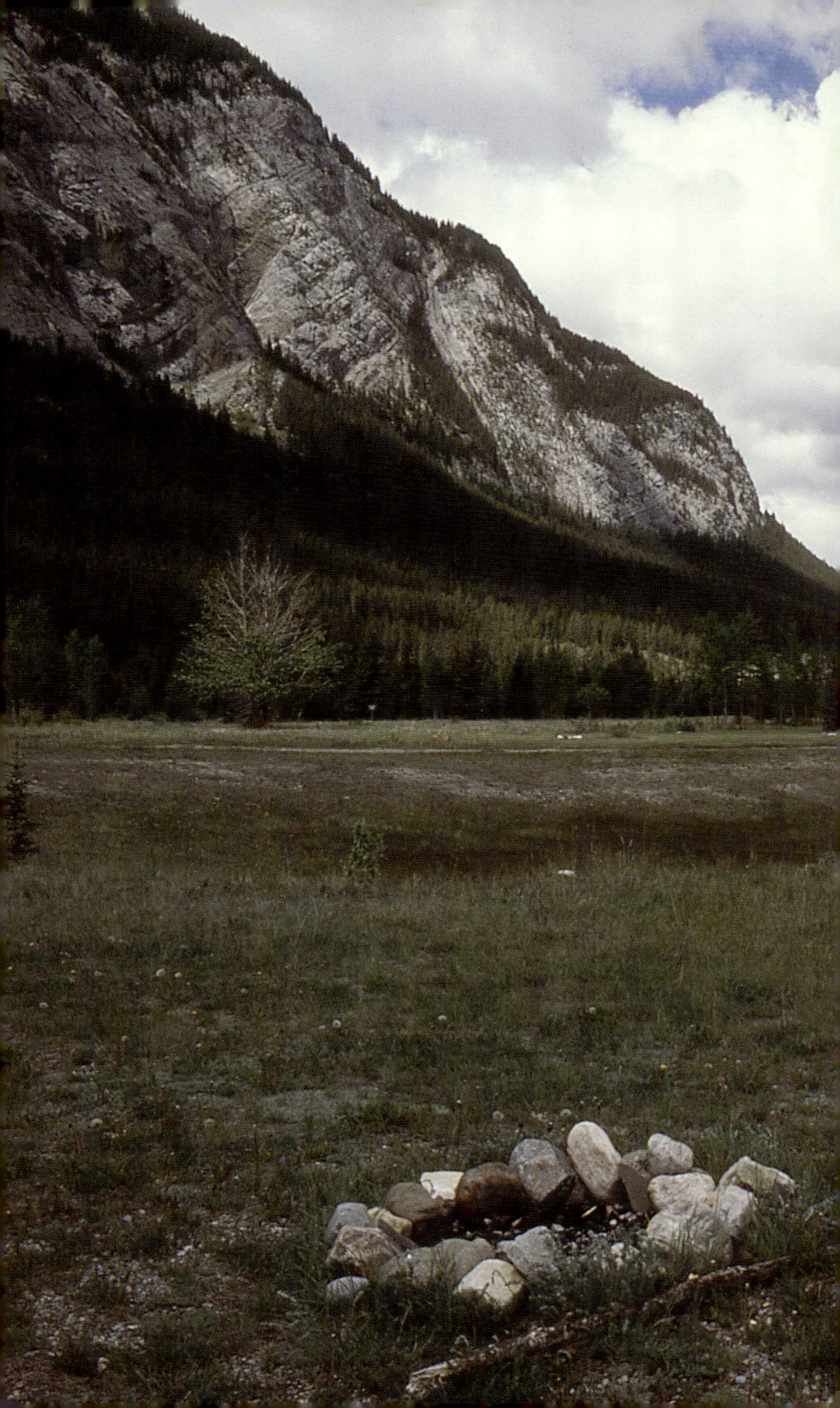

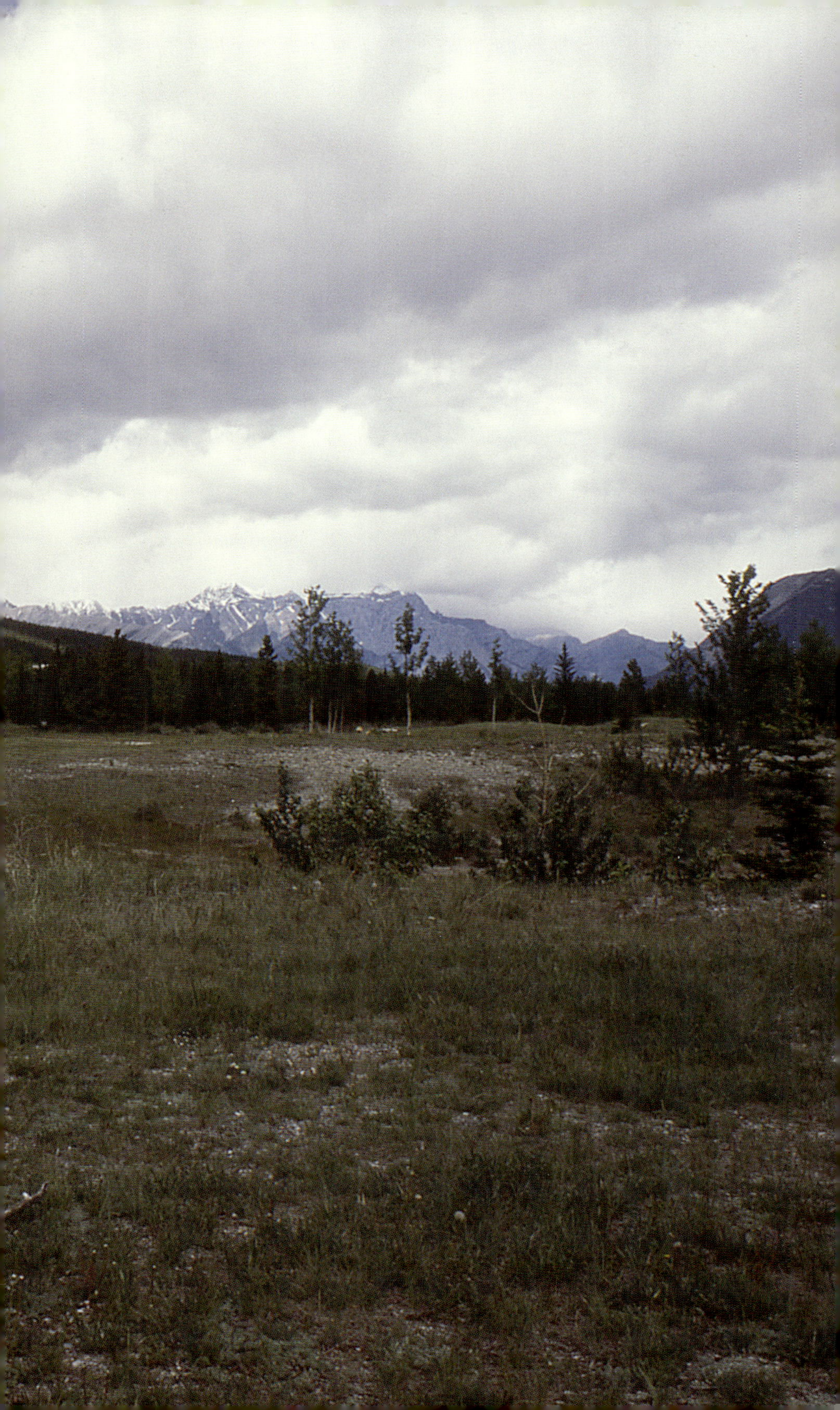

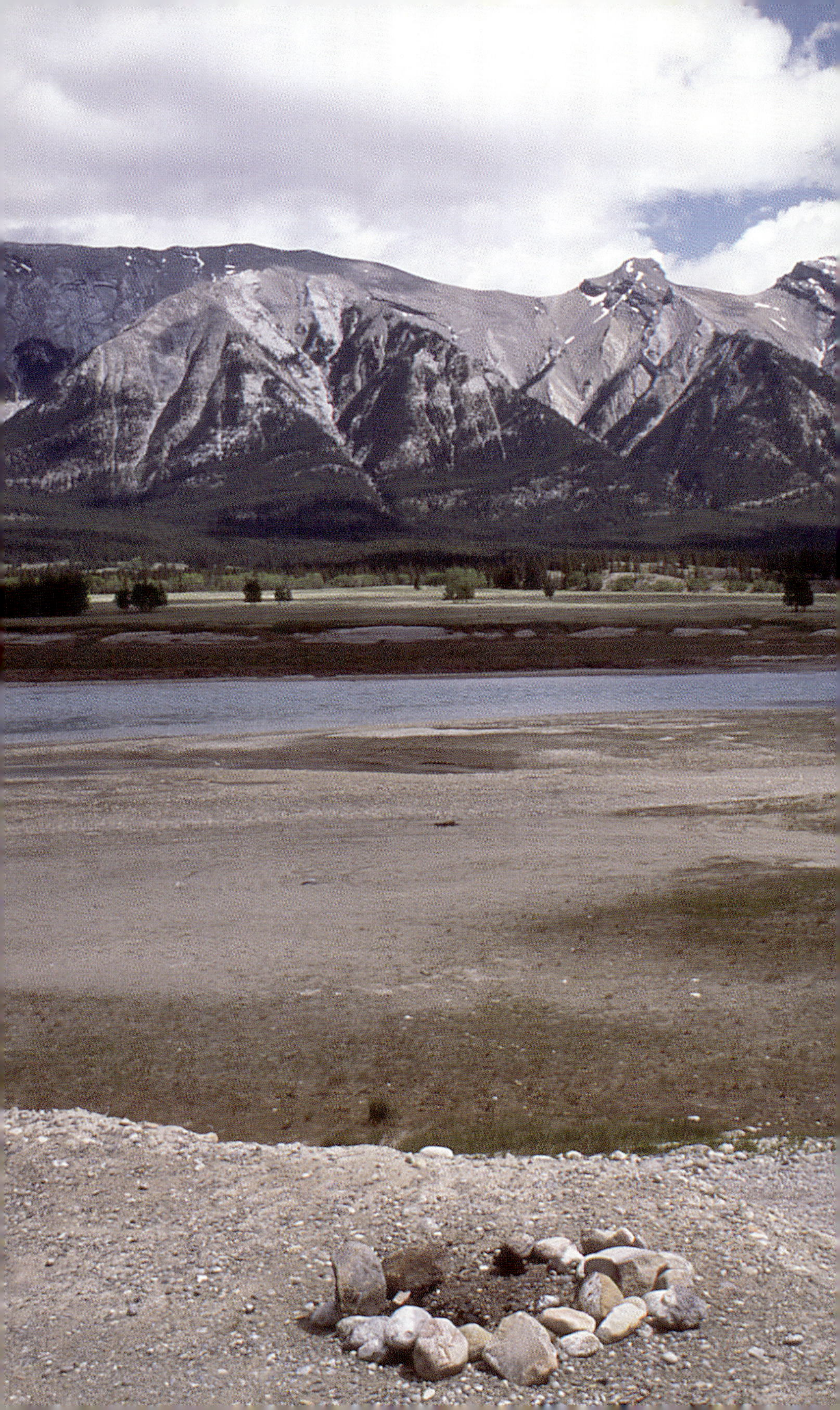

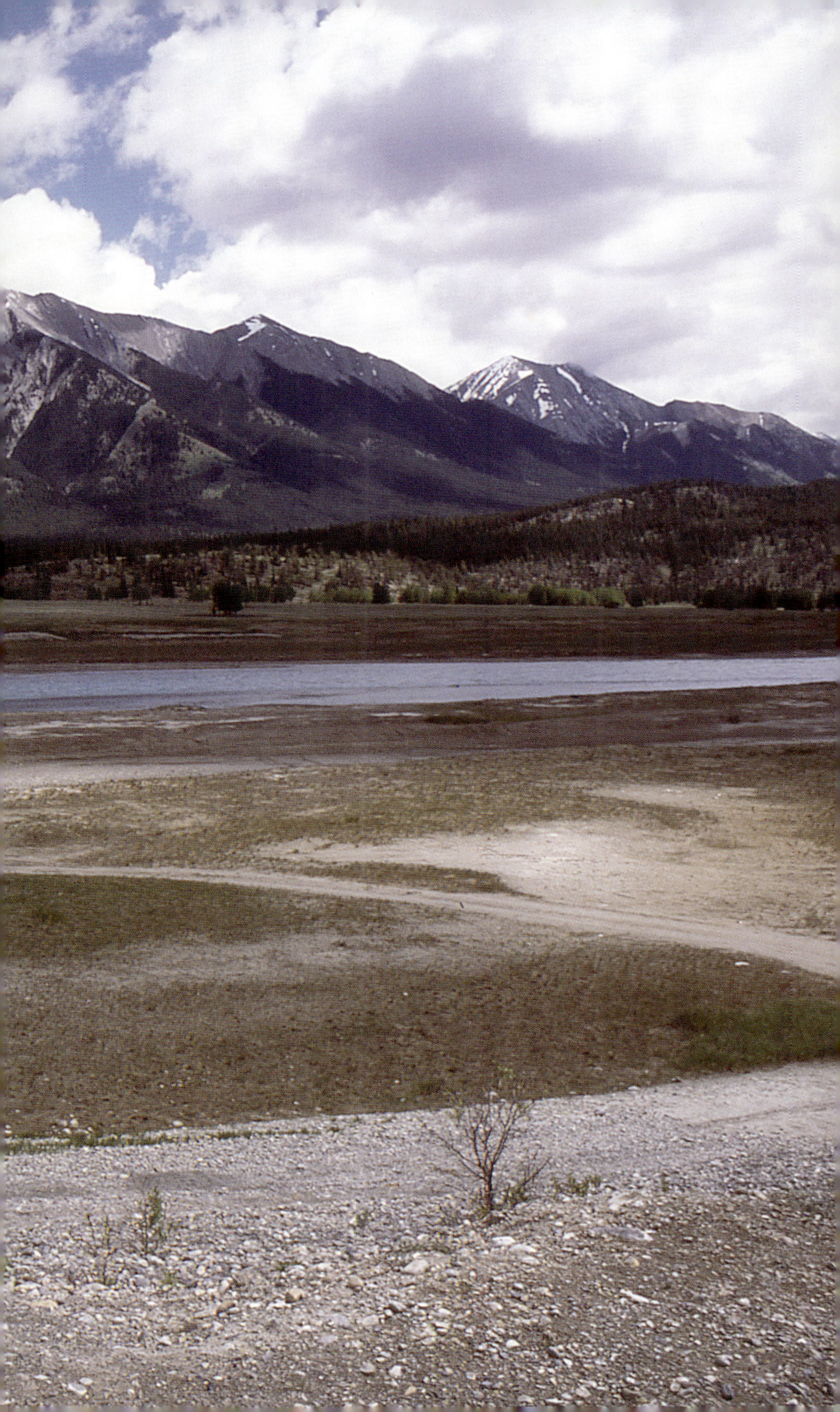

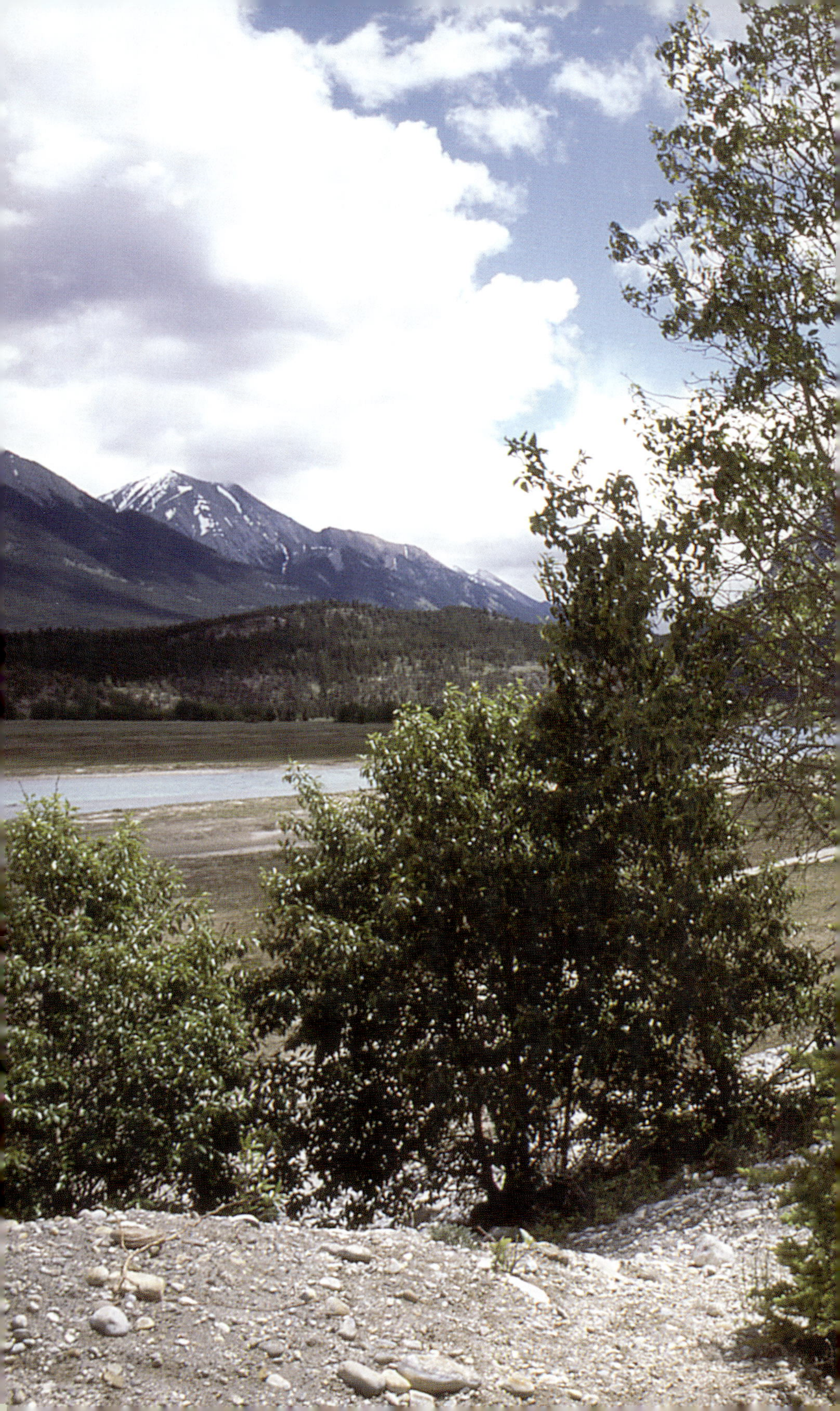

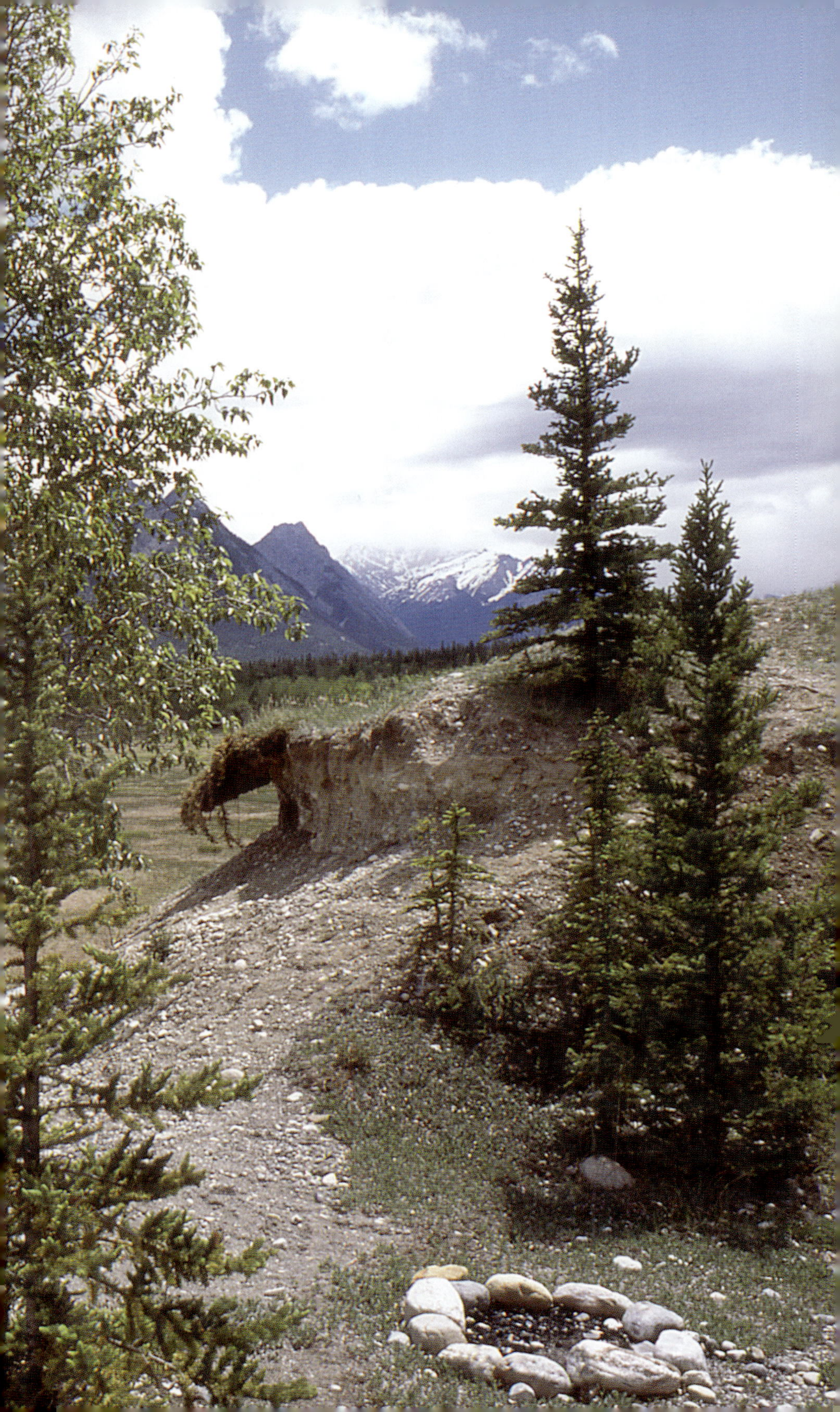

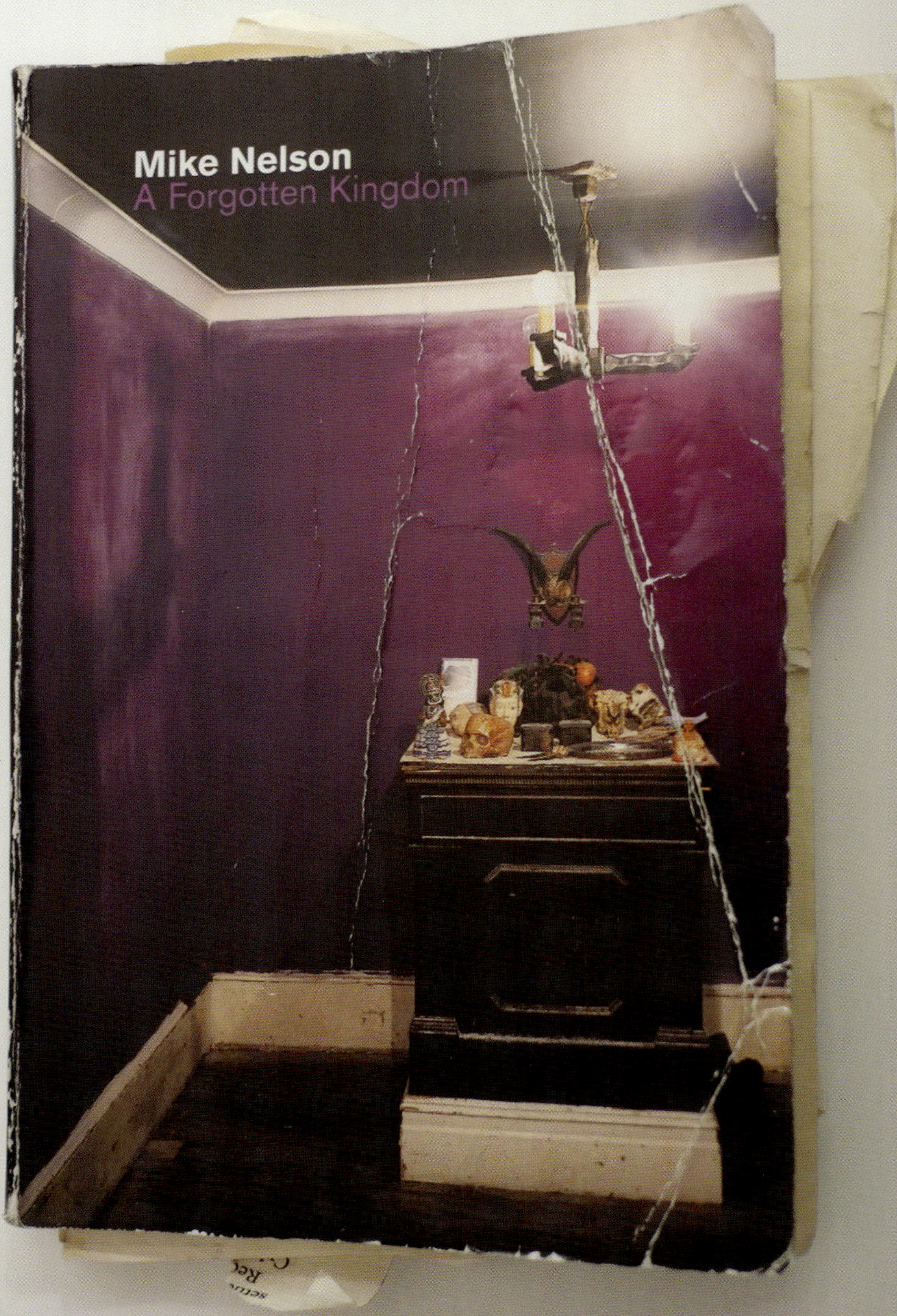
Mike Nelson
A Forgotten Kingdom

The Trapper and the Fall: An Amnesiac's Diary

Dick Hebdige

"I would define the baroque as that style that deliberately exhausts (or tries to exhaust) its own possibilities, and that borders on self-caricature."
JL Borges Preface to *A Universal History of Iniquity*, 1954

Fabricate vt **1.** to make by art and skill and labor
2. to construct or manufacture something especially from prepared components
3. to devise or invent (a legend, lie etc.)
4. to fake, forge (a document, signature etc.)

Composite On-Line Dictionary

Thursday, January 30: DESCENDING

The plane is running at least an hour late out of LAX due to ice on the runway at Toronto, and I've spent the flight trapped inside a centre aisle seat, and the involuted confines of *Mike Nelson: A Forgotten Kingdom*, the book the artist put together to accompany his exhibition *Nothing is True. Everything is Permitted*, at the London ICA in 2001. (It opened late September, a fortnight after 9/11.) According to the artist's own account published in *Artforum*, the exhibition comprised a nest of indeterminate spaces: "a dingy video arcade… a cross between a seedy gym and torture chamber", and "a reading room with shoestring travel guides" built into the ICA's ground floor corridor connecting the museum's book shop to the gallery and bar.[1] Part institutional critique, part disorienting dérive, part literal and figurative diversion ("more than slightly reminiscent", one reviewer put it, "of the ghost train at a funfair"), the exhibition was a temporary spatial (time-space) intervention within a pre-existing structure: a build within a build.[2]

Far from performing the conventional catalogue functions of interpretation and critical exegesis, *Mike Nelson: A Forgotten Kingdom* mirrors the effect of dislocation in print, producing vertigo by other means, so that book and installation form an interlocking set turned back upon itself like the Ouroborus symbol that recurs in Nelson's work. The book consists of extracts, including a title page, contents page, epilogue and index lifted wholesale from prior published works by more than 20 writers including JG Ballard, Hakim Bey, Borges, Burroughs, Conrad, Kafka, Stanislaw Lem, HP Lovecraft, Poe, the Strugatsky brothers (Boris and Arkady), Jules Verne and Sir Leonard Woolley (archaeologist and author of *A Forgotten Kingdom,* 1953, a survey of excavations at the Sumerian capital of Ur in what is now southern Iraq). The extracts are un-attributed, though there's a key to who wrote what at the back of the book. The original titles/chapter headings at the top of each page provide additional clues for readers unfamiliar with the source works who don't like feeling lost, though losing track of where you are is clearly half the point. Sandwiched in the middle under the heading "Illustrations" are 52 grey and white photographs of unnamed Nelson installations with captions like "Along the central corridor", "At the foot of the stairway" and "Third room (to the right)".[3]

As I've yet to stand inside a Mike Nelson installation, sitting inside one at 30,000 feet is the closest I can get for now to primary research.

If the artist's singular approach to fabrication has a starting point or source then it is here at the intersection of craft and speculative sci fi, travel writing, horror, pirate lore, the colonial Orientalist archive, Occidental wilderness projections and recursive meta-fiction. Nelson's circular perambulations start and end here in the literary equivalent of the boondocks—in Helmland, the Antarctic, Chernobyl or the moon, in Alamut, Algonquin Park or Loughborough (the artist's actual point of origin)—places, on the face of it, remote from the metropolitan biennales and glossy art world hubs through which, nonetheless, his ghostly jangling caravan regularly passes.

I've already read the book from cover to cover months ago, when I first got it, and it's beginning to fall apart; the paperback cover is dog-eared and creased, the spine is cracked, the pages slide out of order like badly shuffled cards. I open it up and page 25 slips out and falls through the narrow crack between my knees. I have to stretch my hand down under the seat in front to retrieve it:

P. 25 "The Departure" (Kafka)

... At the gate the servant stopped me and asked 'Where is the master going?' 'I don't know', I said, 'just out of here, just out of here. Out of here, nothing else, it's the only way I can reach my goal'. 'So you know your goal?' he asked. 'Yes', I replied, 'I've just told you. Out of here—that's my goal.'

The seat belt signs are on, and we begin the final approach into Toronto as the pressure in the cabin precipitously dips, and we start to buck and shake, corkscrewed in the torque, hurtling down through the dark toward the fallen snow banked up along the line of lights veering up to meet us.

. . . .

Then it seemed like falling into a labyrinth: we thought we were at the finish, but our way bent round and we found ourselves as it were back at the beginning, and just as far from that which we were seeking at first. ... Thus the present-day notion of a labyrinth as a place where one can lose [one's] way must be set aside. It is a confusing path, hard to follow without a thread, but, provided [the traverser] is not devoured at the mid-point, it leads surely, despite twists and turns, back to the beginning.

Plato's *Euthydemus* (*Dialogue*), Kerenyi, *Dionysos*, p 92.

. . . .

Wednesday, October 30, 1996: DEVOURED AT THE MID-POINT

ENGLISHMAN MAY HAVE BEEN BLOWN OFF GLENCOE MOUNTAIN BY 80 MPH WINDS. ARTIST FALLS 400 FT TO DEATH WHILE CLIMBING IN STORM

An artist whose works have been exhibited in galleries across Europe has been killed in a climbing accident on one of Scotland's most notorious mountains.... The body of Mr Erlend Williamson, 31, originally from Blackpool, was recovered by members of Glencoe mountain rescue team. It appears Mr Williamson slipped and fell 400 ft on to rocks as he attempted to scale the 3345 ft Buachaille Etive Mor in atrocious weather conditions. Strong winds prevented the rescue helicopter from reaching the mountain but searchers discovered Mr Williamson's body at the bottom of Crowberry Gully on the mountain's east face at 7.30 pm on Monday, almost six hours after the alarm was raised.... Mr Williamson's death is the seventeenth fatality on Highland mountains this year."

Herald Scotland, 30 October, 1996.

Friday afternoon January 31: PREVIEW

I arrive at The Power Plant for a first look at the show to find a gallery walk-through with the artist for staff/docents has just started and decide to tag along. Below is a transcription of my telegraphed notes of Mike Nelson's commentary and responses to questions with my own comments in parenthesis. (NB. I joined the tour as the artist was beginning his remarks on the *Eighty Circles* half of the *Eighty Circles through Canada (the last possessions of an Orcadian Mountain Man)* installation and so missed his gloss on the possessions part).

80 CIRCLES

80 slides of camp fire rings photographed on road trip thru BC (British Columbia? Before Christ?) Ready-made stone circles cf. Richard Long. 80 found fire rings = low key land art vs. Robert Smithson's "imperial gesture" (Spiral Jetty as big footprint Earthwork cf. "*Double Negative*"= reference to Michael Heizer's NV dig).

Q. Why 80?

A. Max. capacity of Kodak carousel.

GANG OF 7

Latest version of *AMNESIACS*, 1996, *Amnesiac Shrine*, 2006 = bike-less biker gang stranded in Berwick-on-Tweed on UK North Sea coast—bleak, depressing-bikers try to 'read' the "language of the sea" by making ritual objects out of flotsam/junk washed up on shore cf. Stanislaw Lem *SOLARIS*; JG Ballard—(beachcomber at edge of terra firma/end of world).

Project under way at time of Erlend Williamson's death—death as interruption/intervention. Life goes on but different—Loss/lost world.

Orange plastic flames made from traffic cones (= memory of fire?)

Major influence = RIDDLEY WALKER—(R Hoban)—1st person narrative set in future UK after nuclear war—post-apocalyptic: language/culture/techno back to Square 1. Lawless scavenge culture/brutal/feral—(LANGUAGE MIRRORS ENTROPY)

making art out of driftwood = "first thing they teach you NOT to do in school": bad art cliché

British art school in the 80s—'terrorism' of Theory/iron rod of political correctness. Art work illustrating theory. Boring.

Nelson's side-stepping tactic—use narrative/fiction as a "disclaimer structure".

Lem, Ballard, Burroughs, Lovecraft etc = outliers (outside academic/art world?): more generative/useful/radical (out there) than 'critical theory'.

QUIVER OF ARROWS
Original install at NYC gallery 2010. Vintage fluorescent street lights from Toronto parking lot key to this install: site-specific.
Quiver = archaic anglo word cf. Robin Hood + merry men but also cowboys + indians. ("1st Nations"). 4 aluminum trailers from 1939/ 48/48/68/ welded 2gether in rectangular formation cf. wagon trains under attack. Linking segments from chopped 1963 Airstream. (Kennedy assassination?) Whole structure mounted on wood trestle w/out wheels. Streamlined/ C20th Retro-Futurism: like arrows on a diagram pointing in different directions/to different poss. futures for US.

UNTITLED: INTIMATE SCULPTURE FOR A PUBLIC SPACE
Erlend W's sleeping bag in perspex box on floor in centre of corridor near entrance. (Egyptian sarcophagus effect.) Slot for donations over turned-back corner where EW's head would be—some coins + small denom. notes. (Martyr's reliquary? Last gasp public art collection box?)

DOUBLE NEGATIVE: THE GENIE
Upper level next to Power Plant offices—7 heavy duty old school office p/copiers (Gang of 7 x 2?) w/cut up blown up xeroxed extracts from artist's travel diary of 90s (?) trip to N China/Tibet spilling on floor. Travel photos + blown up images of Ace of Spades + diary entries noting multiple sightings of Ace card turning up uncannily en route. (IS THIS FOR REAL?) Back home MN processes film—1 roll doubly exposed. Last shots M took in his studio with Erl W (the genie?) in the background overlaid w/clichéd tourist shots of Buddhist temples/mountains etc.

Later that evening: THE OPENING

Lorna said to me, 'You know Riddley theres some thing in us it dont have no name.'
I said, 'What thing is that?'
She said, 'Its some kind of thing aint us but yet its in us. its lookin out through our eye hoals... It aint you nor it don't even know your name. Its in us lorn and loan and sheltering how it can... Tremmering it is and feart. It puts us on like we put on our cloes. Some times we dont fit. Some times it cant find the arm hoals and it tears us a part.'
Russell Hoban, *Riddley Walker*, Jonathan Cape, 1980.

Monday, March 3: INTRODUCTION TO ESSAY (1ST PASS)
One way to tackle a Mike Nelson installation is to approach it from the inside out as a labyrinth embedded in a larger network of interlocking labyrinths or Chinese boxes/Russian dolls—each iteration designed (though not to scale) to fit inside the next—like Donald Judd on acid....

Friday, Feb 21–Sunday, Feb 23: GANG OF SEVEN: FURTHER NOTES
Group of 7 = Algonquin School of early C20th Canadian landscape painters (inc. 3 British émigrés)—met while working at Grip design Co. in Toronto—together fixed Canadian national image as pristine rugged wilderness minus people. Tom Thomson, an affiliate, drowned in mysterious circs. in canoe accident on Canoe Lake, Algonquin Park, Ontario in 1917, see "Death on a Painted Lake: The Tom Thomson Tragedy".
http://www.canadianmysteries.ca/sites/thomson/home/indexen.html

Nelson's *Gang of 7* = inverted voodoo mirror image—natural world made out of junk picked up on Vancouver beaches: animals + heroic 7 made from old tires/driftwood/plastic containers (flotsam from Great Pacific Gyre). *Gang of 7* vs. Group of 7 cf. punk band Gang of 4 (Madame Mao etc) cf. Superman's doppelganger: Bizarro:

> I was striving... for that mirror-image, that opposite. And out of a machine which would reveal the negative Superman, came the mirror image—always remembering that in a mirror everything is reversed.... The times were such that one-dimensional characters, your standard superheroes, even in comics, seemed rather simplistic, like paper cut-outs. What was demanded was the full dimensional personality—a figure that carried a shadow, if you like. I was certainly inspired to some degree also by CG Jung's archetype of "the shadow...".
>
> Alvin Schwartz quoted in Mike Conroy, *500 Comicbook Villains*, Collins & Brown, 2004.

Margaret Atwood, *Death by Landscape*: short story re: young girl (Lois) unjustly blamed for disappearance/death of friend (Lucy) on organised 'Indian-themed' canoe trip 'up there' (i.e. in wilderness) at 60s Ontario summer camp. Trauma recollected by girl in old age in lakeside retirement Toronto apt filled + 2 Tom Thomsons + 3 AY Jacksons + 1 Lawren Harris + 1 Arthur Lismer + 1 JEH MacDonald + 1 David Milne (Jackson, Harris, Lismer, MacDonald all members of Group of 7).

She turns away from the window and looks at her pictures. There is the pinkish island in the lake with the intertwisted trees. It's the same landscape they paddled through that distant summer.... How could you ever find anything there, once it was lost? ... And these paintings are not landscape paintings. Because there aren't any landscapes up there, not in the old, tidy European sense. ... Instead there's a tangle, a receding maze, in which you can become lost almost as soon as you step off the path. There are no backgrounds in any of these paintings, no vistas; only a great deal of foreground that goes back and back.... She looks at the paintings, she looks into them. Every one of them is a picture of Lucy.... Everyone has to be somewhere and this is where Lucy is. She is in Lois' apartment, in the holes that open inward on the wall, not like windows but like doors...".

Margaret Atwood, *Death by Landscape*, 1990.

. . . .

The dead body drifted along in the breeze... farther beyond the reach of ideology, nationality, hardship, inspiration than he had ever been in life.

Brian Aldiss, *Earthworks*, 1965, [opening lines]

. . . .

Tuesday, March 4: INTRODUCTION TO ESSAY (2ND PASS)

One way to tackle a Mike Nelson installation is to approach it as a Rubik's Cube, the 3D puzzle patented in 1975 by Budapest-based logician, Erno Rubik, then smuggled to the West in 1979, and marketed globally throughout the Cold War's final decade and beyond by the Ideal Toy Company of New York City. The Rubik's Cube sits with Nelson's analogue time machines on the threshold of the digital era, prefiguring, in its reliance on nimble finger work and rapid pattern recognition, the advent of the internet. The analogy holds to a certain degree with this proviso—unlike Rubik's toy there are no solutions to Nelson's puzzles, the permutations go on running forever like computer script generated by malfunctioning software....

Monday, March 10: INTRODUCTION TO ESSAY (3RD PASS)

Nelson's installations are slowly ticking time bombs primed to go off some time after the visitor has left the premises. The initial plunge into the slightly fetid aura that emanates from Nelson's set-ups feels at first relatively risk-free if not exactly sanitary or wholesome, like watching a reenactment of the Tate-La Bianca murders on TV, or taking a dip in Lake Ontario. It's only later when the silt has settled back down in the bottom of the tank and the phantasmagorical infusion has begun to permeate the system that the full spectrum of effects—breathlessness, insomnia, discombobulation, paranoia, abnormal reasoning, delusions of reference, thanatophobia, involuntary laughter—start kicking in....

Sunday, March 2: EIGHTY CIRCLES—FURTHER NOTES

Rocky mountain landscapes/densely clouded northern skies cf. Scottish highlands. Nature views bisected in camera view finder—'majestic' untamed background vs. domesticated 4ground + fire rings like Neolithic Natural History dioramas with cave men cleared away. Sketchiness of human purchase on planet—brevity of history/culture vs geological time scales. Nature mediated/passed over/made over. Hinterland infrastructure pushing in from edges of frame—a truss bridge in 1 corner/freight train in another shot/mown grassy knoll bordering hydroelectric dam + generator + pylons + Flintstone-like stone ring in 4ground. 1 shot of dappled clearing next to dry river bed + jumble of rocks thrown down in heap as if by ape-like hominid. Others look like Land Art 101—Richard Long pieces redone by Bigfoot. Some circles = light grey + symmetrical like elegant smoke rings. Others hover in 4ground like ancient astronaut flying saucers.

Roadside Picnic, a Soviet era sci fi novel, 1971 by Arkady + Boris Strugatsky (cf. Tarkovsky's *Stalker*, 1979) sampled in *Mike Nelson. A Forgotten Kingdom* takes place in the aftermath of an extra terrestrial event called 'the Visitation':

Aliens have visited the Earth and gone away again, leaving behind them several landing areas (now called Zones) littered with their refuse. The visitors from space, if they noticed us at all, were evidently uninterested in communication.... The picnickers have gone; the pack rats, wary but curious, approach the crumpled bits of cellophane, the glittering pull tabs from beer cans, and try to carry them home to their holes.

Most of the mystifying debris is extremely dangerous. Some proves useful... but the scientists never know if they are using the devices for their proper purposes or employing (as it were) Geiger counters as hand axes and electric components as nose rings. They cannot figure out the principles of the artefacts, the science behind them. An international Institute sponsors research. A black market flourishes; 'stalkers' enter the forbidden Zones and, at risk of various kinds of disfigurement and death, steal bits of alien litter, bring the stuff out, and sell it, sometimes to the Institute itself... (T)he children of the stalkers are genetically altered until they seem scarcely human.... The setting appears to be North America, perhaps Canada, but the characters have no particular national characteristics...

Ursula K LeGuin "Foreword" to A & B Strugatsky, *Roadside Picnic*, Gollancz, 2012.

One of *Roadside Picnic*'s characters, Dr Valentine Pilma, a xenologist (xenology = sci fi + formal logic) provides the analogy which furnishes the novel's title in a conversation with an engineer called Noonan:

Imagine a picnic.... Picture a forest, a country road, a meadow. A car drives off the country road into the meadow, a group of young people get out of the car carrying bottles, baskets of food, transistor radios, and cameras. They light fires, pitch tents, turn on the music. In the morning they leave. The animals, birds, insects that watched in horror through the long night creep out from their hiding places. And what do they see? Gas and oil spilled on the grass. Old spark plugs and old filters strewn around. Rags, burnt-out bulbs, and a monkey wrench left behind. Oil slicks on the pond. And of course, the usual mess—apple cores, candy wrappers, charred remains of the campfire, cans, bottles, somebody's handkerchief, somebody's penknife, torn newspapers, coins, faded flowers picked in another meadow.
(Noonan) 'I see. A roadside picnic.'
'Precisely. A roadside picnic, on some road in the cosmos...'

NB. cf. Paul Thek's *Personal Effects of the Pied Piper*, 1975–1976: miniature bronze castings of camping paraphernalia including a fire ring. Also cf. *Untitled: intimate sculpture in public space* + Thek's *Tomb: Death of a Hippy* 1967.
Paul Thek motto: "Afflict the comfortable; comfort the afflicted."

Friday, March 21: INTRODUCTION TO ESSAY (4TH PASS)
"The oldest and strongest emotion of mankind is fear and the oldest and strongest kind of fear is fear of the unknown."
HP Lovecraft, *"The Supernatural in Horror"*, 1927.

Given the central role assigned to libraries and books in Nelson's oeuvre, it is fitting that the artist's alma mater should be Reading (pron. Redding).[4] While the material and sensuous qualities of the sculptural forms are often highlighted, if only as a potential health hazard—(one day after the opening a mold advisory was posted at The Power Plant at the entrance to *Quiver of Arrows*)—the primary impulse comes across as semiotic: the assemblages are presented as texts, albeit texts which are only partially legible and which resist or evade a definitive read.

Walking through a Nelson installation is like wading through a water damaged three-dimensional folding book laid out on the gallery floor for inspection by an insurance adjustor or through a movie set or scene in which the actors have been vaporised or airbrushed out. (Time on Nelson's watch is strictly analogue and cyclical; Photoshop has yet to be invented.) What remains is the closeness of unventilated space and the "scrupulous chaos" of carefully positioned object-clues enclosed within an envelope of menace.[5] As with Conan Doyle's fictionalised description (relayed by journalists as fact) of the undisturbed interior of the *Mary Celeste*, the Canadian-built brigantine found drifting off Gibraltar in 1872, what matters to the reader is less the question of veracity than the mounting sense of apprehension—apprehension as in foreboding: fear or anxiety of some impending evil; apprehension as in grasp or understanding: the apprehension of the art work....[6]

. . . .

For thousands of years mankind lived by hunting. In the course of endless pursuits hunters learned to construct the appearance and the movements of an unseen quarry through its tracks—prints in soft ground, snapped twigs, droppings, snagged hairs or feathers, smells, puddles, threads of saliva. They learned to sniff, to observe, to give meaning and context to the slightest trace. They learned to make complex calculations in an instant, in shadowy wood or treacherous clearing. ... (The) characteristic feature (of hunter's lore) was that it permitted the leap from apparently insignificant facts, which could be observed, to a complex reality which—directly at least—could not. And these facts would be ordered by the observer in such a way as to provide a narrative sequence—at its simplest, 'someone passed this way'. Perhaps indeed the idea of a narrative, as opposed to spell or exorcism or invocation, originated in a hunting society, from the experience of interpreting tracks.

Carlo Ginzberg, "Morelli, Freud and Sherlock Holmes: Clues and Scientific Method", *History Workshop Journal*, Issue 9, 1980.

. . . .

Tuesday, June 10–Friday, June 13: (BREAKTHROUGH!?)—APPREHENSION OF THE ARTWORK/THE TRAPPER AND THE FALL

Hide **vt** from old English *hydan*—to hide, conceal, preserve, hide oneself, bury a corpse

n **1.** the pelt or skin of one of the larger animals (buffalo, bear, moose etc) **2.** (British) a camouflaged shelter used to get a close view of wildlife cf hunting blind.

Composite On-line Dictionary

AMNESIAC HIDE: The title itself is a riddle and a trap however cautiously you approach it and from whatever angle. Any attempt on the part of an amnesiac to locate a hidden item is, by definition, doomed; the quest, no sooner launched, founders on a question: not just *where* is it but *what* is it we're looking for? Is the titular amnesiac bagged game—the trophy pelt hanging on the wall—or the hunter lurking unseen in his blind, sighting his unwitting prey?

The hunting motif is encoded not just in the title of the present exhibition but at the core of Nelson's project in the element of calculation: the baiting of the set-up and the lure with staged effects and misdirected detail.

Every work of art that works is like this, a trap or snare that impedes passage; and what is any art gallery but a place of capture, set with… 'thought traps', which hold their victims for a time, in suspension?
Alfred Gell

The drama of entrapment is key to Alfred Gell's definition, elaborated in his work on the agency of objects, of the artwork as a "complex of intentionalities" available to the viewer through abduction—what ancient Arab scientists called "'firasa'—the capacity to leap from the known to the unknown by inference (on the basis of clues)".[7] In a carefully constructed argument that closes round the unsuspecting reader like a snare, Gell sets out in his essay "Vogel's Trap" to demonstrate that traps can be seen as artworks just as artworks can be seen as traps.[8] For Gell, writing as an anthropologist as inclined as his surrealist forebears to put ethnology on an equal footing with contemporary art, a West African device for trapping chimpanzees provides a far more profound and telling portrait of its maker than any carving ("which only shows… the outward lineaments"…) ever could. As the material embodiment of a particularly complicated nexus of devious and lethal, but legible (though camouflaged) intentions, the 'primitive' hunting trap becomes, in Gell's analysis, not just a diabolically ingenious tool, but the archetypical artwork i.e. a contrivance primed "to achieve—something complex, allusive, hard to bring off".

"It's about entrapment and escape… of course, escape often leads to entrapment…."
Mike Nelson in Robert Enright, "Space Stories: An Interview with Mike Nelson", *Border Crossings*, issue 124, December, 2012.

The trap is both a model of its creator ("a subsidiary self in the form of an automaton") and its victim (anticipating "in negative contour... parameters of the animal's natural behavior"), while, at the same time, it embodies the dramatic nexus that binds these two protagonists together through action-at-a-distance in a time that is to come: "the catastrophe that will ensue as the trap closes". Traps, for Gell, are tropes freighted with metaphysical significance, embodying, and exposing, as they do, through their sequential mode of operation, the tragic parameters of existence as ordered by an absent Maker/God; the Faustian predicament of knowledge: idling curiosity, hubris and nemesis... the gradient and the fall.

What Gell discerns as the 'point' of a work like Damien Hirst's *A Thousand Years* "which actually incorporates a working trap device" (i.e. decaying cow's head + maggots + flies + insect-ocutor sealed inside a glass box), and the point of the arrow waiting to be triggered in the African arrow trap illustrated elsewhere in Gell's essay converge on a common trajectory:

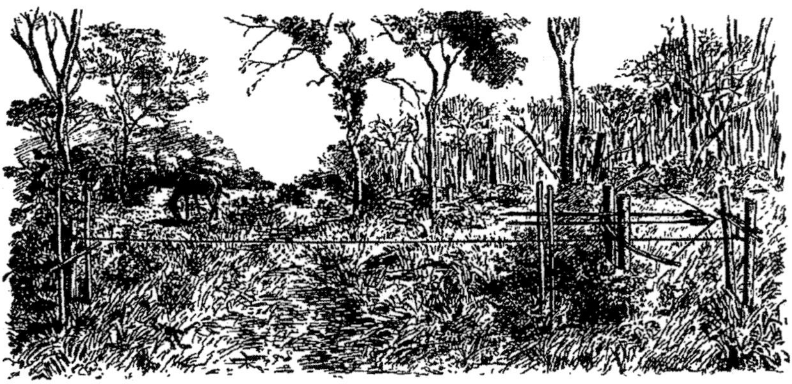

Figure 6.4 Arrow trap, central Africa; sketch by Weule

Now imagine encountering the arrow trap, not (one hopes) as the victim is going to encounter it, but as a gallery-goer encounters an 'installation' by the latest contemporary artist. In those circumstances, and without additional context, what might the sensitive gallery-goer intuit as the thought, or intention, in this artwork? A representation of human-being-in-the-world as unthinking, poised violence which is not perhaps a pretty thought, but not for that reason an untrue or inartistic one. Initially a trap such as this communicates a deadly absence—the absence of the man who devised and set it, and the absence of the animal who will become the victim. Because of these marked absences, the trap, like all traps, functions as a powerful sign. ... The static violence of the tensed bow, the congealed malevolence of the arrangement of sticks and cords, are revelatory in themselves....[9]

Saturday, June 14: AIRSTREAM ARROW TRAP

'*Quiver of Arrows*' is... a must-see installation: it will leave you with an experience you will never forget! ... Mike Nelson: Amnesiac Hide will leave you with an eerie feeling and will give you another take on interactive art!
Façade Academy of the Arts, 5 Feb 2014 http://facadeacademy.com/2014/02/mike-nelsons-amnesiac-hide-now-at-the-power-plant/

Suddenly, the clouds rose to a great height, rimmed with a blinding crimson glare; the lurid sky became grey, distant and flat; everything was blotted out; I was falling in a spin...
I heard the mechanical voice from the control center:
"Station Solaris. Zero and zero. The capsule has landed. Out..."[10]

The most structurally coherent, and monumental of the four component installations, *Quiver of Arrows* functions as the seedy-splashy main attraction in *Amnesiac Hide*. Reassuringly circular and self-contained, it functions as the exhibition's crowd-drawing centre piece, supplying in the retro-futurist syntax of its four conjoined vintage airstream trailers, the closest thing on offer to a fairground ghost train ride.

The gallery-goer ascends the stairs and steps onto the walkway, advancing from room to room along a Möbius strip of interlocking tableaux. The narrow concave interior, obliquely lit, and painted dark room red or muggy blues and greens appears recently occupied. Someone left the lights on and a fan is whirring noisily (to no discernible effect) somewhere further on. Dirty dishes are piled up in the sink(s.)

...I found myself inside a vast, silver funnel.... I turned round. The ventilation shafts were roaring, sucking in the poisonous gases from the planet's atmosphere which had infiltrated when my capsule had landed inside the Station. Empty, resembling a burst cocoon, the cigar-shaped capsule stood upright, enfolded by a calyx mounted on a steel base. The outer casing, scorched during flight, had turned a dirty brown. I looked around me, a little uncertain, waiting for someone to appear; but there was no sign of life. Only a

neon arrow glowed, pointing towards a moving walkway which was silently unreeling. I allowed myself to be carried forward….

We're back inside the Amnesiacs HQ again—the now familiar dusty mirrored labyrinth, bereft, as always, of living human presence (except, that is, our own). A combination storage locker—living space, Nelson's corroded aluminum 'Quiver' is stuffed with his phantom bikers' oceanic gleanings: a trove of trailer trash imbued by years of human handling with abject occult power.

A rusting Schlitz (Tall Boy) can stands guard over empty metal boxes marked with the initials of the US Marine Corp alongside football helmets, Arab language books and video tapes, and a square-faced 1960s portable TV… the ghost of Cassius Clay flashes an indignant stare from an old b/w studio portrait lodged inside an arabesque filigree shrine… a polished table spoon glints in the half light next to an antique ('oriental') set of scales and a cigarette lighter… a verdigris bald eagle stamped at the centre of a metal tray looks like it's done underwater service… moth-eaten sofas, improvised bedding, rope mats and bead curtains…

…The moving walkway set me down at the far end of the gallery, on the threshold of a dome. Here there was an even greater disorder. A pool of oily liquid spread out from beneath a pile of oil-drums; a nauseating smell hung in the air; footprints, in a series of glutinous smears, went off in all directions. The oil-drums were covered with a tangle of tickertape, torn paper and other waste. Another green arrow directed me to the central door. Behind this stretched a narrow corridor, hardly wide enough for two men to walk side by side, lit by slabs of glass let into the ceiling. Then another door, painted in green and white squares, which was ajar; I went in…

… Audio cassettes lie in stacks underneath a loop of worry beads… a Turkish language poster for *Dag Adami (The Mountain Men)* starring Charlton Heston is pinned by a doorway next to an amulet designed to ward off the Evil Eye… a cocoa sack from Ghana does double duty as a makeshift seat cover… a pamphlet on Kropotkin lies on a metal table next to an assortment of machine parts in front of a dilapidated stove… a battered rubber Uncle Sam grins up at the ceiling in a window casement while farther on (or farther back) a Bugs Bunny doll grins up into the ceiling from the edge of a knock-off 'Persian' rug…

On completing the circuit, the visitor emerges from a silent guided tour through a wilderness of mirrors along the unsecured perimeter of the faltering

US empire in the helter-skelter slipstream of an "American century" that definitively ended one year late on 9/11… the outer edges folding in toward the detonated centre in the wake of that event… a hinterland on every doorstep… the assassin at the gate…

A squared off, dented metal Ouroboros squatting under yellow sodium lights, Nelson's Quiver trap swallows the line of curiosity-seekers one by one as they file up the rough plank steps at monitored intervals before spitting them out again, one at a time, several minutes later, through the same aperture with something alien and ill-assorted sticking to the bottom of their shoes.

The dates of manufacture of the constituent parts weigh into the concoction… the suffocating fog of history:

1939—(Platt Tandem)—Ist world science fiction convention opens in NYC; outbreak of WW2 (for Europe).

1948—(Zimmer Mobile Home)—Berlin Blockade/escalation of the Cold War; Communist Party seizure of power in Czechoslovakia; R-1—first Soviet launch into space; Manchuria and Northeast China fall to Mao Zedung's People's Liberation Army (PLA); founding of Israel/first Arab-Israeli War.

1948—(Spartan Mansion)—House Un-American Activities Committee (HUAC)—Alger Hiss hearings televised; start of negotiations to establish NATO alliance; first chimpanzee astronaut launched into space from White Sands, NM; Hells Angels motorcycle gang founded in CA.

1963—(Airstream Safari [chopped])—the JF Kennedy assassination—(the articulating segments/unifying thread of paranoia).

1968—(Streamline Empress)—Tet offensive, mass student protests, Martin Luther King assassinated; race riots across US cities; Robert Kennedy assassinated; My Lai massacre; *Planet of the Apes + 2001* released in theatres; Apollo 7 and 8 launched; Richard Nixon elected US President; rise to power of Saddam Hussein's Ba'ath party in Iraq.

Dumped this side of the 49th Parallel like some off-world relic of the Cold War space race abandoned in the Inter-zone, *Quiver of Arrows* looms up into the frozen North like a shadow on the moon.... The ruins of the forward-facing US Jetson era repurposed as a living space for the Rag and Bone Faction (RBF)... the International Blowback Brigade (IBB)... the irradiated desert rats... the stalkers... the drudges and the drones.

The detail is the torn apart (from French detailer ([1600]—cut to pieces). Big Bang shrapnel, wreckage from the Fall. There is no going back...

... The cabin had concave walls and a big panoramic window, which a glowing mist had tinged with purple. Outside the murky waves slid silently past. Open cupboards lined the walls, filled with instruments, books, dirty glasses, vacuum flasks—all covered with dust. Five or six small trolleys and some collapsible chairs cluttered up the stained floor....

. . . .

I remain very concerned about what we are not seeing.

FBI Director, Robert Mueller testifying before the Senate Committee on Intelligence, Feb 16, 2005.

. . . .

Wednesday, March 26, 2014: FOG OF "HISTORY"

History was launched on January 1, 1995 as The History Channel, ... On February 16, 2008, a new logo was launched on the US network as part of a major rebranding effort. While the trademark H was kept, the triangle shape on the left acts as a play button for animation and fly-outs during commercials and shows. On March 20, 2008, as part of that same rebranding effort, The History Channel dropped the "The" and "Channel" from its name to become simply 'History'.

Wikipedia entry for "History" (TV Channel), accessed 3/26/14

Partial list in alphabetical order of series and TV specials available from A&E Network's "History" web-site (accessed 16/3/14):

After Armageddon; *American Hoggers* ("reality"); *American Pickers* ("reality"); *Ancient Aliens*; *Ancient Mysteries; Ancients Behaving Badly*; "Apocalypse Man"; *Appalachian Outlaws* ("reality"); *Ax Men* ("reality"); *Beyond the Da Vinci Code*; "The Bible Code—Predicting Armageddon"; *Billy the Exterminator* ("reality"); *Brad Meltzer's Decoded*; *Celebrity Ghost Stories* ("reality");"Comets: Prophets of Doom"; *Conspiracy? The RFK Assassination*; *Countdown to Apocalypse* (inc. "Four Horsemen"; "The

Mayan Messengers"); *Decoding the Past* (inc. "Mayan Doomsday Prophecy", "The Other Nostradamus"); *Digging for Doomsday 2012* (50% off); *Duck Dynasty* ("reality"); "Exorcism: Driving out the Devil"; *Extreme History with Roger Daltrey*; *Fear Files*; "God vs Satan"; *History's Mysteries* (inc. "Crop Circle Controversy"); *Holy Grail in America*; *Ice Road Truckers* ("reality"); *Incredible but True?;* **"I Know What I Saw"**; *In Search of History* (inc. "Curse of the Monkey Man"; "Frankenstein", "The Oracle at Delphi"; "Riddles of the Zodiac"; "Secret Brotherhood of Freemasons"); "JFK's Assassination: The Definitive Guide"; "The Kennedy Assassination: 24 Hours After"; "The Kennedy Assassination: Beyond Conspiracy"; *Life After People*; "Live from '69—Moon Landing"; *Lost Worlds—The Real Dracul*a; "Manson"; *Mega Disasters*; *Moonshiners* ("reality"); "Moonshot"; *Monster Quest* (inc. "Abominable Snowman", "Ohio Grassman", "Real Hobbit", "Sasquatch", "Stalin's Ape Man","Swamp Beast"; "Unidentified Flying Creatures"); ***Mountain Men* ("reality")**; *Mud Men* ("reality"); *Mysteries of the Freemasons*; *Nostradamus Effect*; *Off the Grid: Million Dollar Manhunt* ("reality game show"); *Opus Dei*; *Paranormal States* (inc. "Demonic Possession"); *Pawn Stars* ("reality"); *Roswell Legacy* (inc. "British Roswell", "Canada's Roswell (Shag Harbor, Nova Scotia),"Mexico's Roswell", "Texas Roswell"*); Sandhogs* ("reality"*); Secret Societies; Shark Wranglers* ("reality"); *Secrets of Kabbalah*; *Secrets of the Founding Fathers*; *Swamp People* ("reality") ; *The 9/11 Conspiracies—Fact or Fiction?*; *UFO Files*: (inc. "Hanger 18", "The Pacific Bermuda Triangle").

I KNOW WHAT I SAW, a documentary guaranteed to change the way we see the universe. Director James Fox assembled the most credible UFO witnesses from around the world to testify at The National Press Club in Washington DC: Air Force Generals, astronauts, military and commercial pilots, government and FAA officials from seven countries tell stories that, as Governor Fife Symington from Arizona stated, will challenge your reality.

"History" web-site http://shop.history.com/i-know-what-i-saw-dvd/detail.php?p=254309 accessed 3/26/14.

Invisibility within art is pretty well done these days, … There's a given imaginative space that traditional conceptual work refers to, a standard perception of something that exists in a space beyond. … (I)t's an accepted mode of production, and we need to steal away from this with another idea of what invisibility can do… a cipher into something you can't see….

Mike Nelson[11]

Sunday, March 22: INTRODUCTION TO ESSAY (5th Pass)

Cipher **n** from Arabic *sifr*, empty.

1. a secret or disguised way of writing; a code: "he wrote cryptic notes in a cipher".

2. something written in a code: "he came across ciphers written on parchment and concealed in a hollow altar pillar"; a key to a code.

3. a zero; a figure 0.

4. any of the Arabic numerals or figures

vt **1.** put (a message) into secret writing; encode: "he left two, as yet uncracked, ciphered messages for posthumous decoding"

2. *archaic* do arithmetic.

Composite On-line Dictionary

(O)ur challenge in this new century is a difficult one: to defend our nation against the unknown, the uncertain, the unseen and the unexpected.

Remarks prepared for Secretary of Defense, Donald Rumsfeld, the National Defense University in Washington, DC; Thursday Jan 31, 2002 www.defenselink.mil/speeches/2002/s20020131-secdef.html

God and devil both are in the details, but the underlying code remains eternally intact, impervious, un-crackable, no matter how fast whose Collider sends the leptons round the track.... Though everything inside the Zone is palpably constructed, nothing whatsoever is nailed down; the itinerary is always circular, the line from a to b loops back through all the other letters....

. . . .

January 12th... Sharik (the dog) can read. He can read (three exclamation marks). ... The surgeon's scalpel has brought to life a new human entity. Prof Preobrazhensky—you are a creator (ink blot)...

Mikhail Bulgakov, *A Heart of a Dog*, 1925 sampled in *Mike Nelson. A Forgotten Kingdom*.[12]

. . . .

Wednesday, March 13th: DOGGED PURSUIT

Anarchist Evening at the Magic Theatre. Not for Everybody. For Madmen Only, Price of Admission Your Mind.

Hand bill delivered to the protagonist of Herman Hesse's *Steppenwolf* by a man on his way to a funeral.[13]

In *Trading Station Alpha CMa*, (Alpha CMa—Sirius—the Dog Star) an early Nelson installation mounted in 1996 at Matt's Gallery (named after gallery owner, Robin Klassnik's dog, Matt E Mulsion) in Bow in East London, the motivating cipher at the heart of the labyrinth turned out to be a dog-man hybrid, a composite deducible from its reading matter, the Strugatsky brothers' *Hard to be a God*, 1964, a copy of which lay secreted in plain sight inside the creature's lair, built into the cluttered shelving of the simulated storage space into which the gallery, (a former werehouse sited 3 miles north of the Isle of Dogs; 7 miles west of Barking) had been converted. According to the artist, the book's title provided a "pivotal clue" to the para-fictional convergence on which the entire fabrication was founded i.e. the moment in *Apocrypha Now!* (1979), when the Kurtz-worshipping "American Photojournalist" played by Dennis Hopper, (to cite the artist's own description) "observes the reversal of 'god' and 'dog'", thereby pairing Coppola's psychoto-mimetic Vietnam war saga and its source work, Conrad's *Heart of Darkness* (1899), with *Stalker* (1979), and the Strugatsky brothers' *Roadside Picnic* (1971), on which the Tarkovsky film is based, thus sealing in an Ouroboric circle ('a wilderness of mirrors') the symmetrically dystopian underground imaginaries of the former Soviet Bloc and its US-dominated NATO adversary-twin.[14]

... Redrick was amazed to see how short his terrible, endless path had been... It was only twenty or thirty yards from one edge of the burnt-out grass to the other, but in his blindness and fear he had crawled in some wild zigzag, like a roach on a hot skillet, and thank God he had at least crawled in the right direction....
Roadside Picnic

Friday June 20: (EIGHTY CIRCLES): LAST POSSESSIONS OF AN ORCADIAN MOUNTAIN MAN

The eighty stone circle slides are projected onto a screen that is exactly coterminous with the wall of shelving made of salvaged plywood and driftwood that holds the last possessions of an Orcadian Mountain Man stacked higgledy piggledy, as in a garage or a garden shed, so that object and image stand back to back like twins, each the mirror to the other's tain. One side haunts and implicates the other: the primal camping scene/the terminal descent.

The contents of EW's estate include:

6 round hairbrushes with strands of hair adhering
camouflage outdoor man headwear complete with regional decals
a red baseball cap with the words *Erl's Tours* picked out in yellow
photo ID cards (one for British Rail)
an opened tube of purple gouache
jack adaptor cable leads
sundry camping supplies
orange rope and climbing gear
camera and tripod
sleeping bag
climbing boots
converse sneakers
audio cassettes,
a collection of mineral samples
welding mask
elastics
hold alls
a bike lock
drawing pads
newspapers
maps
several pairs of glasses
old leather wallets
a compass
a ball of string
a few generic prints

A *Tin-Tin*-era illustration of a Bedouin on a camel with palm trees and a pyramid is propped up at one end of the unit. Towards the other end, a lurid orange sunset is stacked behind a stylised painted anime (self?) portrait of an androgynous youth—a flat white face in ¾ profile framed by flat black hair that merges with the background positioned on its side, the mouth obscured by a military kepi placed in front, one black eye turned toward the viewer, the whole flat 2D head hovering at an unnatural angle over the collar of the grey-white tartan dressing gown hanging from a hook in the wardrobe compartment directly underneath, like a poltergeist in a Japanese horror film—a ghost with a broken neck looking back at us looking blankly, blindly back at him, as he hangs there camouflaged among the mouldering belays and caribiners—the tackle and the fall.

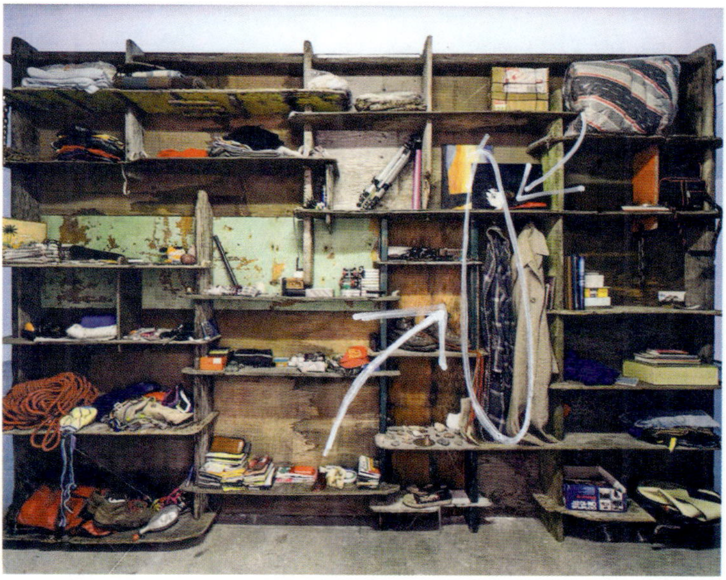

Et in Orcadia Ego

a parcel bound in string and ready to go sits on the shelf above.[15]

Friday, August 1, 1997: "Back in no time"

William Burroughs' last words (quoting Brion Gysin), spoken to Pat Connor, a friend, as the author was being loaded into an ambulance outside his house in Lawrence, Kansas after suffering a heart attack.[16]

. . . .

The original version of this exercise (the walking routine) was taught me by an old Mafia Don in Columbus, Ohio: seeing everyone in the street before he sees you. [...] Generally speaking, if you see other people before they see you, they won't see you. I have even managed to get past a whole block of guides and shoeshine boys in Tangier this way, thus earning my Moroccan moniker: 'El Hombre Invisible'...

William S Burroughs

. . . .

Saturday morning February 1: TORONTO DIM SUM TIME

Jenifer steers the car onto a street in Chinatown just as Mike Nelson veers into view on foot coming from a different direction and another thick flurry begins drifting down onto the mock pagoda roofs and the slush-encircled mounds of dirty snow piled up along the sidewalk. As we pull past I watch Mike threading his way forward on the other side of the street—a compact self-contained figure with a backpack advancing with the practiced, focused gait of the seasoned independent traveler who's accustomed to avoiding eye contact on the street with strangers, oblivious alike, or so it seems, to hazardous conditions underfoot, heavy snowfall, stumbling, hurrying crowds, and the car load of acquaintances gliding past to his right. Despite the villainous full black beard and matching beanie combo worthy of a pirate of the Caribbean, an outlaw biker from a 1960s Roger Corman movie or a Pashtun Imam from a madrassa on the Pakistan-Afghani border, Mike Nelson abroad on the Toronto streets in 2014 blends into the backdrop with the spectral aplomb of his literary forebear, William Burroughs, the original el hombre invisible, the man who turned hiding in the light into an art form:

> … Disguise is not a false beard, dyed hair and plastic surgery.… Disguise… is clothes and bearing and behavior that leave no questions unanswered… American tourist with a wife he calls 'Mother'… old queen on the make… dirty beatnik… marginal film producer… Every article of my luggage and clothing is carefully planned to create a certain impression. Behind this impression I can operate without interference.…
> William Burroughs, *Wild Boys*, Grove Press, 1971.

We find a spot and park, then all pile out and stand for a moment in a huddle looking for the restaurant rendezvous point. Mike stops in front of a place diagonally opposite, opens the door and disappears inside and we start heading over as a clash of cymbals heralds in the Chinese New Year (again) and a team of dancers in dragon masks spills out onto the street to a raucous prerecorded 'traditional' accompaniment, the snow gusting in eddies round their brightly costumed torsos. It's the year of the Horse again in Toronto/China/Tibet, the setting for the staging of *Double negative (The Genie)*, the artist's recapitulation of uncanny encounters at the end of the world—Erl's last tour—the handling of the death card. Somewhere in the laden clouds an ace of spades is hanging upside down waiting to drop.

Saturday afternoon, February 1: SCREWED

While I tag along on a group trip to some bunker in the heart of the University complex to see a conceptually driven art-as-espionage exhibition (CounterIntelligence at the Justina M Barnicke Gallery—sample panel: "Site-Specific/Non-Site/Black Site")[17], Mike Nelson takes off on foot in the teeth of another blizzard to scour army surplus and vintage clothing stores for a military issue Korean War era (1950–1953) coyote trimmed Arctic parka similar to the one he's already wearing. Later in a crowded fair trade coffee shop in Kensington Market, I sit at the table taking mental notes as Mike engages an artist from Vancouver in an extended discussion of the virtues and drawbacks of the Canadian square recess Robertson screw (patent #116463 lodged in 1909 by PL Robertson of Milton, Ontario).

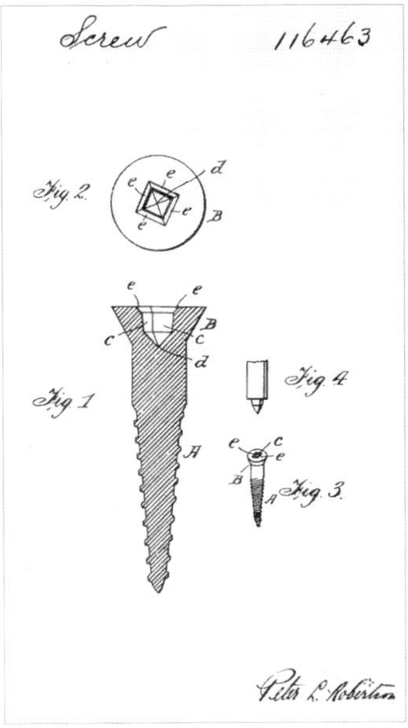

Virtues and Drawbacks of the Robertson screw

+ non-slip/ ergonomically efficient/can be used with one hand

- while standard issue in Canada, distribution elsewhere is uneven/unreliable, ergo always pack a Robertson driver in the tool box before heading for Heathrow.

. . . .

The old writer couldn't write any more because he had reached the end of words, the end of what can be done with words. And then? 'British we are, British we stay.' How long can one hang on to Gibraltar, with the tapestries where mustached riders with scimitars hunt tigers, the ivory balls one inside the other, bare seams showing, the long tearoom with mirrors on both sides and the tired fuschia and rubber plants, the shops selling English marmalade and Fortnum and Mason's tea... clinging to their Rock like the apes, clinging always to less and less.

In Tangier the Parade Bar is closed. Shadows are falling on the Mountain.

'Hurry up, please. It's time.'

William Burroughs, *The Western Lands*, 1987 [closing lines].

Notes and references

1. Nelson, Mike, "A Thousand Words: Mike Nelson talks about his work", *Artforum* 1 February, 2002.

2. Cumming, Laura, "Almost Infamous", *The Observer,* 14 October 2001.

3. Bradley, Will, ed *Mike Nelson. A Forgotten Kingdom*, London ICA, pp 249, 2001 with texts by JG Ballard, Hakim Bey, Jorge Luis Borges, Richard Brautigan, Mikhail Bulgakov, William Burroughs, Albert Camus, Joseph Conrad, Philip K Dick, Franz Kafka, Stanislaw Lem, Peter Linebaugh & Marcus Rediker, HP Lovecraft, Ed Sanders, Arkady & Boris Strugatsky, Theodore Sturgeon, *The Thousand and One Nights* (trans. Sir Richard Francis Burton, Jules Verne, Sir Charles Leonard Woolley). For an insightful reading of the compositional symmetries between Nelson's installations and artist books, see also Helen Hughes, "An editorial approach: Mike Nelson's corridors and *The Deliverance and The Patience*", *emaj*, issue 6, 2011—12 (available on-line—http://emajartjournal.files.wordpress.com/2012/11/hughes-an-editorial-approach2.pdf).

4. Mike Nelson graduated from the University of Reading with a BA in Fine Art in 1990. See, for instance, Jorge Luis Borges, "The Total Library", 1939, "The Library of Babel", 1941, "The Book of Sand", 1975, Kurd Lasswitz, "The Universal Library", 1901, and Robert Burton, *The Anatomy of Melancholy*, 1621 for depictions of the library as a model for infinity. Borges' version has become paradigmatic: "The Library is a sphere whose exact center is any one of its (numberless) hexagons and whose circumference is inaccessible" though another of Borges' somewhat less well known dictums: "Nothing is built on stone. All is built on sand but we must build as if the sand were stone" dovetails more directly with Nelson's bibliophiliac approach to installation-as-analogous translation/building-as-back-to-front-bildungsroman/reading-as-the-Ur-immersion. ("I'm interested in my work being read not purely in the here and now, but also in retrospect, through memory—characteristics that are employed in both film and literature." Mike Nelson).

   For more particularised insights on the centrality of the library/book shelf to Nelson's work, see his interview with Andrew Hunt conducted on the beach at Westcliff-on-Sea (Thursday 11 July 2013) in which the artist discusses a recent work entitled *An Invocation: Five Hundred and Thirty Books from Southend Central Library*. For this installation, Nelson rescued de-accessioned/remaindered volumes scheduled for pulping or re-sale from the about-to-be demolished local public library in South–on-Sea. The covers of the salvaged books reproduced in a compendium which Nelson describes as " the mirror image of *A Forgotten Kingdom"* is currently available through Amazon.com. The interview with Hunt is also reproduced in the book. The hidden connector with *A Forgotten Kingdom*, according to the artist, is the walled-up cat in Edgar Allen Poe's short story *The Black Cat*, 1843, which was reprinted in the latter volume along with HP Lovecraft's *The Rats in the Walls*, 1925. See also documentation of Nelson's installation, *To the memory of HP Lovecraft*, 1999, based on Borges's short story "There are more things (to the memory of HP Lovecraft)"(1975), in which the artist invoked the Beast Within by hacking holes in the walls of the about-to-be-refurbished Collective Gallery in Edinburgh at a constant height and distributing piles of 'excrement' made out of the extruded material on the gallery floor to produce a supernatural/sculptural intervention in white cube space. In the interview with Hunt, Nelson refers to the anachronistic "generosity" of the idea of the public library, unthinkable in the current neo-liberal economic era, and recalled the time in the early 1990s when he worked at London's Central Books, then partly funded by the Soviet Union, while studying at Chelsea College of Art after graduating from Reading. The artist's 1996 installation, *Trading Station Alpha CMa* at Matt's Gallery appears to be a hypnogogic rendition of the bookshop's storage area and another piece, *Taylor*, 1994, "which referenced the marooned astronaut in the film *Planet of the Apes*, 1968 … consisted of a raft built from boxes that had arrived from the Soviet Union (containing) copies of books by Marx and Engels". See *An Invocation: Five Hundred and Thirty Books from Southend Central Library* Focal Point Gallery, Southend-on-Sea, pp 1056, 2013.

5. In 1884, a short story loosely based on the abandonment of the *Mary Celeste,* penned by Arthur Conan Doyle, then a little known part-time author, appeared anonymously as a firsthand account under the title "J Habakuk Jephson's Statement" in the January issue of the *Cornhill Magazine*. Among the details fictionalised in Conan Doyle's story were the ship's name which he Gallicised to *Marie Celeste* and the undisturbed state of the ship's interior (when boarded off the Strait of Gibraltar, the *Mary Celeste* was waterlogged, nine of the 1701 barrels of alcohol in the cargo hold were empty, and its life boat, log, sextant and chronometer were missing).

"A bobbin of silk was found standing upon the sewing-machine, though the least roll of the vessel would have precipitated it to the floor. The boats were intact and slung upon the davits; and the cargo, consisting of tallow and American clocks, was untouched."
"J Habakuk Jephson's Statement", 1884

Both the ship's name and mysteriously intact interior became key signifiers in the popular 'ghost ship' legend that developed round the incident after the story was reported as fact in several newspapers, including the *Boston Herald*.

6. Enright, Robert, "Space Stories: An Interview with Mike Nelson", *Border Crossings*, issue 124, December, 2012.

7. Ginzberg, Carlo, "Morelli, Freud and Sherlock Holmes: Clues and Scientific Method", *History Workshop Journal,* no 9, 1980. In a bravura demonstration of inferential reasoning, Ginzberg proposes links between Neolithic hunter lore, Mesopotamian divinatory practices, palmistry, legal discourse/case law, epidemiology, connoisseurship in art, psychoanalysis, detective fiction and forensic science. In the process he sets out to isolate and define a 'conjectural', 'divinatory' or 'semiotic' paradigm of knowledge which he counter-poses as a form of popular or intuitive, experientially-rooted epistemology against the generalising power of Platonist abstraction and Gailiaean science favoured by modern elites. The legend of Serendip (later morphing into Voltaire's *Zadig*) is cited as the codification in narrative (via "retrospective prophecy") of the appeal (and the incidental dangers) of conjectural logic:

Three brothers (runs a story from the middle east told among Khirgiz, Tartars, Jews, Turks and so on) meet a man who has lost a camel (sometimes a horse). At once they describe it to him: it's white, and blind in one eye; under the saddle it carries two skins, one filled with oil, the other of wine. They must have seen it? No, they haven't seen it so they are accused of theft and are brought to be judged. There follows the triumph of the brothers: they immediately show how from the barest traces they were able to reconstruct the appearance of an animal they'd never set eyes on.
Ginzberg, 1980.

8. Gell, Alfred, "Vogel's Trap. Traps as Artworks and Artworks as Traps" in Eric Hirsch, ed, *Alfred Gell, The Art of Anthropology. Essays and Diagrams*, London School of Economics Monographs on Social Anthropology, no 67, Oxford, New York: Berg 2006. All Gell quotations in this section come from this essay.

9. Alfred Gell, op cit, 2006.

10. Lem, Stanislaw, *Solaris* originally published in Poland, 1961, English trans Joanna Kilmartin and Steve Cox, London: Walker & Co, 1970. All quotes in italics in this section come from Lem's novel:

"Science fiction almost always assumed the aliens we meet play some kind of game with us the rules of which we sooner or later may understand.... However I wanted to cut all threads leading to the personification of the Creature, ie the Solarian Ocean, so that the contact could not follow the human, interpersonal pattern—although it did take place in some strange manner. The method I used in the novel to demonstrate this was the particular outcome of the interest of people, who for over one hundred years have been studying the planet 'Solaris' and the ocean covering its surface....

... The Solarian globe was not just any sphere surrounded by some jelly—it was an active being (although a non-human one). It neither built nor created anything translatable into our language that could have been "explained in translation". Hence a description had to be replaced by analysis—(obviously an impossible task)—of the internal workings of the Ocean's ego. This gave rise to 'symetriads', 'asymetriads' and 'mimoids'—strange semi-constructions scientists were unable to understand; they could only describe them in a mathematically meticulous manner, and this was the sole purpose of the growing Solarian library—the result of over a hundred years' efforts to enclose in folios what was not human and beyond human comprehension; what could not have been translated into human language—or into anything else."

Stanislaw Lem, *The Solaris Station*

http://english.lem.pl/arround-lem/adaptations/soderbergh/147-the-solaris-stationThe?start=1

11. Mike Nelson, op cit, 2013.

12. In *A Heart of a Dog*, 1925, Mikhail Bulgakov's satire on the Bolshevik revolution's attempt to reform human nature, Sharik, the stray dog protagonist is turned into an uncouth slovenly homunculus—a Frankensteinian travesty of the Soviet New Man after undergoing a human pituitary gland and testicle transplant performed by his adoptive surgeon-master, Professor Preobrazhensky. (An extract from the novel—a lab technician's scribbled notes—appears in *Mike Nelson. A Forgotten Kingdom)*. Bulgakov's fictional conceit fits seamlessly inside the documented history of xeno-transplantation experiments alongside the efforts of pioneering bio-engineers like Serge Voronoff who in the 1920s performed "monkey gland' rejuvenation' grafts on (wealthy) men, and Ilya Ivanov who, at Stalin's behest set out in the same decade to breed a Red Ape Army by inseminating female human subjects with orang utang and chimpanzee semen. It seems likely that Bulgakov is the primary reference (if there is one) rather than, say, William Wegman or Joseph Beuys' *How to Explain Pictures to a Dead Hare*, 1965 in Nelson's 1996 performance / exhibition *No can Teach A Dog Old Tricks New* at the Academia De Arta, Bucharest in which the artist attempted (unsuccessfully) to teach a local canine to recognise basic geometric figures—a square, a triangle, a circle.

13. Hesse, Herman, *Steppenwolf* (originally published in Zurich and Berlin 1927 trans into English 1929, Penguin Classics New Edition, 2001). Part stage set for metamorphic acting out, part hall of mirrors and screen for fearful/ desiring projections, Pablo's Magic Theatre provides another literary corollary for Mike Nelson's immersive environments:

> We got up. With a smile Pablo led. He opened a door and drew a curtain aside, and we found ourselves in the horseshoe-shaped corridor of a theater, and exactly in the middle. On either side, the curving passage led past a large number, indeed an incredible number, of narrow doors into the boxes. 'This', explained Pablo, 'is our theater, and a jolly one it is. I hope you'll find lots to laugh at.' He laughed aloud as he spoke, a short laugh, but it went through me like a shot.... 'This little theater of mine has as many doors into as many boxes as you please, ten or a hundred or a thousand, and behind each door exactly what you seek awaits you.'

14. Mike Nelson interviewed by Michele Robecchi, *Flash Art*, no 262, 2008.

15. I have no idea whether the figure/cipher I purport to have found among the last possessions of an Orcadian Mountain Man is actually there or not.

16. For a detailed blow-by-blow account of Burroughs' last 24 hours see Barry Miles, *Call Me Burroughs: A Life*, Twelve, 2014.

17. Curated by Charles Stankievech.

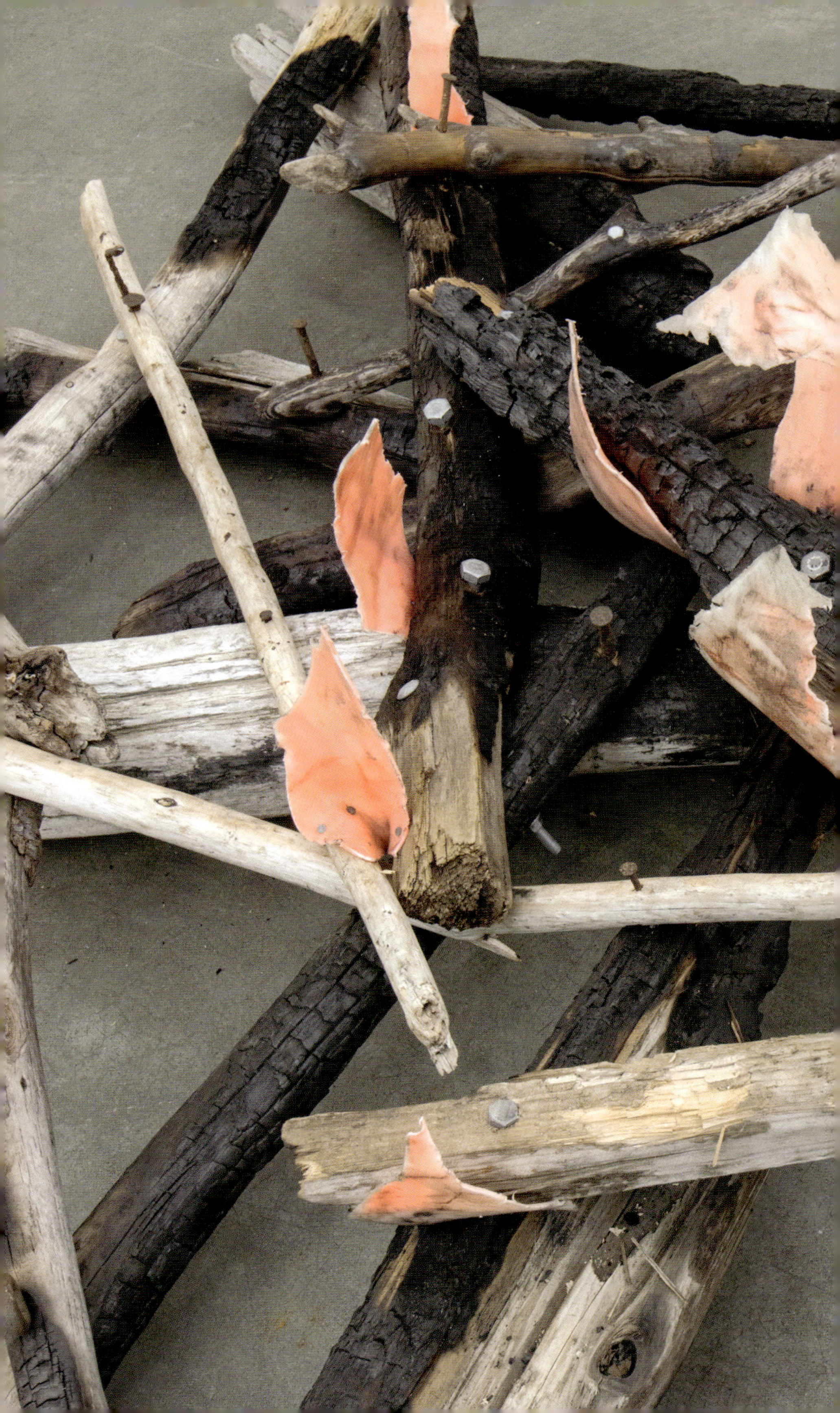

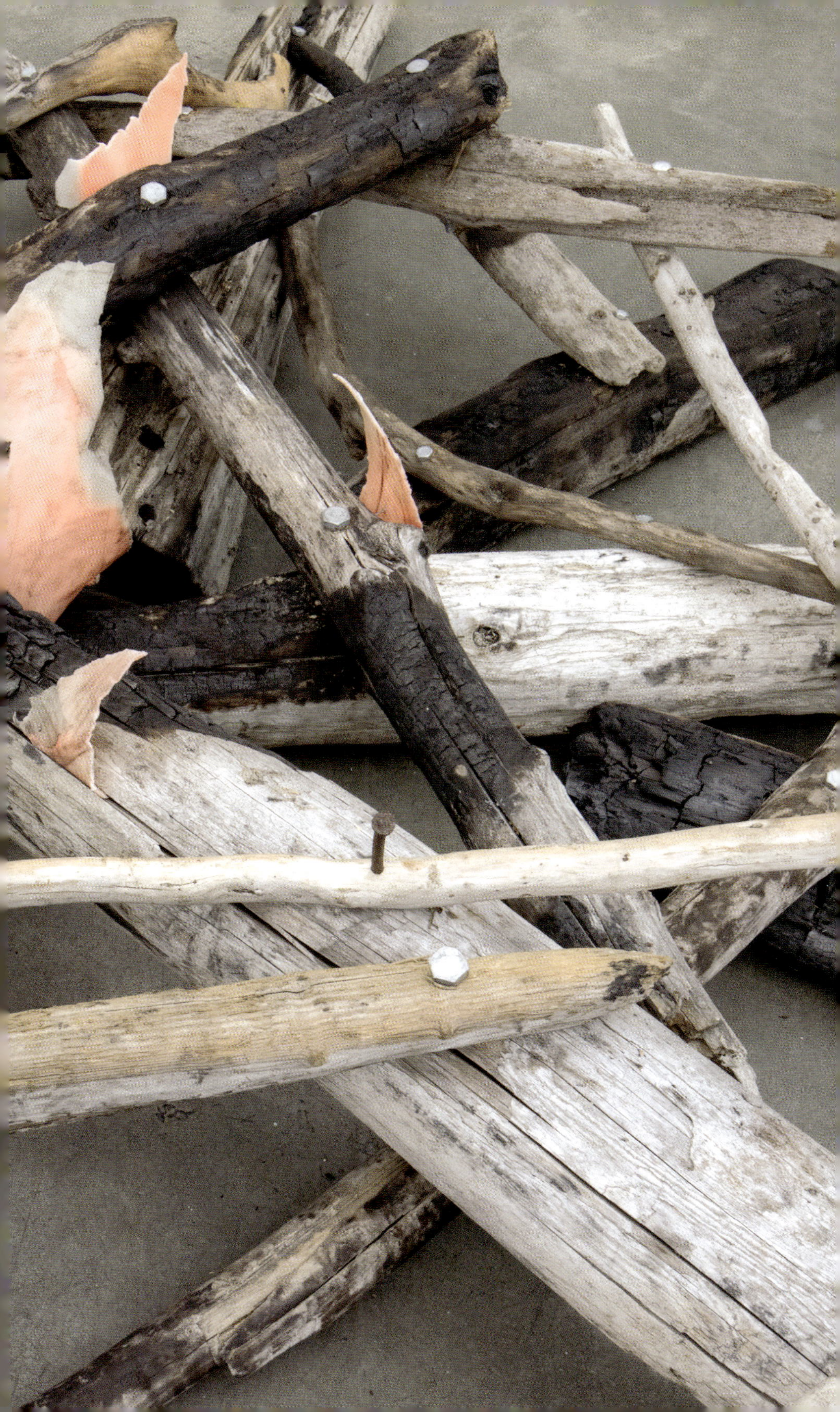

West Wind of Loss

Jenifer Papararo

A SENSATIONALIST!
I COULD BECOME a PLAGIARIST!
A SITUATIONIST—NAAH, I LIKE SPECTACLES TOO MUCH!
70s REVIVALIST—PERHAPS A BIT TOO EARLY 90s!
I SHOULD REALLY BECOME A CAREERIST!
NIHILIST—UH, AND JOIN THE FUCKIN FASHION BRIGADE!
I COULD GET OUT OF THE WHITE CUBE AND DO SOME FUNNY FLUXES STUFF!
MAYBE AN ENTERTAINER OF SOME KIND!
THEN AGAIN, SOME SORT OF ARCHEOLOGIST!
APPROPRIATION, UMMM A BIT TOO 80S!
PERHAPS I'LL JUST GO TO THE PUB!

Erlend Williamson[1]

Prelude: In Memory

Erlend Williamson was a particular artist who integrated the way he lived with his art-making, marking his travels with pink squares or temporarily posting short narratives within the places he passed through. Descriptions of his apartment have it filled with pink boxes of things he collected from his walks around London. The stuff he amassed was not necessarily typical of what you might imagine an artist to select from discard on the streets like unwanted signs or broken furniture—although he did that too, it was more the daily make up of garage—the nasty bits and pieces from tinfoil scraps to used condoms.[2] These objects formed stories, documenting the places

1 Williamson, Erlend, British Export, ELBA: Nijmegen, The Netherlands, 1994, exhibition handout published for the exhibition British Export.

2 Irvine, Jaki, "Somewhere: Talking with Mike... Thinking about Erlend", *Scum + Junk*, Retrieved 1 March, 2014. http://bak.spc.org/scumjunk/somewhere/index.html#heart.

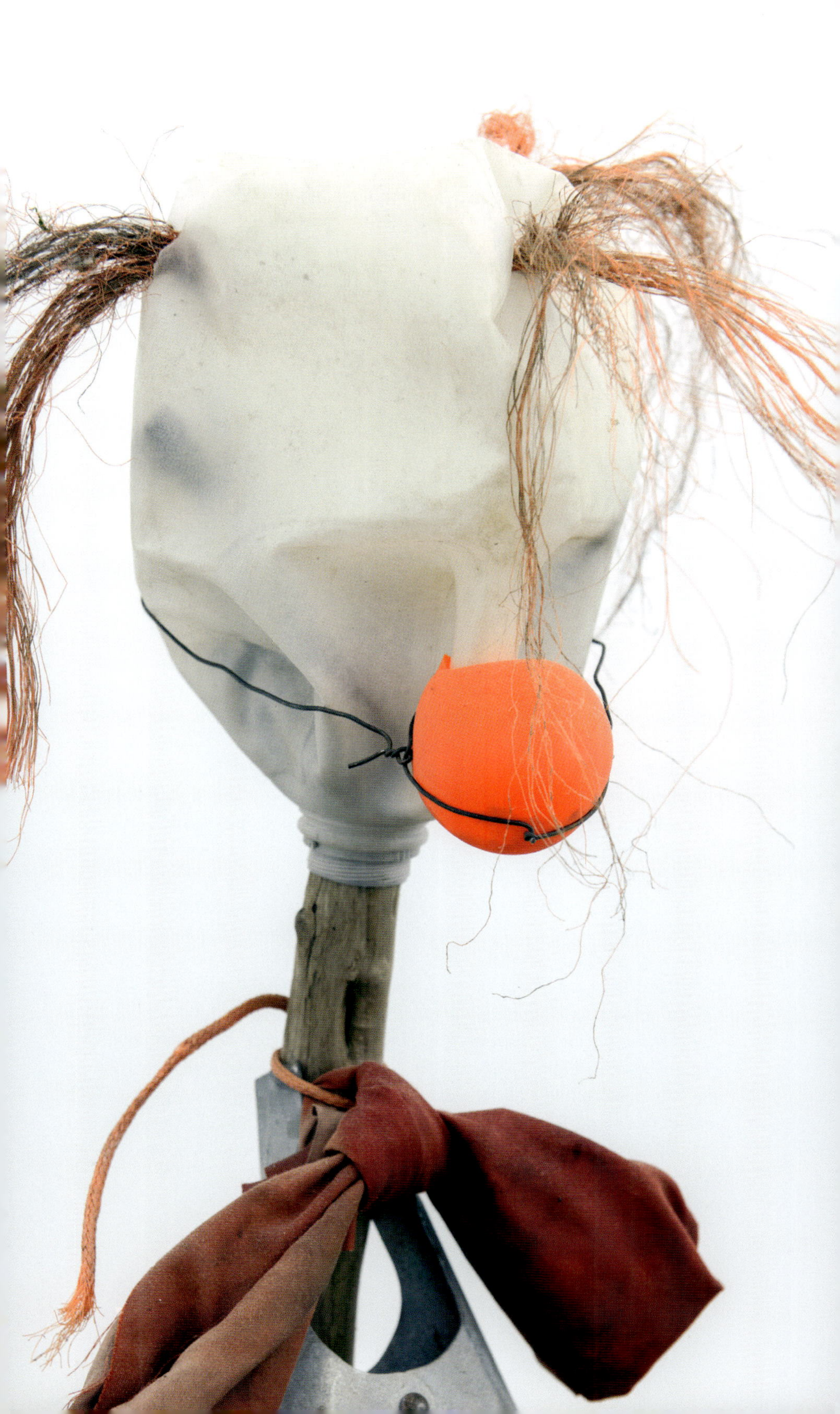

he traversed and functioned as evidence of how these places were used. The items were accumulated in recollection and anticipation of the arbitrary and planned journeys he'd take.

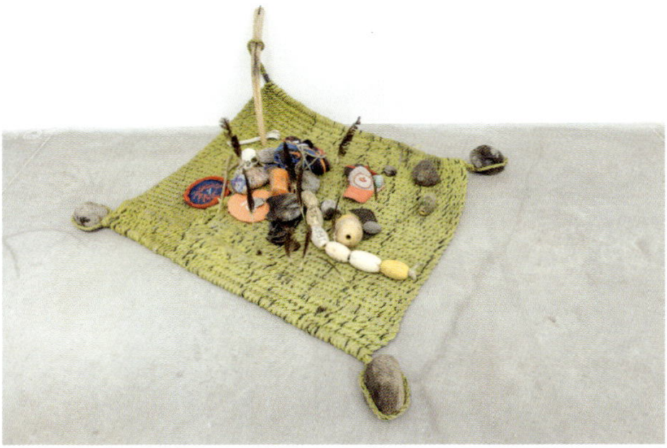

William Gilpin, a sculptural work by Williamson exhibited at Transmission Gallery, Glasgow in 1995 was a reconstructed minivan covered in hand-painted signs selling guided tours through South East London council estates and announcing crimes of racial and class violence mainly centred around car theft. The van was emptied of all seats but one and its windows were blacked out. On a monitor inside the van was a transferred super8 film of the artist touring the Scottish Highlands. Images of Williamson climbing mountains or snowboarding stood in contrast to the reassembled rickety vehicle covered in odd bombastic slogans, stating that their tours were "packed with adventure, enlightenment and sociological insight". A cassette played a loop of Williamson describing possible tours. While listening to his promotions one could read headlines proclaiming news such as "Bagshot Street Drive By" or "Violent Incident in the Dole Queue". There were also more detailed narratives that blamed the dull and soulless existence of living in Southeast London as the cause for car theft, joyriding, vandalism and death. This odd almost evangelistic vehicle, was truly destined for somewhere, but not necessarily a specific place. In an artist statement about this piece, Erlend states that the imagined tours are of... "[a] place that has become a nagging rootless placelessness permanently in recession."[3]

3 Williamson, Erlend, *Erl's Tours*, London, UK: Self-published pamphlet, 1995.

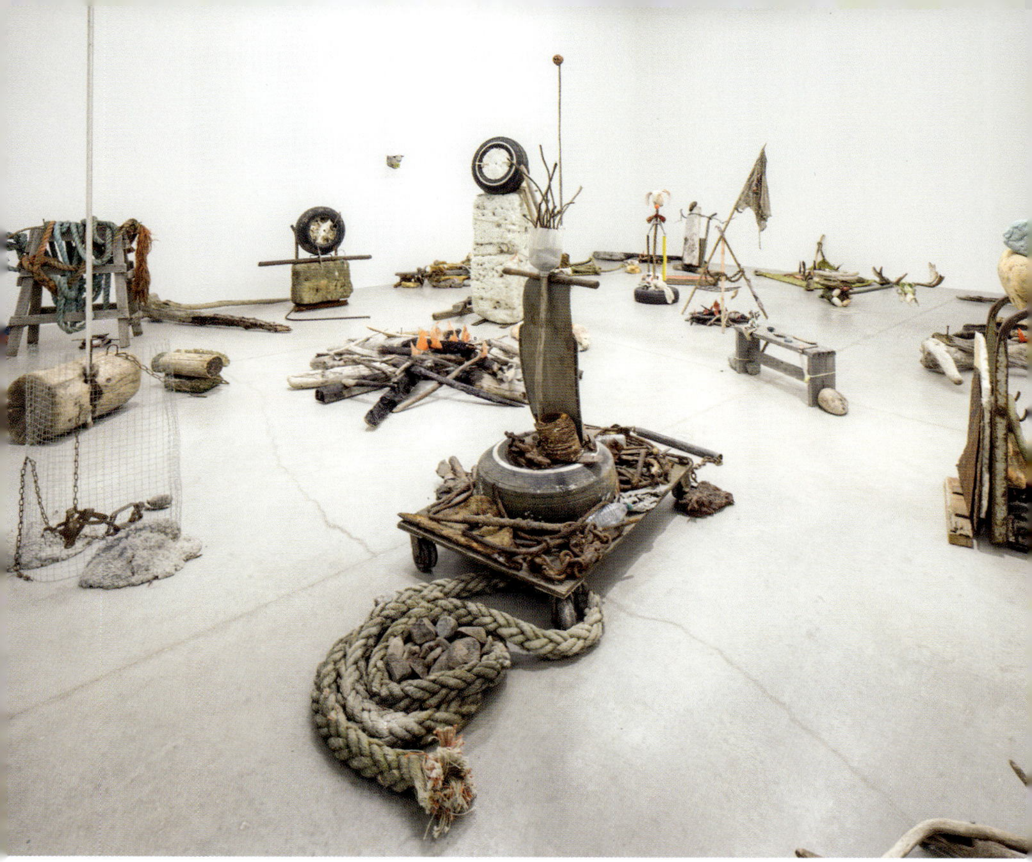

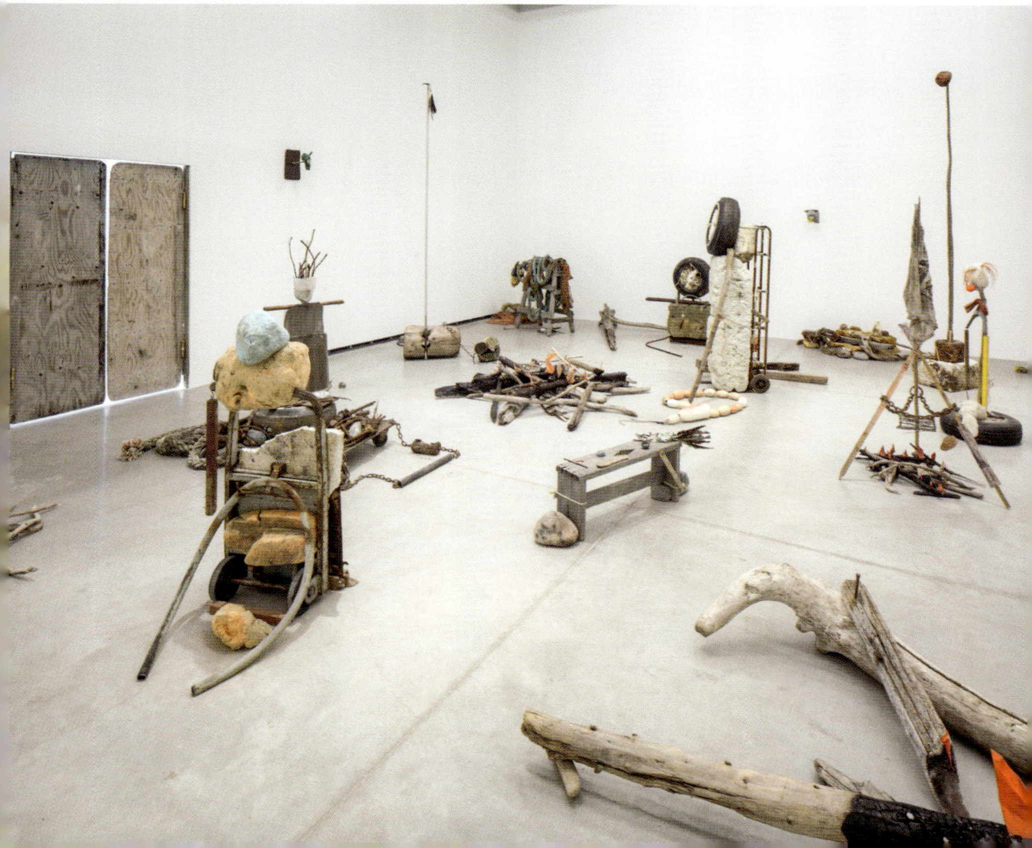

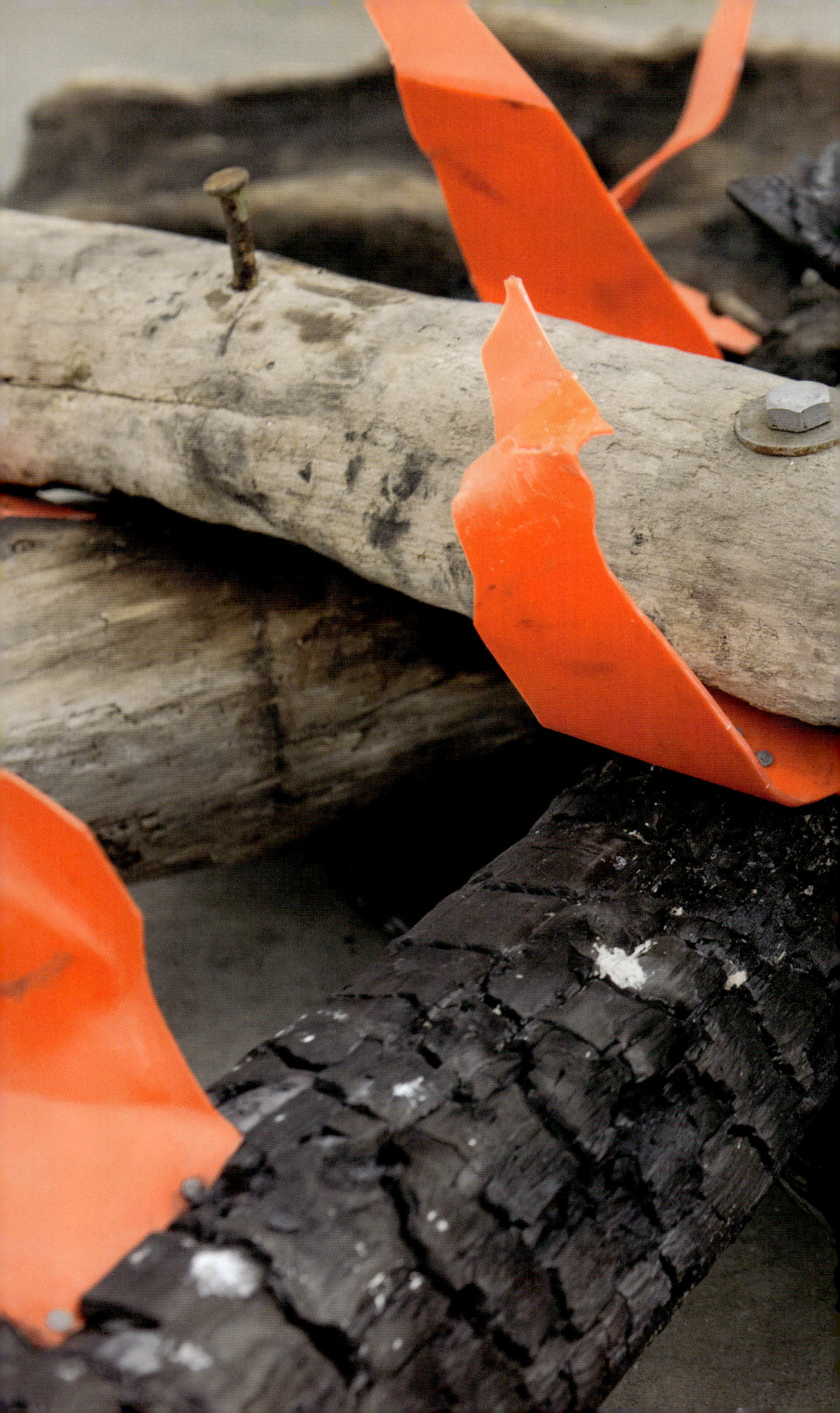

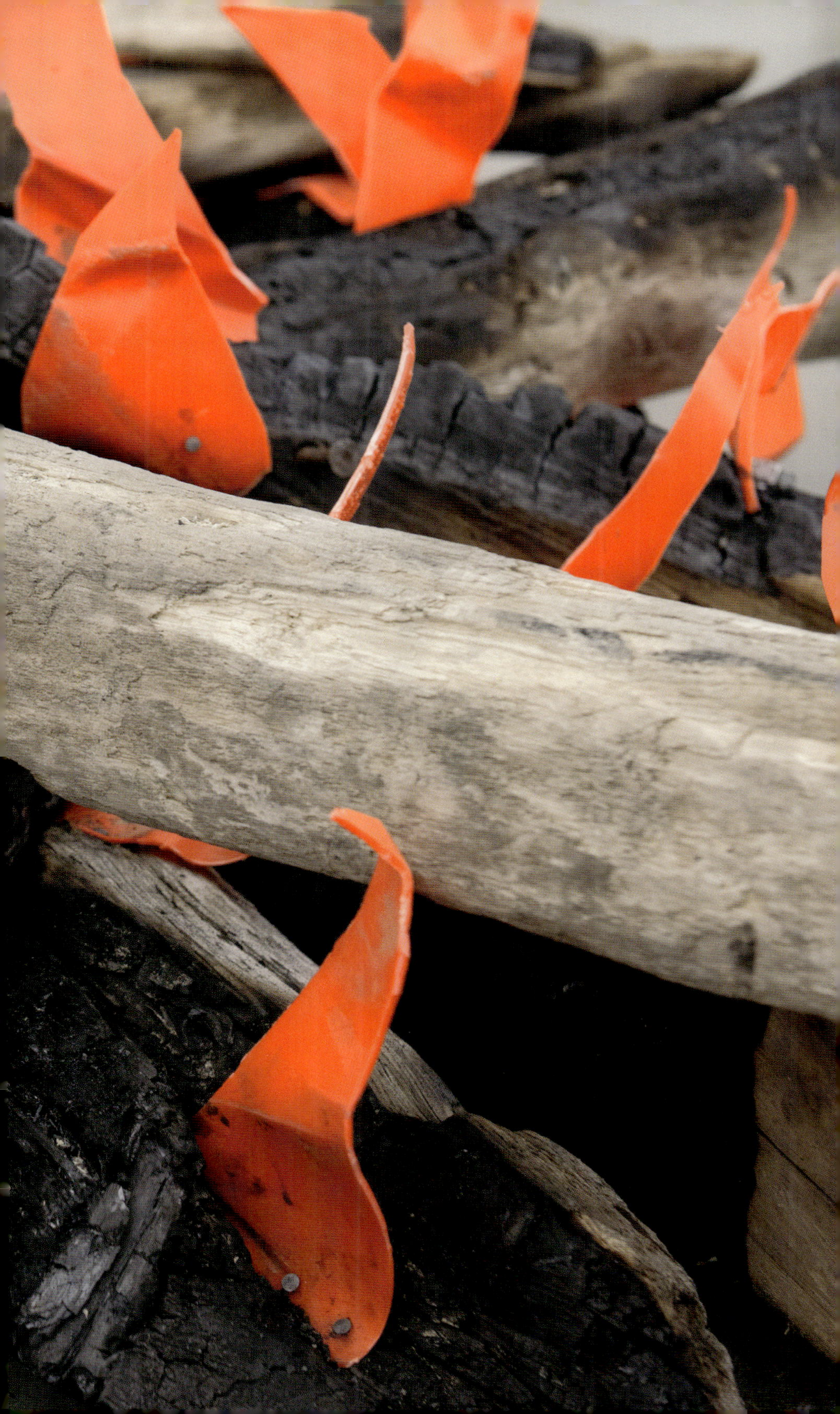

Erl's Tours were always going "somewhere"—a reoccurring theme and name of his tour van. In a pamphlet he made promoting his tours, he had mocking images of dreary tower blocks, a burned out car and a portrait of himself in a diaper with beer in hand. He offered a series of packaged tours from "Rear Window", which came with binoculars and the promise you'd witness violence and crime, to "You Fucking Little Shit", which ended in abuse and obscenities. His humour is apparent, but it is grounded in the realness of what he saw as London his home—a place he brought with him as stories of delinquency and death even when he left the city.

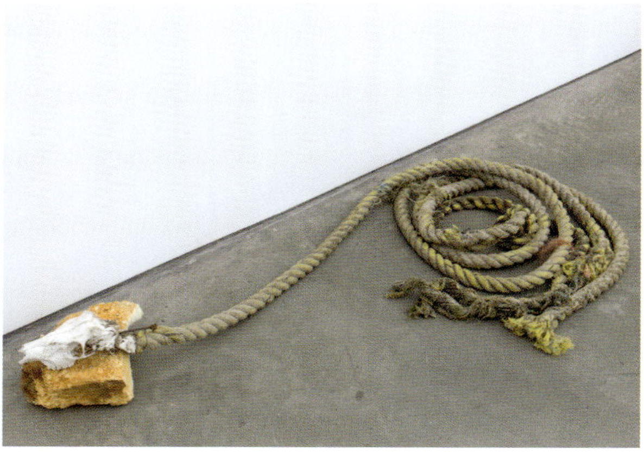

He was an avid climber and on his treks into the wilderness he would take time to adhere stories to rocks, signs, or barbwire fences using masking tape. He intentionally disrupted the serenity of the scene, making discord between experiences of being in nature with short, sometimes gruesome narratives that were most often fatally linked to vehicles. For example, "Nick was still unused to the powerful acceleration of the Golf GTI. He was even less accustomed to the incredibly narrow, winding roads of the remoter parts of the Scottish Highlands. The steep hairpin proved too much and Nick's first and only joyride ended in an uncontrollable descent into a dark hellish ravine where his broken and battered body lay unnoticed for several days." Stories such as Nick's, would temporarily sit out of place, unlikely to be encountered by anyone before the elements would degrade the tape, but this disjointed clash between expansive view and dark, mostly urban centred stories articulated—even if only briefly—a significant antagonism that prodded at the way space and place were consumed by tourists as leisure versus experiences born from boredom, poverty and failing municipal infrastructures.

This shift in context situates place and story in opposition. The picturesque, a term coined by the eighteenth century British art historian William Gilpin, and the characters, such as Nick, Suzie, Stephen or Jenny that run across Williamson's various works or situations that appear in his narratives cannot easily reconcile. Suzie's skill at stealing Porches, BMWs and Mercedes cars in relation to the Scottish Highlands or vacation tours in council blocks seem antithetical. They are at odds but unified as experiences by Williamson for an end that is incongruous and unclear. How do the calamities of theft and joyriding acquiesce with adventures into the wilderness? To what end did Williamson collide them? Like many of his Southeast London characters whose lives come to a tragic end, veering off winding roads at full speed or in head-on collisions of fatal car accidents, Williamson's life ended suddenly. The artist died while climbing *buachaille etive mor* in the Glencoe region of Scotland. It is believed that harsh winds blew him off the mountain where he fell 400 feet to his death.[4]

West Wind: Of Loss

I have not seen Williamson's work in person having come to know it through Mike Nelson who was his dear friend and colleague. Williamson was on his way to visit Nelson before his unexpected death. The two were part of a tight community of artist friends, having studied and previously exhibited together. Nelson speaks of Williamson as a collaborator and someone with whom he was in close dialogue. While grappling with the loss of his friend Nelson began production on *The Amnesiacs*, a complex narrative-based work that transformed into an ongoing sculptural project. The expression of his grief became intertwined with this new body of work, as a generative means for coping but also as a method to sort through, and cope with the general inability to share this experience of loss through language beyond platitudes and truisms. If we start to look at this work through its title, we are confronted with loss immediately, but it implies a notion of loss that is removed, somewhat fictional in itself. It is not a personalised loss, grander than forgetfulness, uncommon and more the credulity of pop fiction. Amnesia is a temporary loss, implying the potential for a return. Maybe it is a

4 Tinning, William, "Artist Falls 400 ft to Death While Climbing in Storm", *Herald Scotland*, 30 October 1996. Herald and Times Group, Scotland. Retrieved 1 March, 2014. http://www.heraldscotland.com/sport/spl/aberdeen/englishman-may-have-been-blown-off-glencoe-mountain-by-80mph-winds-artist-falls-400ft-to-death-while-climbing-in-storm-1.429008

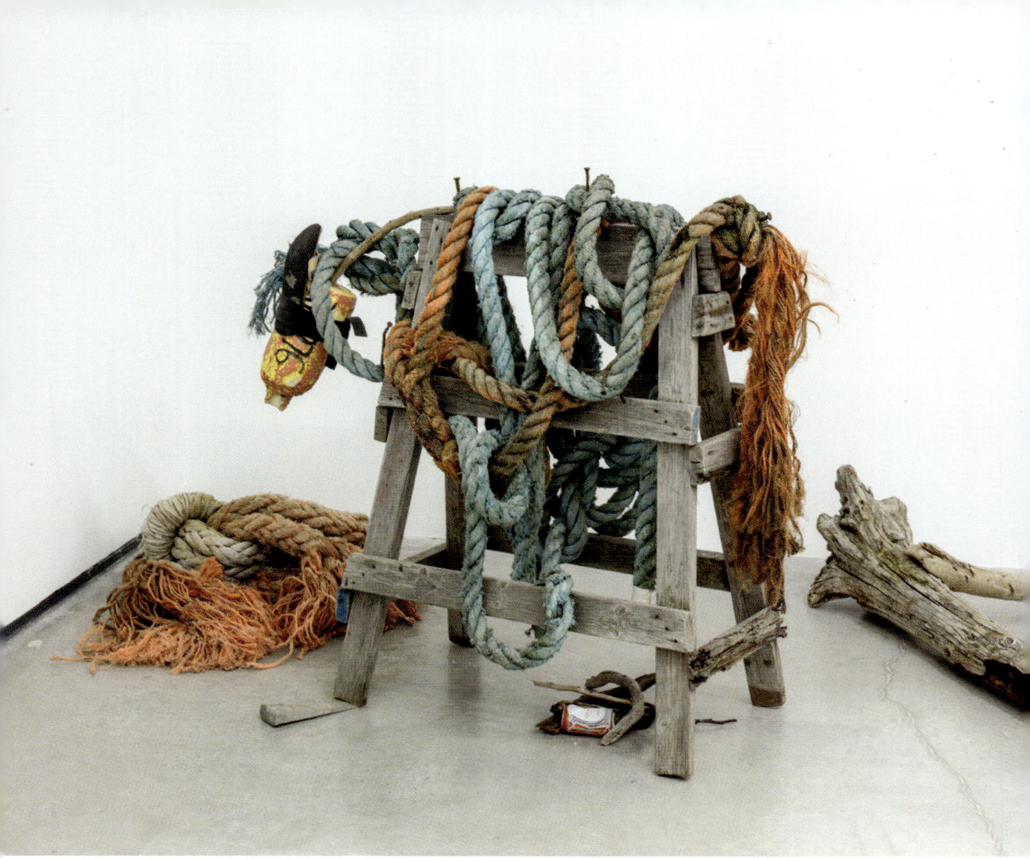

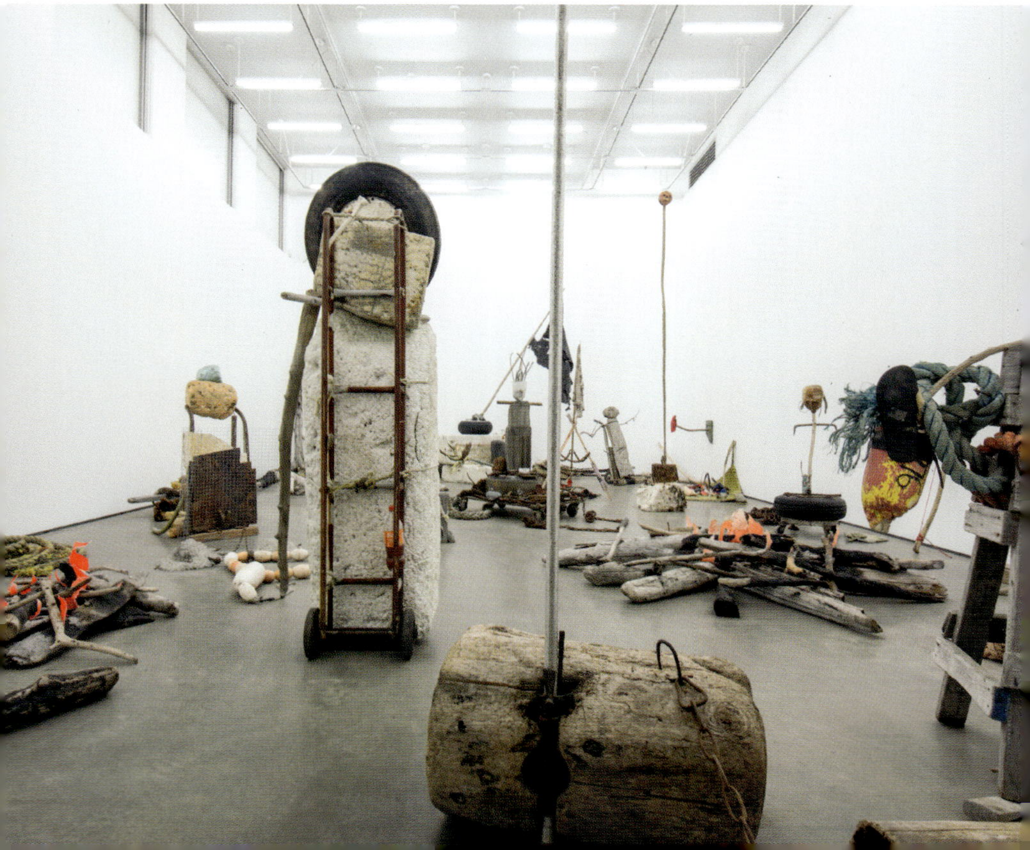

condition Nelson desired for himself in his bereavement, which he projected on to the work that expanded in form and content as he encountered the limitations of language to express such all-consuming emotions.

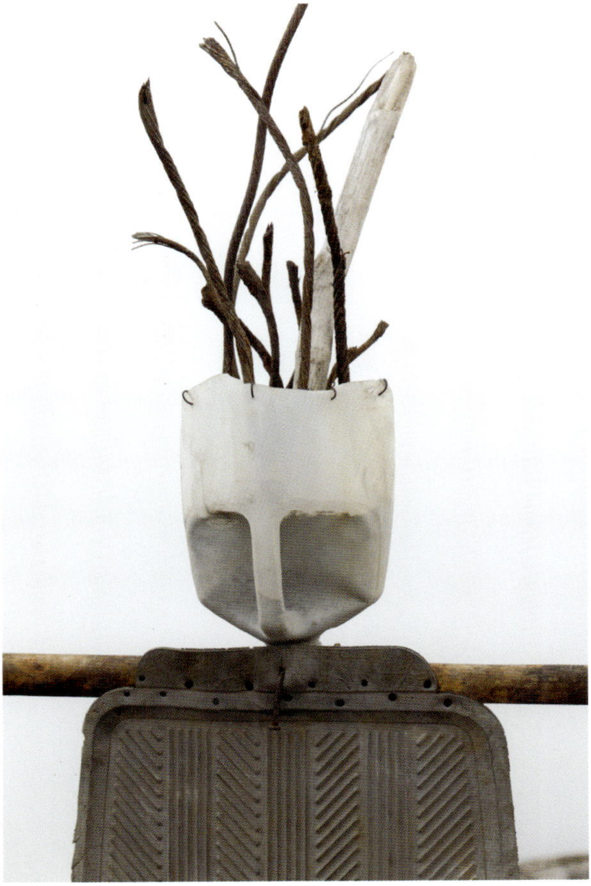

Before Williamson died, Nelson had a basic conceptual frame for a new body of work that started with a lone beachcomber, who the artist describes "as if plucked from a JG Ballard text, scouring the coastlines, interpreting the material cast out by the ocean like huge sentences". The underlying narrative borrowed heavily from the early 1960s science-

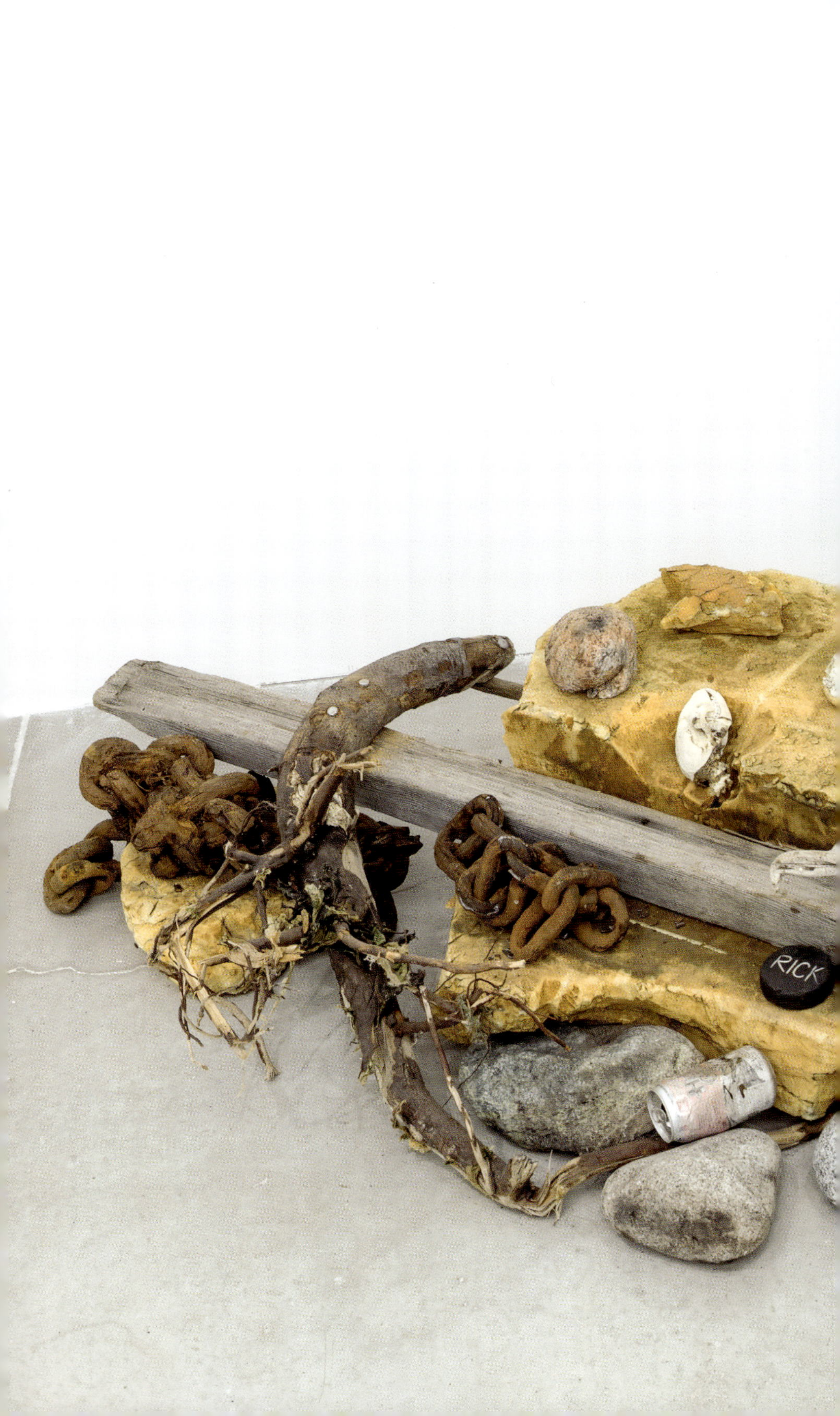
RICK

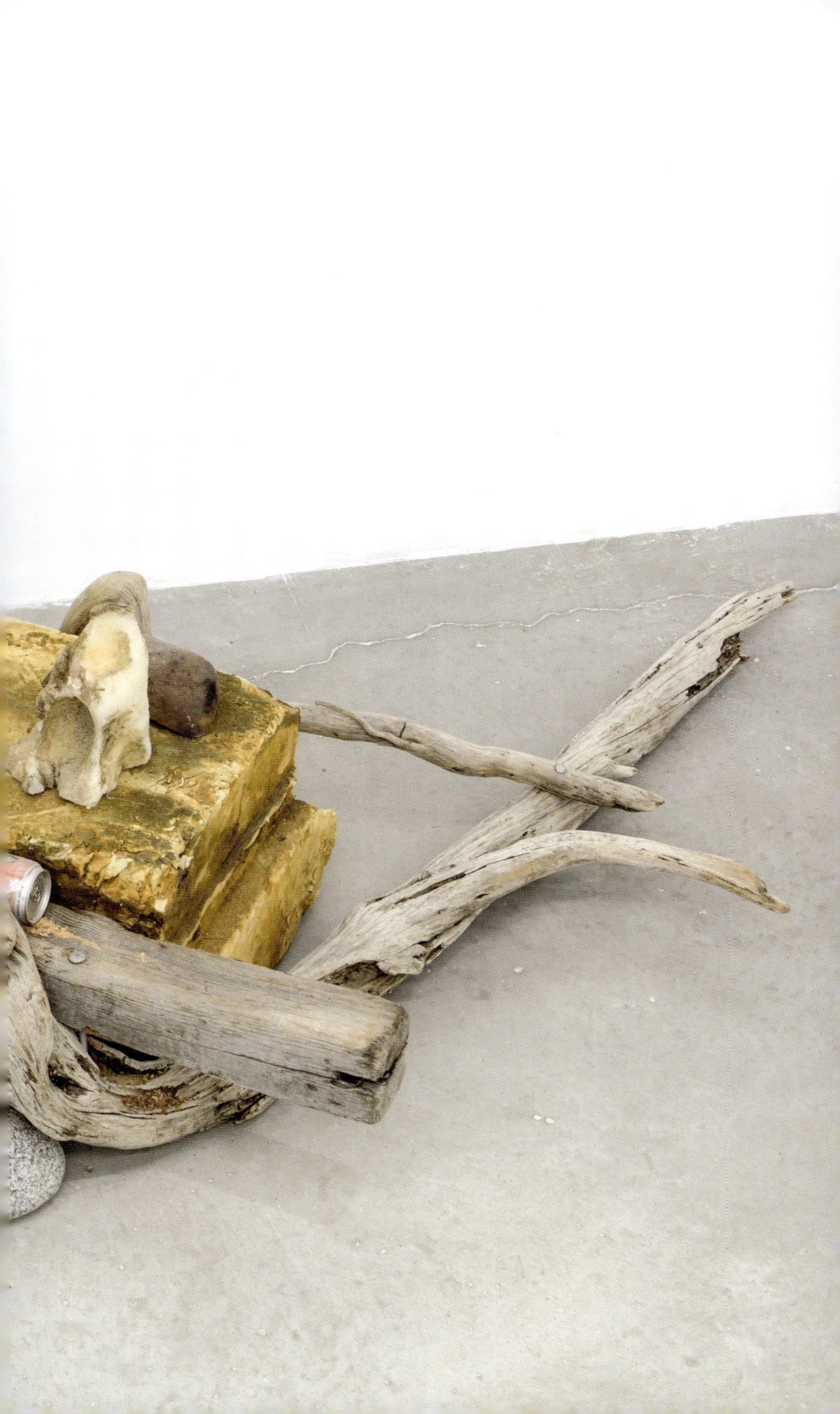

fiction novel *Solaris* by the Polish writer Stansilaw Lem. The original story is centred on the scientific observation of a planet that is mostly formed of a large oceanic mass. After decades of categorical research and only thorough aggressive means scientists learn that the water-like mass is a living sentient being. Yet, even after they recognised the oceanic form as intelligent, the scientists were unable to communicate with it. The potency of Lem's philosophical drive, which posits a barrier between human understanding and that of other beings, is taken up by Nelson as a metaphor for mankind's broader struggle to communicate.

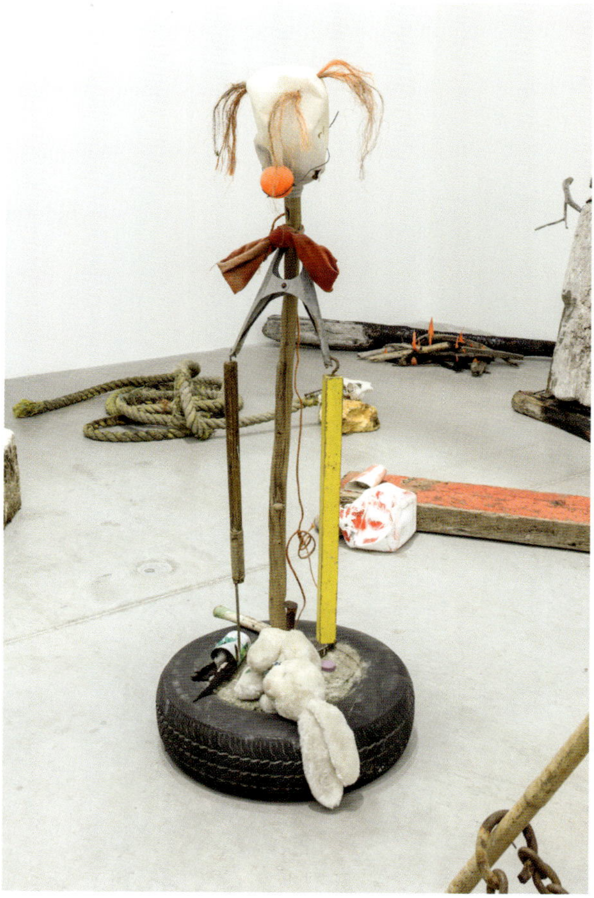

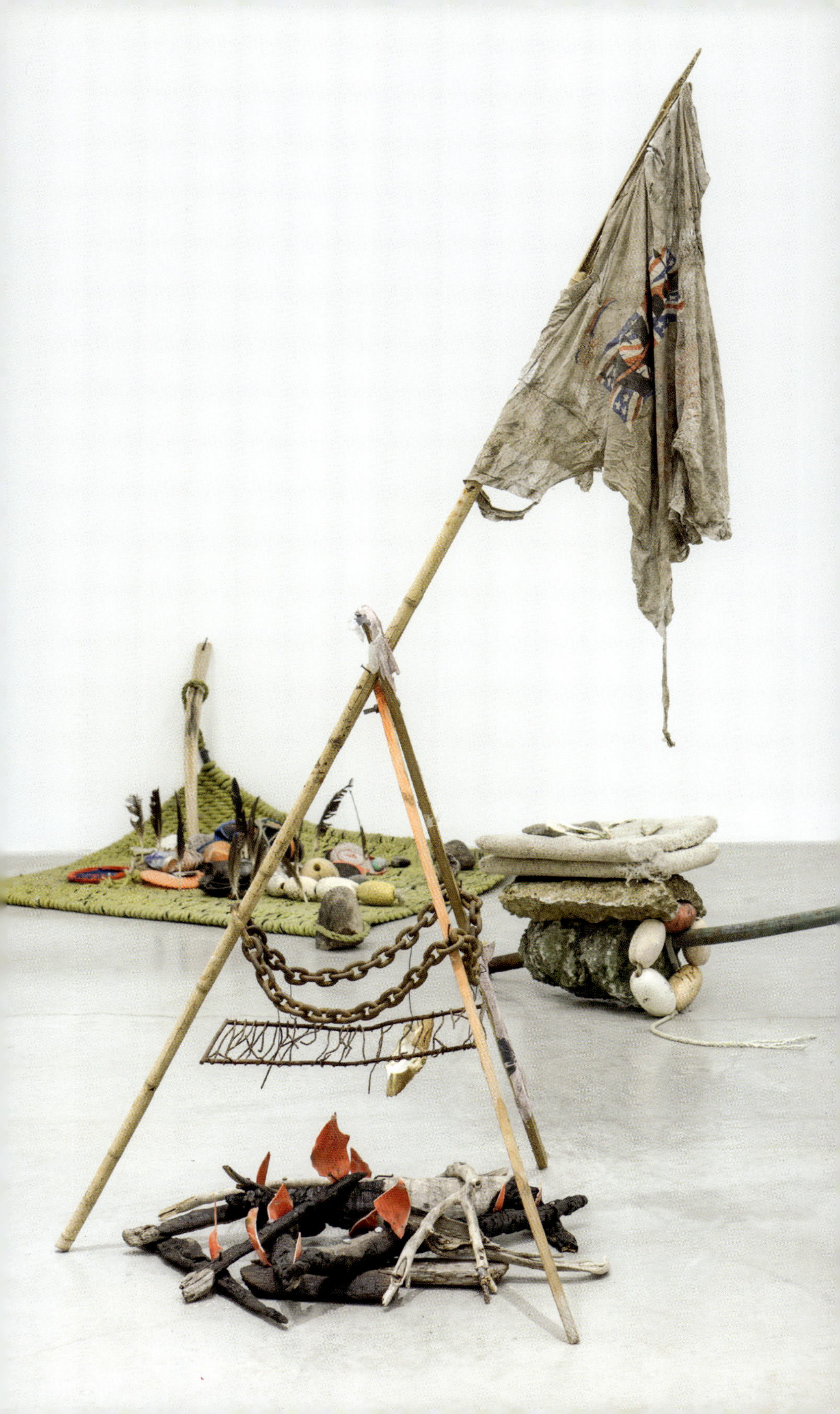

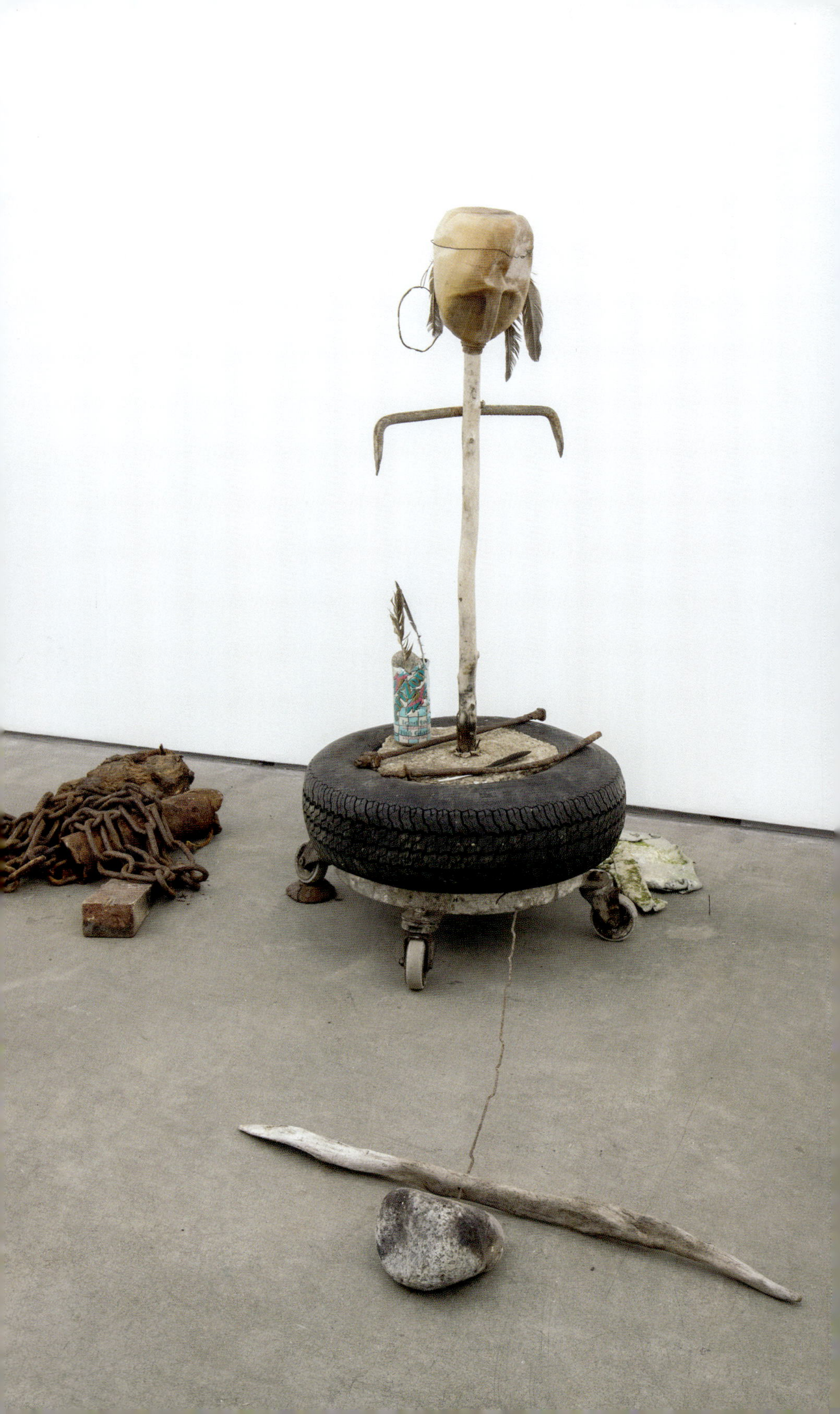

After Williamson's death *The Amnesiacs* were born. Nelson filtered the clichés of language into an odd cast of equally stereotypical characters who he banded together as interrupters, inciting a composite

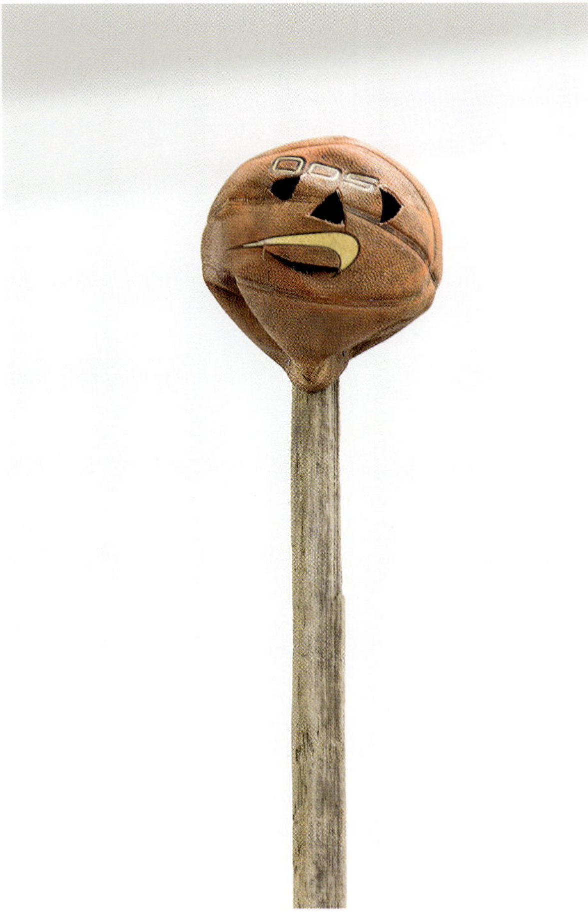

crew reminiscent of nomadic fur trappers, earlier American pioneers, beatniks and bikers. They were assembled in order to connect and decode the solitary beachcomber's debris. Nelson envisages these historically wrought wanderers as tackling the failure of syntactic language to interpret and express experiences of daily life from its monotony to its apexes. In *The Amnesiacs* words, sentences, paragraphs are mere generalisations unable to convey the complexity to uncover truths about our contemporary world and our place within it, rejecting language for its inadequacies. Instead of words these characters form assemblages of combined objects that when united reveal hidden meaning. It is through these objects, which have intent of their own, that understanding can begin. In giving shape to this mystic world of subcultures, Nelson is looking for indirect insight into his experiences that can't be paraphrased. There is no summation for *The Amnesiacs*'s task because it is constant and can only be built on, assembled and expanded. They are and their work is inexhaustible.

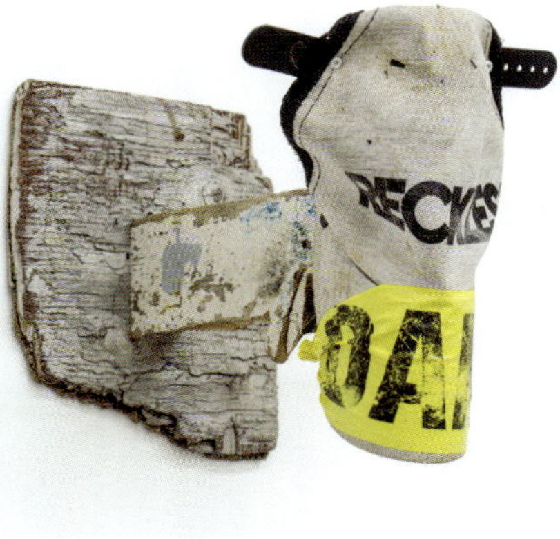

Since 1997, this work has taken many forms. [5] *The Amnesiacs* have assumed figurative shape, been housed in temporary chicken wire shelters filled with makeshift traps and cooking devices and warmed by bright pylon fires. They have had motorbikes, canoes and rafts. Shrines have been built for them. Some minimally constructed of wire, wood and plaster while others covered with detritus empty cans, used books, dirty dolls surrounded by crushed light bulbs. There is a repeating formal language that follows through *The Amnesiacs*, from wall mounted baseball hat animal head trophies, abandoned tires, driftwood fires, animal skeletons and frayed rope to simple constructions, stacked assemblages and basic

5 The series beginning in 1997 with the exhibition *Master of Reality* at Berwick Gymnasium Gallery, Berwick-upon-Tweed, UK and then as *The Amnesiacs* at Campbell's Occasionally, Copenhagen, Denmark.

figures whose form can be as simple as a leaning stick with a customised motorcycle helmet propped upon it.

For *Gang of Seven*, 2013, Nelson's latest revisiting of *The Amnesiacs* project he densely packed a generic white-cube gallery with a scatter of sculptural forms made from debris collected off the shores of British Columbia. In this new work he predicated the installation on figures who became the gang of seven—a parody and nod to the famed Canadian landscape painters. The Group of Seven, who like other North American subcultures typical to Nelson's frame of reference were romantic wanderers into the wild albeit a bit more tidy and tame, are commonly known to have trekked into the deep wilderness for their subject matter. Nelson's gang is definitely more ragtag than the historical group and less distinct than the early biker Amnesiac, but still rough and weather worn—more the type of the trapper and the pioneer. One gang member seems to have come directly from horror films made from a found red ball, upside down empty milk jug, some sticks, string, a metal hook and a tire filled with concrete.

These characters stood among several driftwood and ripped pylon fires now signature of *The Amnesiacs*. Nelson built several assemblages placing them around the room, one centred at the back was distinctly an iceberg made from blocks of ocean worn polystyrene foam. On it is was a large black flag hanging diagonally with a penguin made from a black and white plastic drum sitting on a yellow rubber glove. Filling the room were small assemblages from a workbench replete with tools and piles of rusty metal to a cooking apparatus for fires made from a tripod of metal rods wrapped with chain and an empty crab shell dangling from it. Three animal-like forms were also strewn about the room: a snake made from a large rope and a found animal skull; a pony fashioned from a wood trestle, mounds of rope with a worn foam buoy face; and a dragon-like creature built from a moldy moose skull and a gnarled signpost with a cement base balanced on stacked bits of carpet. All these elements positioned densely in the room created an even distribution of forms and shape that were unified in their material and proximity—the tight formation making viewers cognisant of their movements as if walking through a crowd.

Nelson's homage to the Group of Seven has a deeper more personal inference than I have stipulated above. There is a sentiment to this reference that brings us back to Williamson and loss. Among the many sculptural forms in *Gang of Seven*, behind the melting iceberg is a canoe. A tattered plank of driftwood tilted slightly with a stick and foam paddle

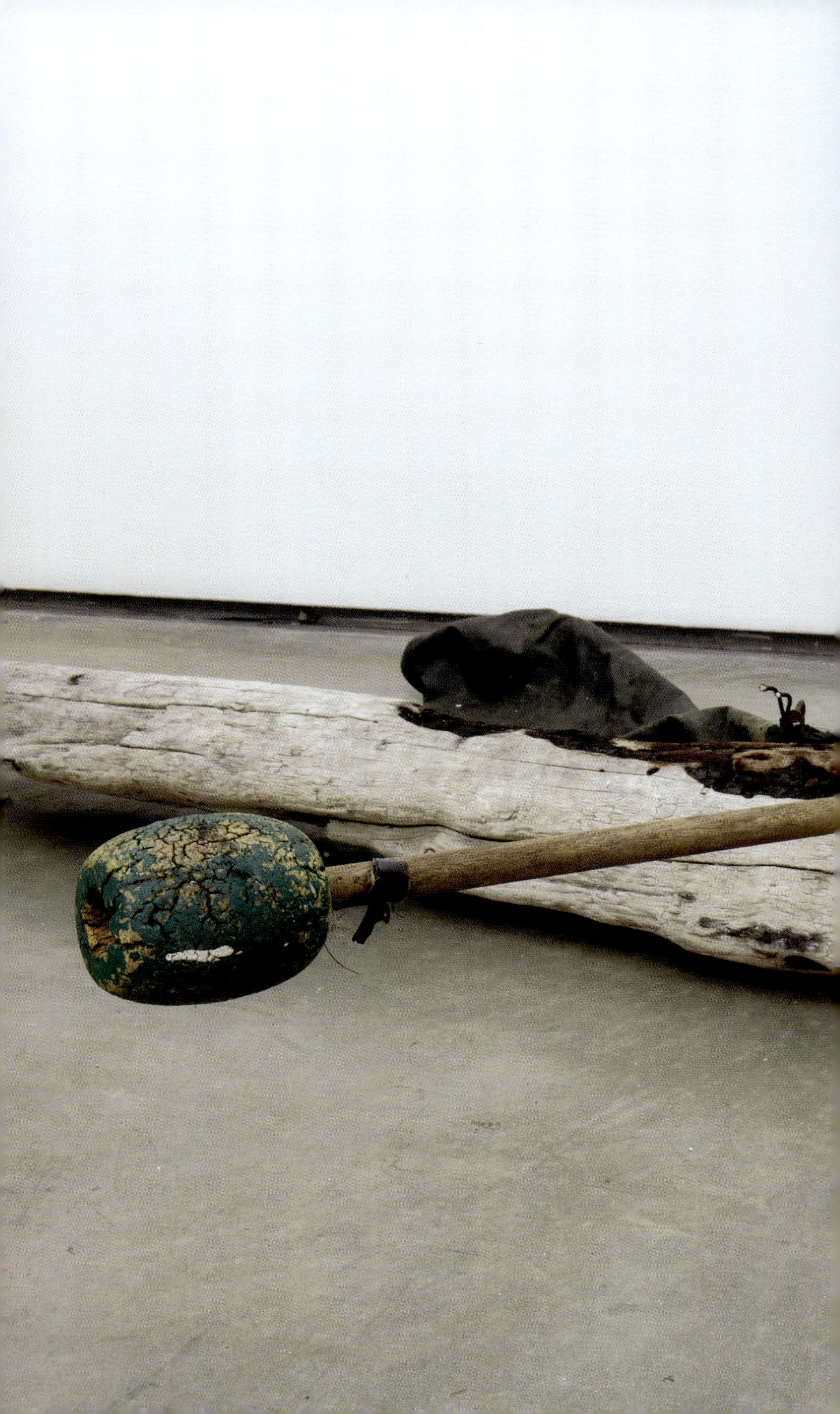

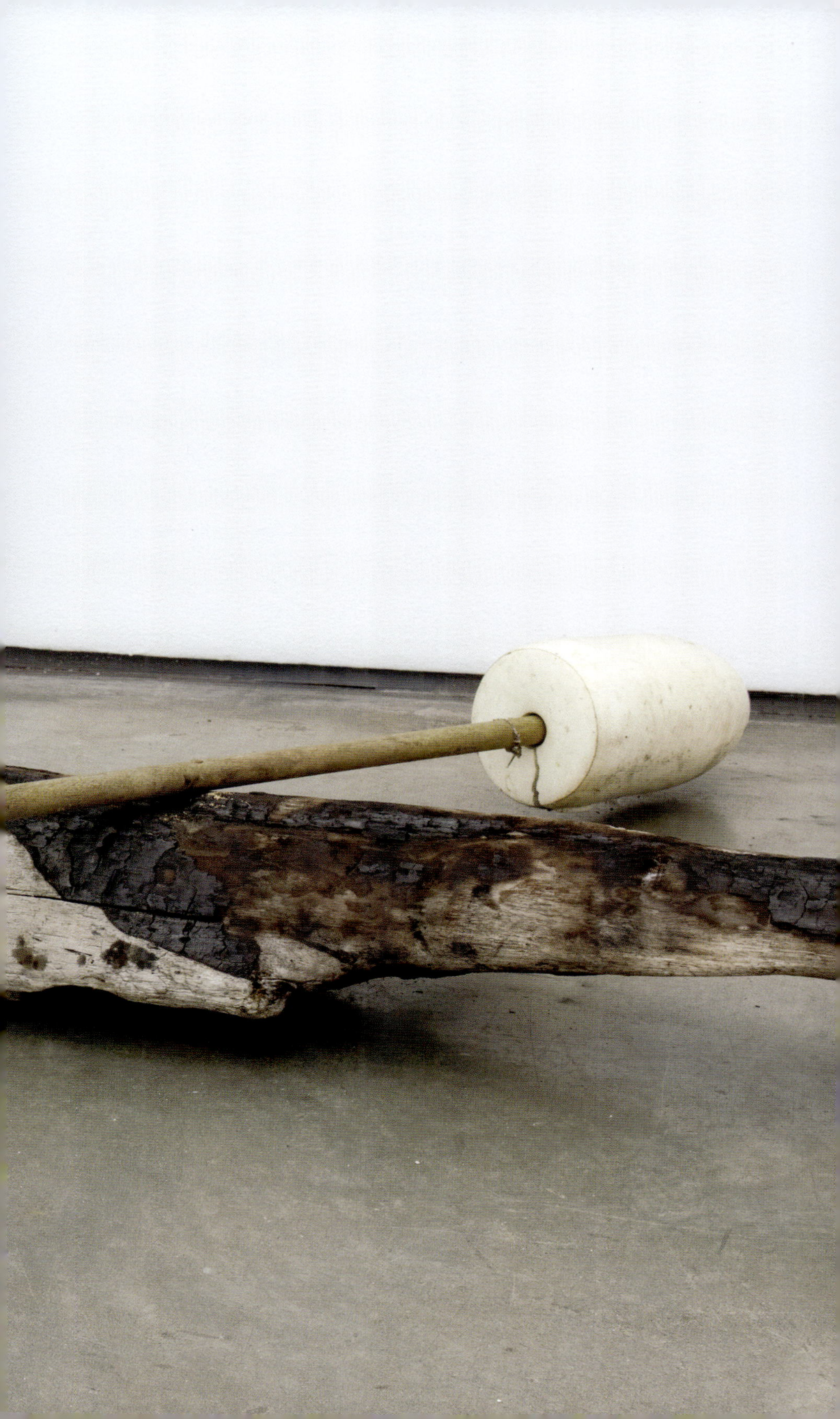

casually placed over it. This sculpture is a work that lay in homage to Tom Thomson, a beloved Canadian painter who even in his short life and only five year career had a great impact on the Group of Seven. He was never a member of the group but was part of its beginnings and influences. He died alone in 1917 in a canoe accident. There was some suspicion around his death, but most plausibly his life was claimed by natural forces.[6]

Several months before beginning production on *Gang of Seven* Nelson received word from the Erlend Williamson Foundation, an organisation established by Williamson's parents as a residency to support emerging artists and curators, that his friend's mother had recently passed away. With no other kin left the Foundation was sorting Williamson's personal effects. His belongings were sited to be destroyed unless a use could be found, which started Nelson thinking and led to his decision to incorporate his friend's possessions into this new incarnation of *The Amnesiacs*. Nelson went to the Orkney Islands, where Williamson's family had orginated and had returned to base the Foundation, to sort through the remnants of his late friend's life. Nelson describes Williamson's mother "as a strong obsessive woman who kept everything of Erlend's after his death", from clothes which included his childhood house coat to fan paintings of album covers he made in high school. For Nelson importing the objects to North America that once surrounded his friend has intimate implications but also goes beyond the personal. Moving these effects from an island off Scotland to Canada has its historical and political connotations of a not so distant colonial past where pioneers and settlers claimed land that wasn't necessarily theirs for the taking. But this time, Nelson incited a posthumous emigration of a person without a body to be raised in memory through a concatenation of objects as an Amnesiac. 13 boxes of Williamson's possessions, including climbing equipment and rope, old hiking boots, stacks of snapshots, old blankets, posters, notebooks and clothing made it to Vancouver, but they never became part of the *Gang of Seven*, instead Nelson incorporated them into another work, which initially sat across from and outside the saloon style doors that acted as the entrance into an Amnesiac's world. These things took on a form of their own, opening a new story and depicting a new fictional character that was conjured from Williamson's belongings but are nevertheless not him.

The objects Nelson collected from Orkney came to rest on a crafted freestanding shelf made up from irregular scraps of sea-beaten plywood, the silvered timber or peeling paintwork planks cut and slotted together and backed by larger oddments of plywood. The possessions lay somewhat casually displayed as if simply arranged on the wall-sized structure's many irregular shelves. For example, tucked up high on a thin and narrow ledge lies a rolled up piece of paper, resting on the shelf below are what appear to be folded curtains with a wool blanket still in its dry-cleaning bag on top of them; other shelves hold an unopened cardboard box, red wool socks, an old Nikon camera and tripod, folded clothes, odd toiletries, a bundle of tooth brushes, half-painted plastic models and fishing reels.... All of these items could still be in use, as if looking at the shelf was entering into the wardrobe of someone's home. Combined in this dimly lit display on the raw handmade structure, the contents portray a character. They seem the belongings of an outdoorsman staged and ordered museologically to represent a type as much as an individual.

No matter how personal the objects on display—whether it's a half used deodorant stick or piles of snapshots—they become codified, reflective of a generalised recluse who lives isolated and remote. They were Williamson's but to me as a viewer they represent him. With this new work Nelson has transformed his friend's possessions into those of an imaginary figure. The other side of this fabricated shelf is a seamless white screen on to which 35mm slides of the Canadian landscape are projected. Within each frame is a customary stone ring once used to contain fire. From Rocky Mountain House in Alberta and throughout southern British Columbia to its coast, Nelson took photographs of used stone fire rings. There is only one ring per photograph, usually sitting in the foreground of the image below the horizon line and often set within a vast landscape. These 80 images together with the shelf/screen and Williamson's belongings form *Eighty Circles through Canada (the last possessions of an Orcadian mountain man),* 2013.

Williamson's personal effects and the fire ring photographs can't be seen together. The viewer must walk around the personal effects or projection to see the other, but they insinuate the other. The man who owned these items and built this shelf took these photographs and vice versa. In a romantic vision the imagined photographer built every one of these rings, lighting a fire within it and laying claim to each site as a temporary hearth. The images ordered as if to trace the route of the photographer. And to take this romance further he is an artist—the aesthetic value of the images moving beyond mere document or typographical research. The fire rings become circles and as repetitive geometric markings in their repetition set in remote places they allude to the work of the British land artist Richard

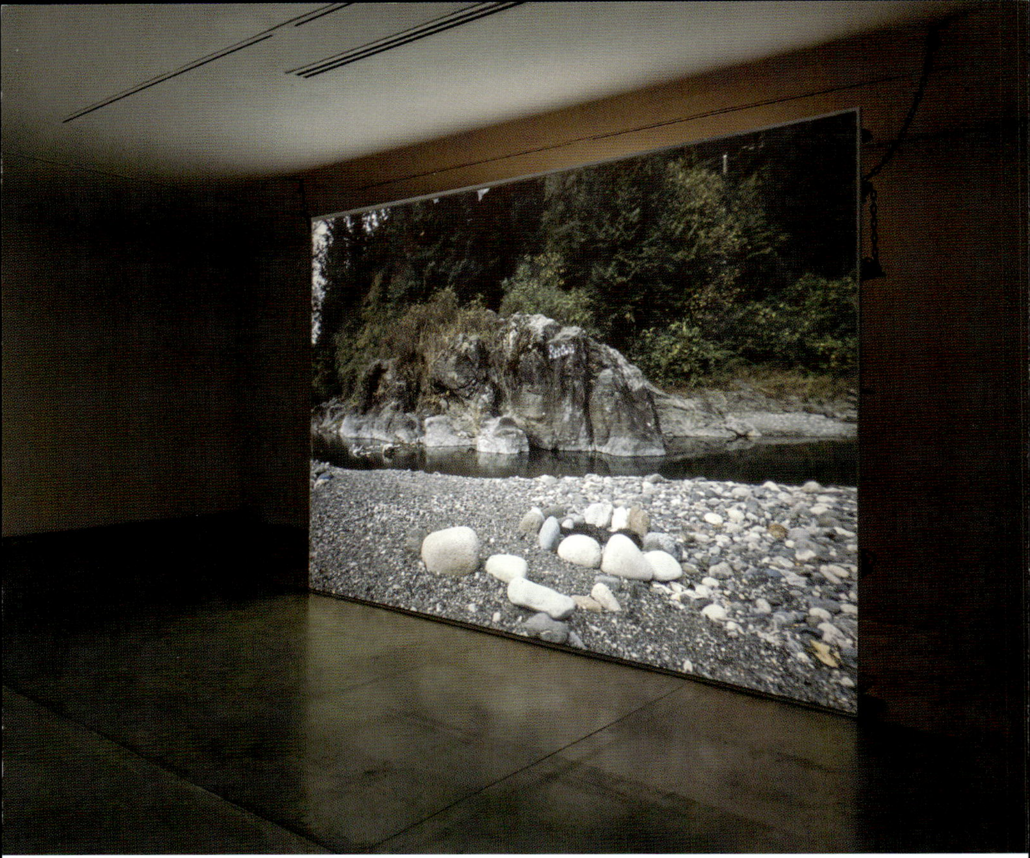

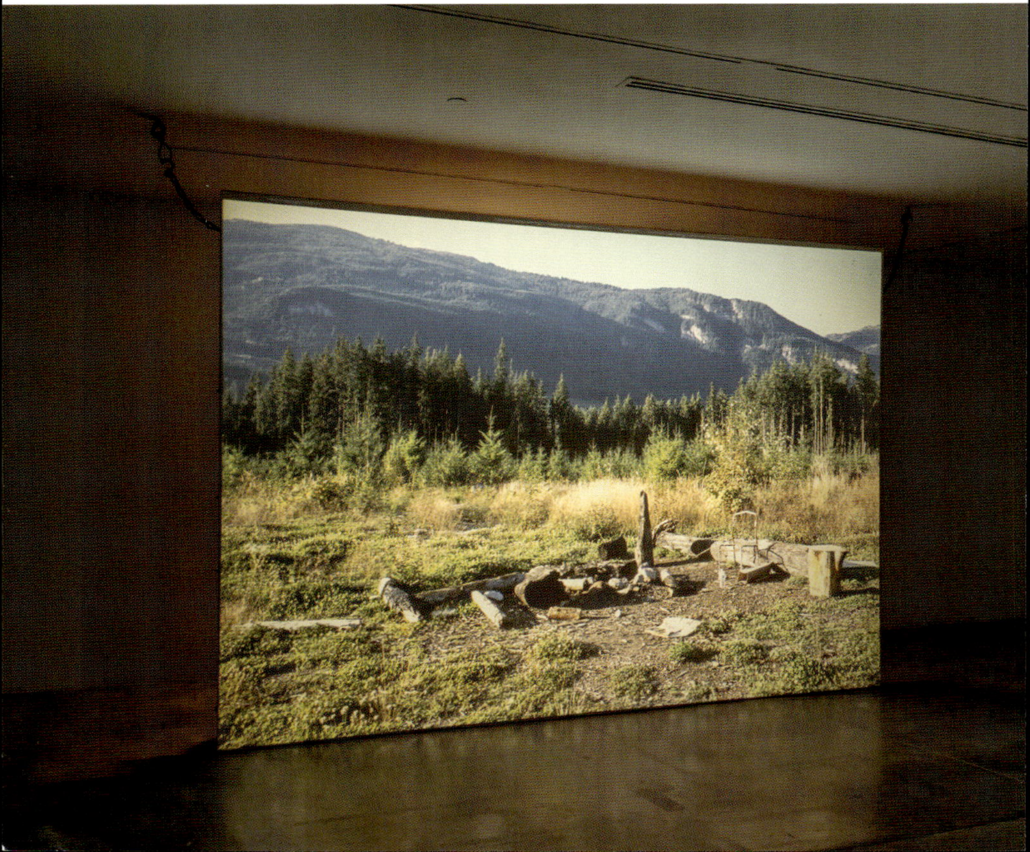

Long. Long often marked his walks into the landscape with distinct geometric forms, photographing them on site as well as collecting materials along his way which he often used to construct basic shapes in gallery and interior spaces. In the case of Long his mark-making affirms the humanness of his scale in the landscape muted yet in control. In Nelson's images the circles capture traces of humans occupying the landscape anecdotal stories almost akin to Williamson's masking tape texts—and remnants of a Gilpinesqe tourism that he would have appreciated. The incentives of Long lies more of a transcendental nature where the specificities of his encounters with the landscape can be universalised, while Nelson and Williamson are grounded in the everyday through storytelling. Nelson's story is formed by the assemblage of staged objects with images, but is not reiterated as concrete. There is no beginning or end. The story is circular like the rings.

The conceptualisation of *Eighty Circles through Canada*... is linked to Long's romance with the landscape and in his need to have influence on it. In Nelson's work there is a utilitarian taming that is connected to the imaginations of early settlers and pioneers—one that prefaces a colonialist claiming of the land. The initial idea to make a 35mm slide work began with a visit to the Museum of Anthropology in Vancouver where Nelson encountered a sequence of slides by the Canadian anthropologist Wilson Duff's family trips across British Colombia between 1957 and 1972. His vacation slides through the coast and interior of British Columbia showed aboriginal festivals or visits to workshops of totem pole carvers. His children were sometimes caught in the frame but rarely the focal point of the images, which tracked the family's holiday but were focused on First Nation's use of the land. Duff's images resonated with Nelson as much if not more than the artefacts in the museum as a language that needed to be unravelled. They were of a time and place—representative of traditions that were tied to the land, but already temporally displaced as a document of a distant present that portrayed the anthropologist's historical research of North West Coast aboriginal peoples. Movement is essential to Duff as its impact on aboriginal culture is the subject of his studies and for Nelson a reflective point on how the colonialist eye is still perceptible; how this documented movement across a vast landscape locates the past while giving substance to the present as one navigates the terrain, intervenes, interprets and lays claim to it. The landscape comes to signify the people who use it.

The reoccurring characters that underlie *The Amnesiacs* are born of North America. The pioneers, settlers, fur traders, loggers, gold rush miners, warring Indians exist from this history or representations thereof. Nelson draws out these stereotypical characters, hyperbolically exemplifying their brutish masculine relationship to the land, overplaying their solitary isolation and drawing them into the twentieth and twenty-first centuries, adding other outsider types such as the biker and survivalists to this odd crew. Grouped together through the filter of a science fictional lens they become unified, somewhat homogenised.

Nelson's omnipresence, his process, the historical references and the memory of a lost friend draw attention to the collision between the real and fictive, making a distinction between the biography of the artist and his friend while perpetuating the imaginations of an elusive character. Whether it is the artist or the outdoorsman traversing the landscape, Williamson is intertwined in these two recent works by Nelson. Connecting them is *Untitled (intimate sculpture for a public space),* 2013, a solitary sculpture made of one of Williamson's old nylon sleeping bags, which lies flat on the ground covered with a customised clear five-sided Plexiglas box. The box sits two feet high with a small slit to one side of the top just big enough to put coins through. As the coins accumulate at the head of the sleeping bag they imply a figure. It is a donation box and an intimate memorial to Williamson. There is a descriptive power in this simple work in its sarcophagus form with its lack of a physical body, but slow collective building of one that balances absence with presence. Nelson's loss of a dear friend surfaces and disappears. For the most part this experience is withheld as other more familiar characters who were defined in different times and under different frames of reference come to the foreground, but in having these three works together Williamson stays floating as a plurality between them, only partially, but in relation to them all.

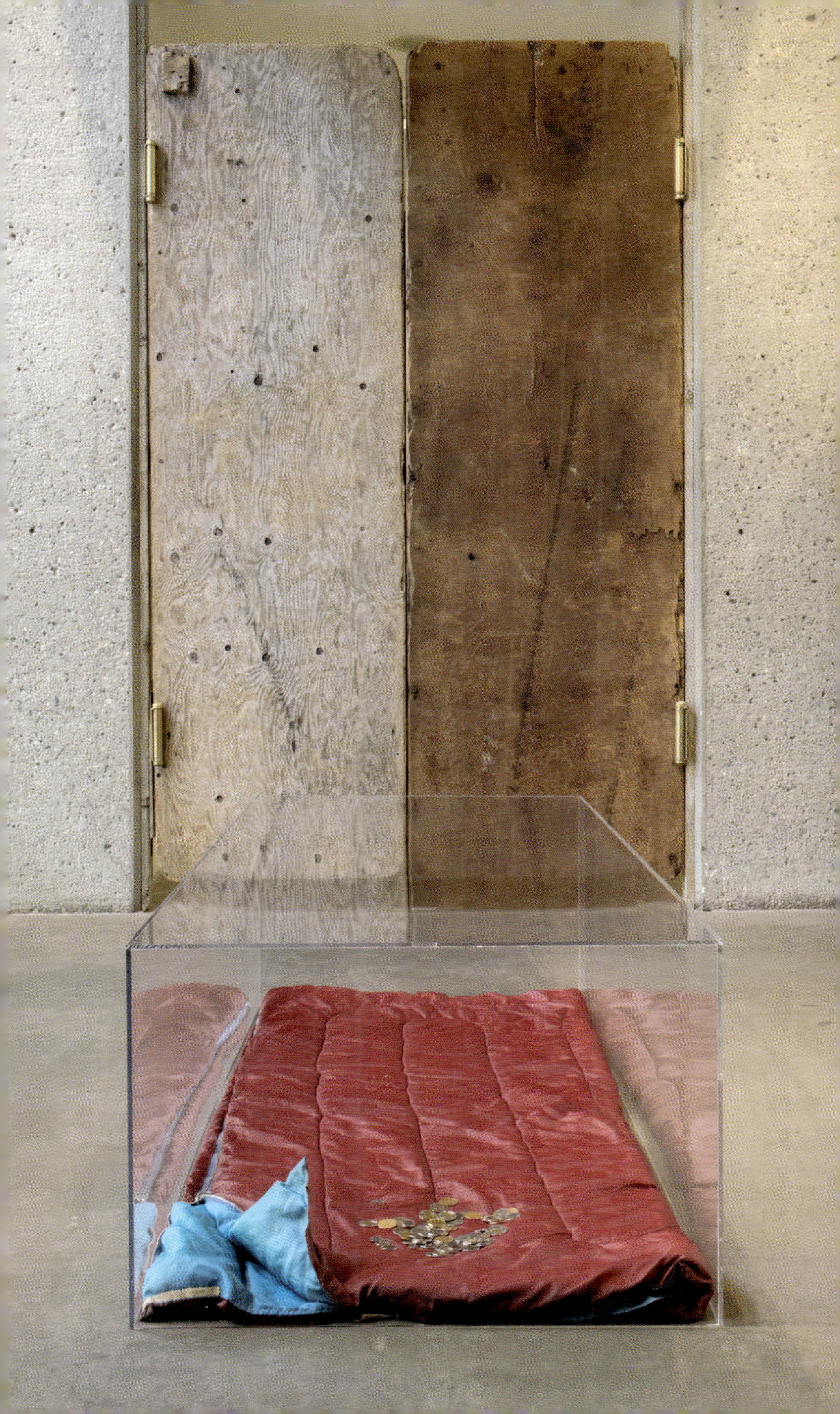

Nelson Algren wrote about them in *A Walk on the Wild Side*, but that story was told before they crossed the Rockies. Dove Linkhorn son of Crazy Fitz, went to hustle for his fortune in New Orleans. Ten years later he would have gone to Los Angeles.

Algren's book opens with one of the best historical descriptions of American white trash ever written.* He traces the Linkhorn ancestry back to the first wave of bonded servants to arrive on these shores. These were the dregs of society from all over the British Isles – bums, misfits, criminals, debtors, social bankrupts of every type and description – all of them willing to sign oppressive work contracts with future employers in exchange for ocean passage to the New World. Once here, they endured a form of slavery for a year or two – during which they were fed and sheltered by the boss – and when their time of bondage ended, they were turned loose to make their own way.

WHILE Texan pioneers and Santa Fe traders were beginning their assault on the Mexican borderlands, another band of frontiersmen—the fur traders—were blazing their trails into the heartland of the Far West. Their hour of glory was brief; the trade flourished only between the mid-1820's and the early 1840's. But during those years the fur trappers played a heroic role in opening the land to more permanent settlers. Theirs was the task of spying out fertile valleys that needed only man's touch to yield bountiful harvests, of spreading word of the West's riches throughout the Mississippi Valley, of pioneering routes through mountain barriers, and of breaking down the self-sufficiency of the Indians by accustoming them to the firearms and firewater of civilization. When their day was done all the Far West was readied for the coming of the pioneer farmers.

It would not be fair to say that all motorcycle outlaws carry Linkhorn genes, but nobody who has ever spent time among the inbred Anglo-Saxon tribes of Appalachia would need more than a few hours with the Hell's Angels to work up a very strong sense of *déjà vu*. There is the same sulking hostility towards 'outsiders', the same extremes of temper and action, and even the same names, sharp faces and long-boned bodies that never look quite natural unless they are leaning on something.

Most of the Angels are obvious Anglo-Saxons, but the Linkhorn attitude is contagious. The few outlaws with Mexican or Italian names not only act like the others but somehow look like them. Even Chinese Mel from Frisco and Charley, a young Negro from Oakland, have the Linkhorn gait and mannerisms.

If the speech of the Mountain Men showed the corrosive influence of their environment, so did their mental attitudes reveal their reversion toward savagery. Their philosophy of life was based on the uncertainty of survival; men could live in the wilderness only by inuring themselves completely to hardship and misfortune. "They become," wrote one who had lived among them, "callous to any feeling of danger, and destroy human and animal life with as little scruple and as freely as they expose their own." [19] Death was so commonplace in a land where danger lurked at every turn that there was no mourning for the dead in the mountains; when a trapper heard that a friend had been killed he would only shrug his shoulders and say, "Poor fellow!

for the dead in the mountains; when a trapper heard that a friend had been killed he would only shrug his shoulders and say, "Poor fellow! Out of luck." Joe Meek, a famous mountaineer, was hunting buffalo when one of the party was thrown from his horse amidst the trampling herd. Joe was told to ride to his friend's rescue.

"What'll I do with him if he is dead?" he asked. - 53

"Can't you pack him to camp?"

"Pack hell," Joe objected. "I should rather pack a load of meat." There was nothing disrespectful in that remark. Joe only reflected an attitude normal among men who lived constantly under the shadow of death. "Live men war what we wanted," he explained to a friend later; "dead ones war of no account." [20]

Algren called them 'fierce craving boys' with 'a feeling of having been cheated'. Freebooters, armed and drunk – a legion of gamblers, brawlers and whorehoppers. Blowing into town in a junk Model-A with bald tyres, no muffler and one headlight . . . looking for quick work, with no questions asked and preferably no tax deductions. Just get the cash, fill up at a cut-rate gas station and hit the road, with a pint on the seat and Eddy Arnold on the radio moaning good back-country tunes about home sweet home, that Bluegrass sweetheart still waitin', and roses on Mama's grave.

Algren left the Linkhorns in Texas, but anyone who drives the Western Highways knows they didn't stay there either. They kept moving until one day in the late 1930s they stood on the spine of a

p. 163 H.A
HST

scrub-oak California hill and looked down on the Pacific Ocean – the end of the road. Things were tough for a while but no tougher than they were in a hundred other places. And then came the war – fat city, big money even for Linkhorns.

When the war ended, California was full of veterans looking for ways to spend their separation bonuses. Many decided to stay on the Coast, and while their new radios played hillbilly music they went out and bought big motorcycles – not knowing exactly why, but in the booming, rootless atmosphere of those times, it seemed like the thing to do. They were not all Linkhorns, but the forced

Half-civilized, half-savage, these were the men of brave and reckless breed who brought the western fur trade to its height—and decline—during the 1830's. Few eras have produced beings as free as they, for neither society nor their consciences imposed restraints upon them. "They had," wrote one who knew them, "little fear of God and none at all of the devil." [27] Utterly the masters of their own lives, they could trap or hunt, sleep or wake, wander or camp, kill or forgive, as the whim of the moment dictated. Yet they had scarcely entered upon the scene when forces began to take shape that would soon degrade them to mere pawns in the hands of men whose might was based on wealth rather than brawn. For the early profits of the trade inevitably attracted to the Far West great capitalists from the East, each anxious to monopolize the traffic in furs and each determined to do so by fair means or foul. 55

The transformation of the Hell's Angels from a motorcycle gang to an international drug traffi-

The transformation of the Hell's Angels from a motorcycle gang to an international drug trafficking network is a masterpiece of business ingenuity greased with sweat and blood. The Angels decide early to concentrate their efforts on LSD, PCP and methamphetamine. They make the drugs in clandestine laboratories and control the distribution network from wholesalers to street-level pushers. It' secure

Yet the fur trade lived on for one brief but romantic interval. Its center, after 1840, was no longer the heart of the Rockies, but in a number of trading posts that were built along the fringes of the moun- 65

[40] Annie H. Abel (ed.), *Chardon's Journal at Fort Clark, 1834–1839* (Pierre, S.D., 1932), pp. 124–125.

[41] Asahel Munger, "Diary of Asahel Munger and Wife," *Oregon Historical Quarterly*, VIII (1907), 395.

p. 65

tain country. Strategically located at points where they could be sup-

The Big Four outlaw motorcycle gangs claim to be the one percent of motorcyclists who won't conform to society's laws and morals. They are guided by their own code of terror. They strive to maintain their reputation as outlaws by instilling in people a fear they interpret as respect. The gangs keep members in line and eliminate the opposition with squads of killers: the Hell's Angels' Filthy Few, the Outlaws' SS, the Pagans' Black T-shirt squad, and the Bandidos' Nomad chapter.

66 Of the 150 posts that were operating or had been recently abandoned in 1843, three played an especially important role in the later history of the trade. One was Fort Hall, which, as the Hudson's Bay Company's principal eastern outpost, dominated the traffic in furs in the western Rocky Mountain country. Another was Fort Laramie on the upper Platte River. Built in 1834 as a way station for caravans by the Rocky Mountain Fur Company, and later used for the same purpose by the American Fur Company, this stoutly built fort for many years controlled the trade of the central Rockies. To the south lay the third outpost, Bent's Fort, which was completed in 1833 near the junction of the Arkansas and Purgatory rivers by the brothers William and Charles Bent and their partner, Céran St. Vrain. The most elaborate of all the posts, Bent's Fort was surrounded by adobe walls fifteen feet high and seven thick at the base, enclosing an oblong court 100 by 180 feet, and surmounted by bastions thirty feet tall. Within the court were trading rooms, warehouses, homes for the officers, and a two-story recreation center containing a billiard room and bar; nearby was a corral enclosed by adobe walls that were planted on the top with cacti to prevent scaling, and an icehouse that was filled from the frozen river each winter.[42]

Reeseman is one of the club's biggest methamphetamine

the frozen river each winter.[42]

Cheeseman is one of the club's biggest methamphetamine producers on the East Coast. He has a moveable lab he alternates between Binghamton and a house on a dirt road in Montrose, Pennsylvania, where he keeps tanks of ether in the chicken coop and $15,000 of glassware in the kitchen. He also deals in cocaine smuggled to Florida in a Dominican Republic diplomatic pouch. He ships his speed across to Canada in cookie boxes.

live."[40] Seldom had the Rockies been so dan- those next months.

Given time, the American Fur Company might have recovered from these disasters, but that was a commodity that was running out. For moving relentlessly in from the west was a rival that could never be absorbed: the Hudson's Bay Company. In 1837 this concern bought Fort Hall from Nathaniel J. Wyeth, thus placing its eastern headquarters in the middle Snake River country, where its well-organized brigades could move easily over the whole Rocky Mountain hunting ground. Nor could the Americans compete with its efficient methods. Able to purchase the British goods that were always demanded by the trade without paying duties on them, and using the Columbia and Lewis rivers to provide cheap transportation, the Hudson's Bay Company caravans could outbid their rivals for the few furs left in the West. From 1837 on the American Fur Company was fighting a losing battle whose outcome was inevitable.

The Hell's Angels' most aggressive expansion takes place in Canada. It begins with the conquest of Quebec when the club takes over the Popeyes in the country's second largest province on December 5, 1977.

The Hell's Angels aren't satisfied with control of Quebec. They want all of Canada. Montreal Angels criss-cross the country in 1980 when the two-year-old war with the Out-

laws cools temporarily. They party with gangs and build alliances. The Angels eye British Columbia. Control of the westernmost province creates a drug and weapons pipeline north from California to British Columbia and across Canada to Quebec. The Satan's Angels monopolize British Columbia's drug traffic. They also terrorize smaller gangs. The club's bylaw #3 reads: "No member will disgrace the club by being yellow." The Satan's Angels cruise the British Columbia coast and make forays into Oregon to strip colors off other bikers like scalps. They embarrass the L'il Devils in Van-

bikers like scalps. They embarrass the L'il Devils in Vancouver, the Devil's Escorts in Kamloops and the Gypsy Jokers in Oregon. They hang stolen colors on the clubhouse wall next to the coats of arms of the Vancouver City Police and the Royal Canadian Mounted Police.

A second pathway into the beaver country began at Fort Vancouver, nestling against the banks of the broad Columbia River in the far Northwest. Built in 1824 by the venerable Hudson's Bay Company of England, this strategic outpost was under the command of Dr. John McLoughlin, a rawboned giant of a man with piercing eyes that gleamed from beneath a disordered patch of prematurely white hair, and "a beard that would do honor to the chin of a Grizzly." Genius of the trade that he was, Dr. McLoughlin helped devise the "brigade system" that allowed his "Honourable Company" to dominate the beaver streams of the Northwest. Every autumn, during the golden era of trapping, several giant processions wound their way out of Fort Vancouver, each containing dozens of trappers with their Indian wives, and each led by a "partisan" who proclaimed his exalted position by wearing a broadcloth suit, white shirt, high collar, and tall beaver hat. Some moved southward into the Sacramento and San Joaquin valleys of California; others tramped eastward along the Snake River to trap beaver in the heart of the northern Rocky Mountains. At the end of the 1820's, when competition with American trappers was reducing profits in the Rockies, Dr. McLoughlin began concentrating his brigades on the Pacific slope, but this withdrawal was only temporary. During the next decade the Americans were to

[1] James Ohio Pattie, *The Personal Narrative of James Ohio Pattie of Kentucky* (Cincinnati, 1831), *passim.* A critical study by Joseph J. Hill, "New Light on Pattie and the Southwestern Fur Trade," *Southwestern Historical Quarterly,* XXVI (1923), 241–254, demonstrates that many of Pattie's statements are not to be taken literally. The best study of the trade in the Southwest is Robert G. Cleland, *This Reckless Breed of Men: The Trappers and Fur Traders of the Southwest* (New York, 1950), *passim.*

[2] Armíjo's brief journal, together with other documents on this trade, are collected in LeRoy R. Hafen and Ann W. Hafen, *Old Spanish Trail: Santa Fé to Los Angeles* (Glendale, Calif., 1954), pp. 131–165.

find to their sorrow that the Hudson's Bay Company was still one of their most formidable foes in the battle for control of the West.[3]

The lower British Columbia mainland has a rapidly expanding drug market within easy reach of the California drug network. BC Angels make most of their money selling cocaine. The four Angel chapters in BC control all outlaw motorcycle gang activity in the province as well as 40 registered companies.

The BC Angels own a campground called Angel Acres in

The BC Angels own a campground called Angel Acres in Nanaimo. The heavily wooded property has a large in-ground swimming pool, trailers and a bandshell. Angels and prospects guard the chained-off roadway into the property, part of which is off limits to anyone but Angels. The BC Hell's Angels host more than 3,000 bikers from across North America at their anniversary party on August 2, 3, 4, 1986. The Para-Dice Riders from Toronto make the event a mandatory one-month run for the club's 39 members during the gang's 25th year. It is unusual for any Toronto gang to show such support for either the Angels or Outlaws.

Y.L

H.A

From that day the rendezvous was a regular feature of the trade. Ashley brought out the trading goods in the 1826 caravan, returning with 123 packs of furs, worth enough to allow him to retire from the mountains forever. Before he left he sold his interests to three former employees headed by Jedediah Smith; during the next few years these partners sent trappers over the whole Rocky Mountain country in their quest for pelts. Forever seeking new beaver streams, Jed Smith led two remarkable expeditions westward, exploring the Colorado and

[3] The best study of the Hudson's Bay Company's strategy on the Pacific coast is in the introduction of Frederick Merk (ed.), *Fur Trade and Empire, George Simpson's Journal* (Cambridge, Mass., 1931). Important documents on the brigade system are in Alice B. Maloney (ed.), *Fur Brigade to the Bonaventura. John Work's California Expedition, 1832–1833, for the Hudson's Bay Company* (San Francisco, 1945), and E. E. Rich (ed.), *Peter Skene Ogden's Snake Country Journals, 1824–25 and 1825–26* (London, 1950).

[4] Harrison C. Dale, *The Ashley-Smith Explorations and the Discovery of a Central Route to the Pacific, 1822–1829* (Cleveland, 1918), pp. 85–90.

43

Gila rivers, trafficking with Mexicans in the interior valleys of California, and pushing northward as far as Fort Vancouver before rejoining his partners at the rendezvous in 1829. He could report few prospects for trade in the lands that he had seen, but he had gained a place in immortality as the most venturesome of all American explorers. A year later he and his partners were ready to retire from the West with fortunes that assured them lives of indolent luxury. At the 1830 rendezvous they sold their interests to a group of traders under Thomas Fitzpatrick, James Bridger, and Milton Sublette, organized as the Rocky Mountain Fur Company. Well was their retirement earned, for they, with Ashley, had devised the techniques that allowed the fur trade to enter its palmiest days.[5]

They had, moreover, conjured into existence a reckless new breed of men: the "free trappers," or "Mountain Men," as they loved to call themselves. These aristocrats of the wilderness spent their entire lives in the mountains, renewing contact with civilization only once each year when they visited the rendezvous to sell their furs and buy the few necessities that the forest could not provide. Calling no man master, and free to move where or when they wished, these Mountain Men contributed more than any other group to the exploration of the

master, and free to move where or when they wished, these Mountain Men contributed more than any other group to the exploration of the West. Their significance in the history of the frontier, however, extended beyond the service they performed as pathfinders or trail blazers. The lives that they led, and the characteristics that those lives forced upon them, illustrated in exaggerated form the corrosive effect of a wilderness environment on transplanted Easterners. On all frontiers, pioneers grappling with the untamed forces of nature cast off the artifacts and institutions and habits of civilization; the Mountain Men, divorced entirely from traditional patterns of civilized life, reverted more completely toward the primitive than any other pioneers. Their pattern of existence illustrated, even in caricature, the extent to which environment transcended hereditary factors in molding the lives of frontiersmen.

H.S.
H.A
p. 121

Anybody who has ever seen the Angels on a run will agree that rural Californians are likely to reject the spectacle as not right for their way of living. It is a human zoo on wheels. An outlaw whose normal, day-to-day appearance is enough to disrupt traffic will appear on a run with his beard dyed green or bright red, his eyes hidden behind orange goggles, and a brass ring in his nose. Others wear capes and Apache headbands, or oversize sunglasses and peaked Prussian helmets. Earrings, *Wehrmacht* headgear and German Iron Crosses are virtually part of the uniform – like the grease-caked Levis, the sleeveless vests and all those fine tattoos: 'Mother', 'Dolly', 'Hitler', 'Jack the Ripper', swastikas, daggers, skulls, 'LSD', 'Love', 'Rape' and the inevitable Hell's Angels insignia.

49

Few among the Mountain Men reverted to such complete savagery, but all slipped far backward from a state of civilization. Certainly in their appearance there was little to distinguish them from the Indians. Gaunt and spare, with skin tanned the color of the red men's by life in the open, they let their unkempt hair hang to shoulder length while their faces were hidden beneath beards that "would scarcely disgrace a Bedouin of the desert." They wore buckskin hunting shirts, ornamented at every seam with colored porcupine quills or leather fringes, and pulled in at the waist by a broad belt. In this was thrust a pistol and tomahawk; from it dangled a scalping knife in a leather sheath and a whetstone in a buckskin case. Their pantaloons were similarly of leather and as carefully ornamented, while their moccasins showed the skillful beadwork of their squaws. On their heads they wore a cap of skins, decorated with animals' tails or braided horsehair. About their necks hung a "possibles sack" containing pipe, tobacco, awl, bullet mold, and other necessities; over their shoulders was slung a bullet pouch and powder horn, while a stubby "Hawkins rifle" dangled from the crook of their arms. Romantic as these clothes were, they could best be appreciated at a distance, for they were never removed from the time they were put on until they were discarded, except, perhaps, when their owner laid them across an ant hill for those busy insects to eat some of the lice.[11]

45r

These are his 'originals', to be worn every day until they rot. The Levis are dipped in oil, then hung out to dry in the sun – or left under the motorcycle at night to absorb the crankcase drippings. When they become too ragged to be functional, they are worn over other newer Levis. Many of the jackets are so dirty that

worn over other newer Levis. Many of the jackets are so dirty that the colours are barely visible, but they aren't discarded until they literally fall apart. The condition of the originals is a sign of status. It takes a year or two before they get ripe enough to make a man 57 feel he has really made the grade.

as did the red men. They gestured frequently and meaningfully as they spoke, for they were adept in the sign language that was the Indians' means of intertribal communication. From the Indians, too, they borrowed a colorful imagery that added spice to their speech. A man was a "child" or a "hoss" or a "coon" or a "nigger." A hungry person was "wolfish" and needed to fill his "meatbag" with "buffler meat" or "cow meat"; one who was thirsty drank to satisfy his "dry." To scalp an Indian was to "lift his ha'r," or "tickle his fleece"; one who had been killed had been "rubbed out" or had "gone under." Phrases such as "hyar's a nigger lifted ha'r that spree," were sprinkled through their conversation! Men was "robe

that reads "DEGUELLO" — no quarter. Mexican General Antonio Lopez de Santa Anna's regimental band plays the Moorish march "Deguello" as his troops march on the Alamo under orders to massacre all defenders of the old mission, including Jim Bowie and Davey Crockett. The patch is the Angels' red badge of courage. It is worn by Angels who violently resist arrest and dates to the early 1960s. About 15 members of the Lowell, Massachusetts, chapter wear it for a 20-minute bloody rumble outside their clubhouse in the late 1960s with 20 police officers. 79.

Shortly after the first of July the caravan of trading goods arrived from St. Louis, equipped by merchants willing to endure the dangers of wilderness travel for profits that sometimes touched 2,000 per cent. The trappers asked eagerly for year-old news first, then watched as the merchandise was displayed: powder from the du Pont works in Delaware, lead from the Galena mines of Illinois, stubby rifles from the shops of Missouri gunsmiths, knives and beaver traps from England's distant factories, beads and trinkets from Italy, coffee and sugar from South America, blankets from New England's textile mills, hanks of tobacco from Kentucky, fiery whisky from Taos, and cask after cask of raw alcohol from the distilleries of Cincinnati. Trading came first as the Mountain Men cheerfully surrendered their "hairy bank notes," the beaver skins, for needed items or scarce-remembered luxuries or gaudy fineries for the squaws. It did not matter that prices were astronomical; why quibble over blankets at twenty dollars, tobacco at three dollars a pound, sugar and coffee at two dollars, and alcohol at five dollars a pint when beaver pelts could be had for the taking and were worth from three to six dollars each?[6]

[6] Osburne Russell, *Journal of a Trapper, or Nine Years in the Rocky Mountains, 1834–1843* (Boise, Ida., 1921), pp. 62–63; Joseph Williams, *Narrative of*

Even at these prices the Mountain Man used only a portion of his year's catch to buy what he needed; the merchants secured the rest after they opened the flat casks of raw alcohol that were universally used in the trade. As kettles of this lethal fluid were passed about, day after day, night after night, the rendezvous was transformed into a scene of roaring debauchery. Some staged races on foot or horseback; some wrestled and fought; some gambled recklessly at cards or the Indian game of "hand" until they had squandered away in a few hours their entire year's earnings, their rifles, their horses, their wives, and in a few cases their own scalps. Neither misers nor repentants could be found among men who risked their lives daily; a trapper who had lost his all would only shrug away his disappointment with a "There goes ha'r and beaver" and take solace in more alcohol. Others stamped through Indian dances amidst barbaric yells of

Hi-Hi-Hi-Hi! Hi-i—Hi-i—Hi-i—Hi-i!
Hi-ya—Hi-ya—Hi-ya—Hi-ya
Hi-ya—Hi-ya—Hi-ya—Hi-ya

The transfo[illegible] begins around San Francisco Bay in 1967; the alchemist's stone is lycergic acid diethylamide. The Hell's Angels are everything the flower children aren't in the mid-1960s: they spell peace with an *ie* and the only beads they have are on gun barrels. The spoiled generation rebels by giving away free love, spurns all-American red meat for veggies, and fries its brains with the most unnatural chemicals. It also latches on — hoping the rebellious image rubs off — to the only true counter culture around: the Hell's Angels. The bikers don't understand why

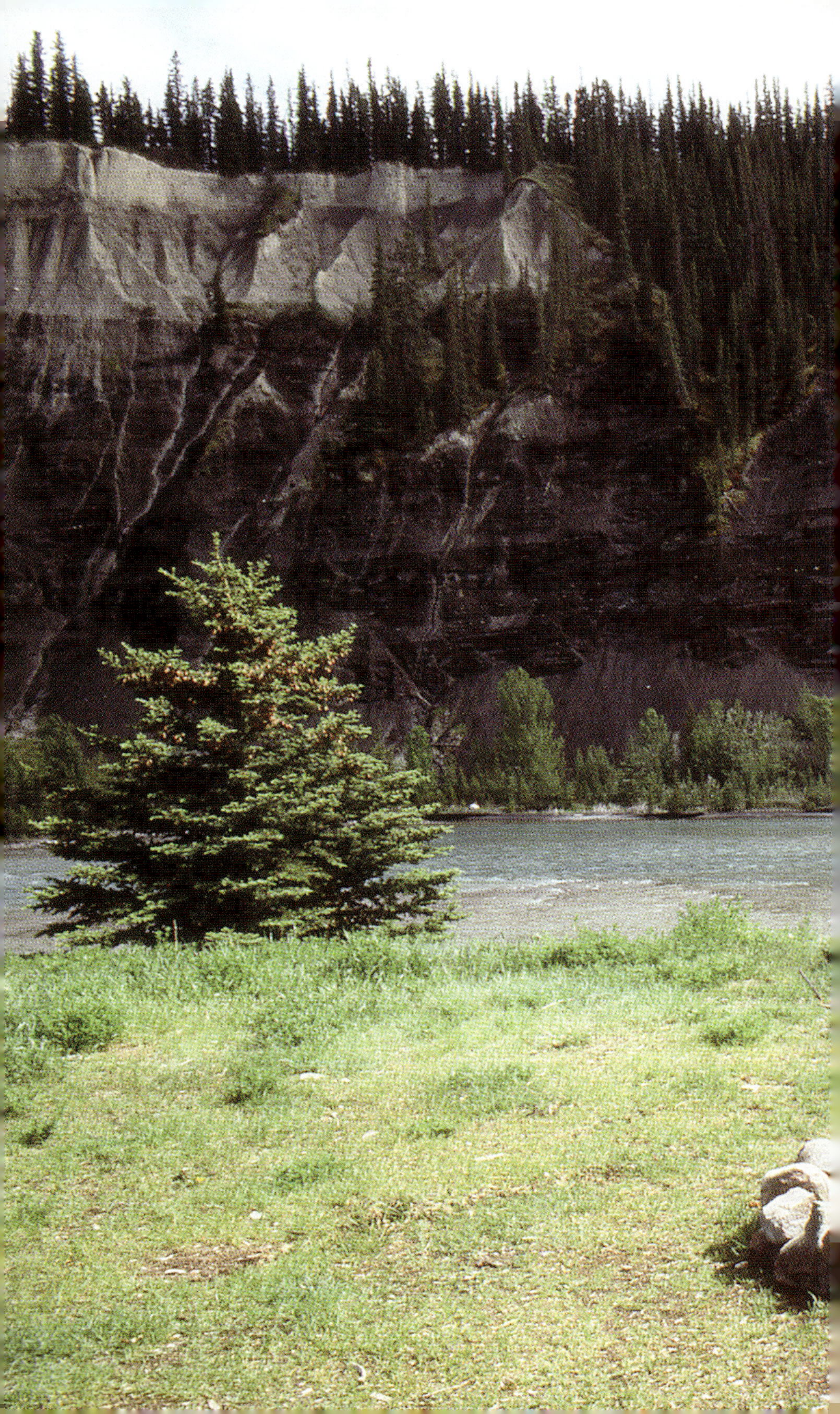

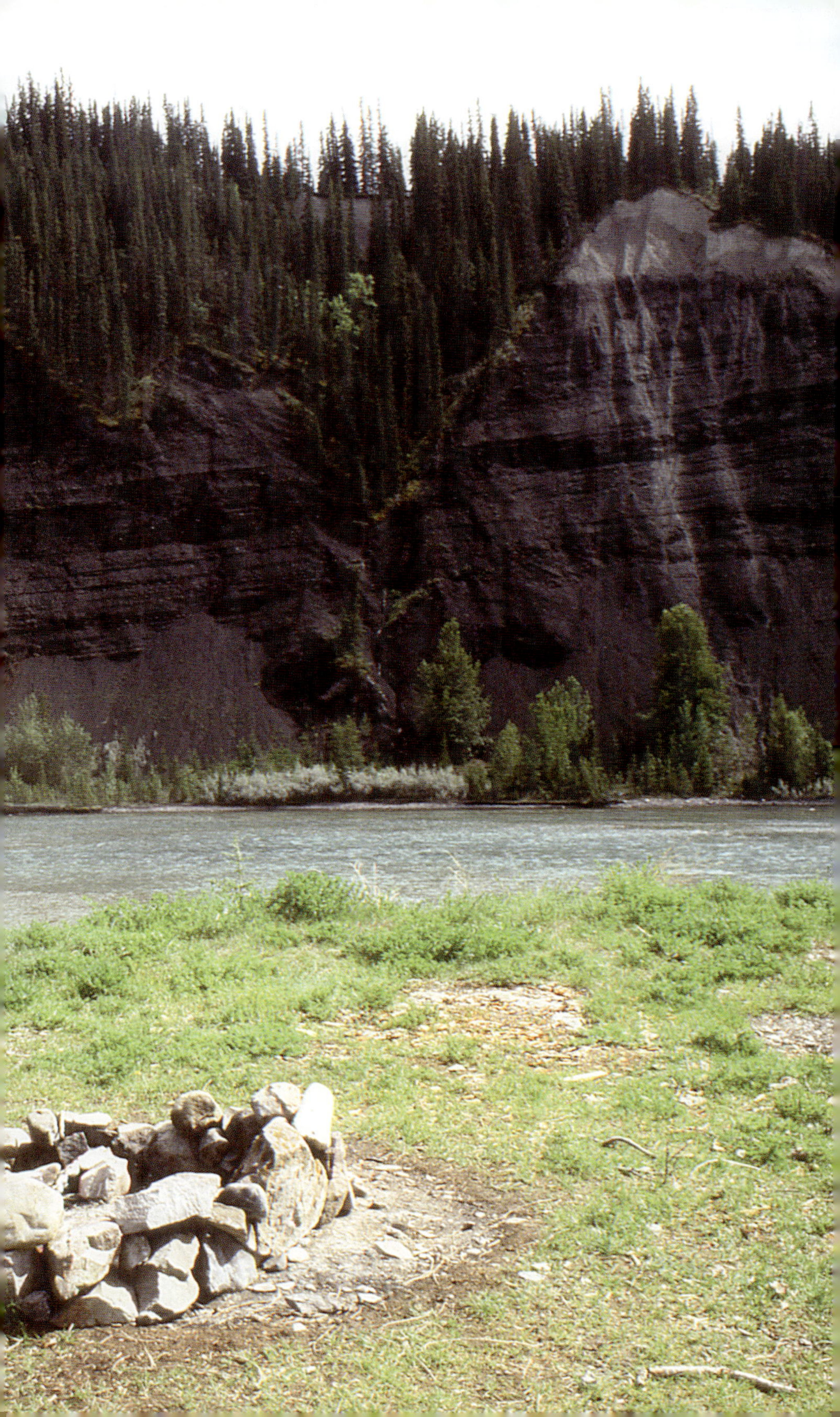

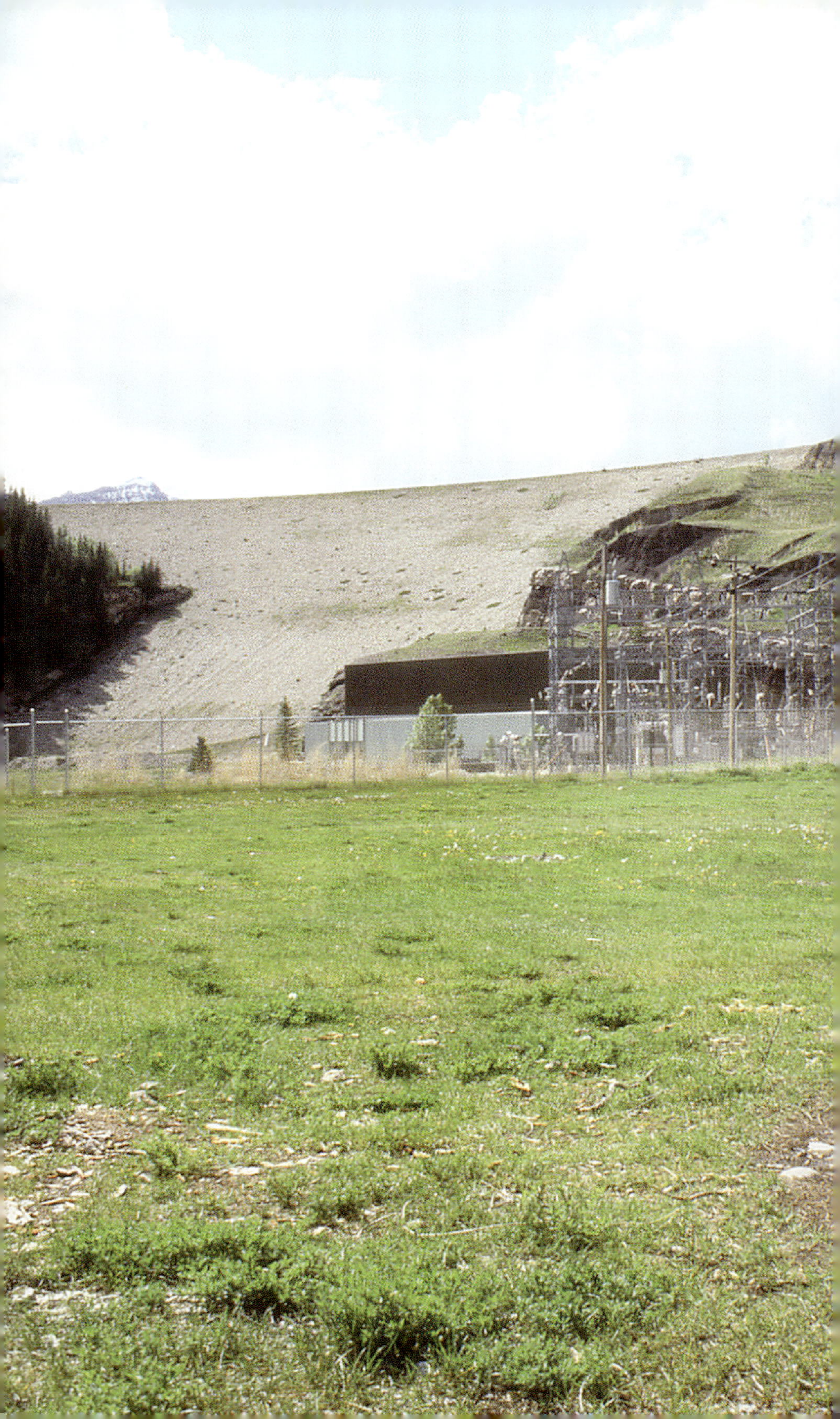

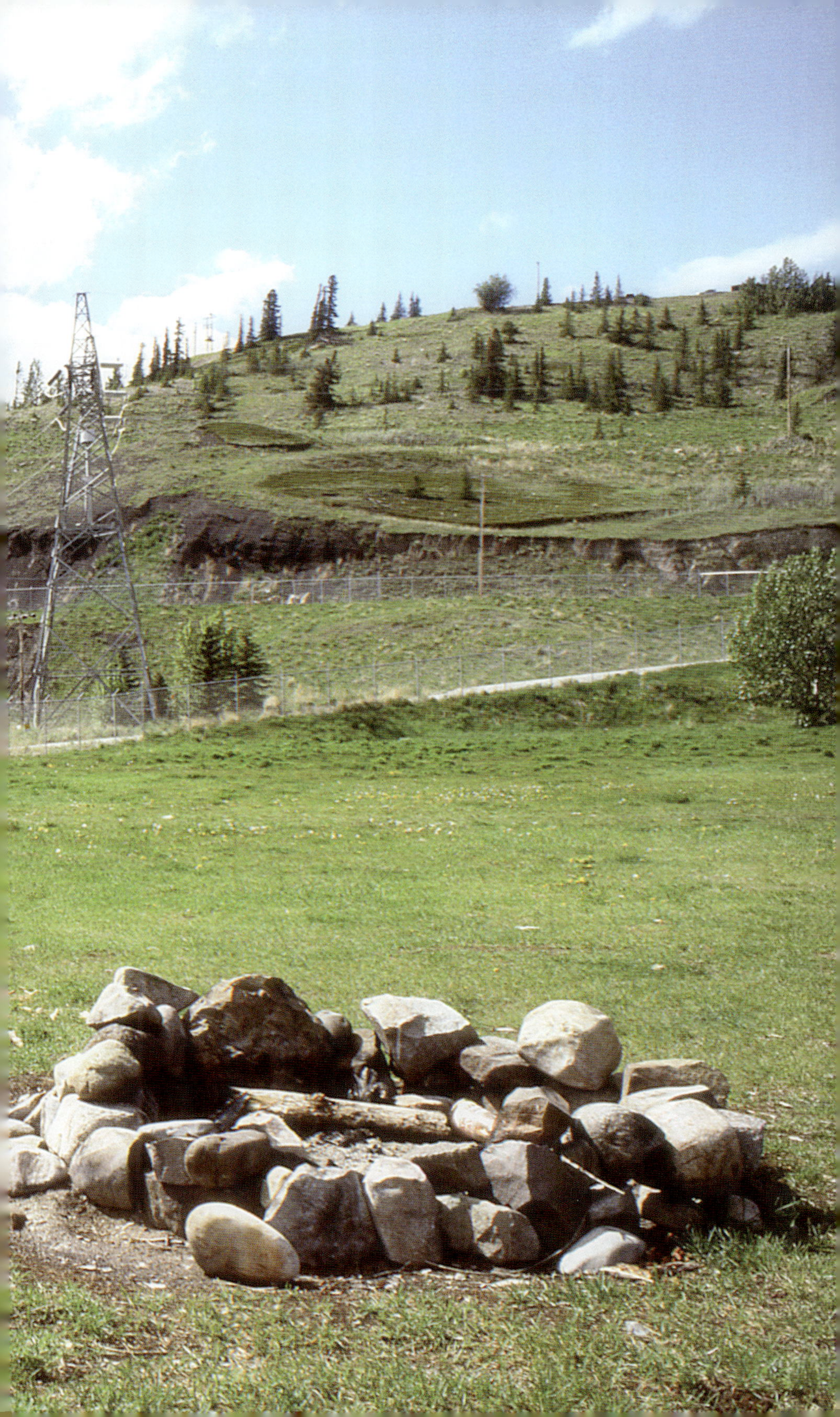

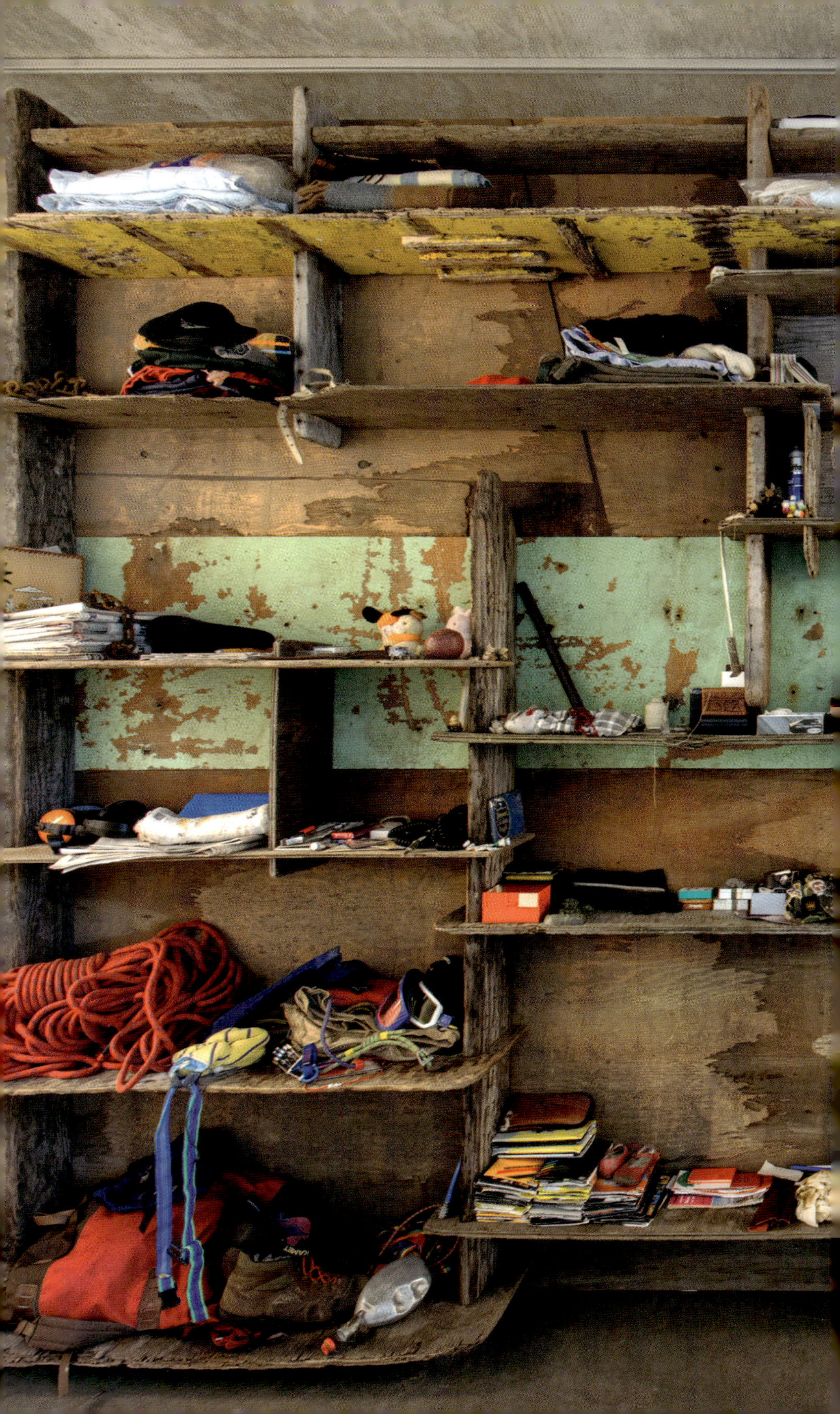

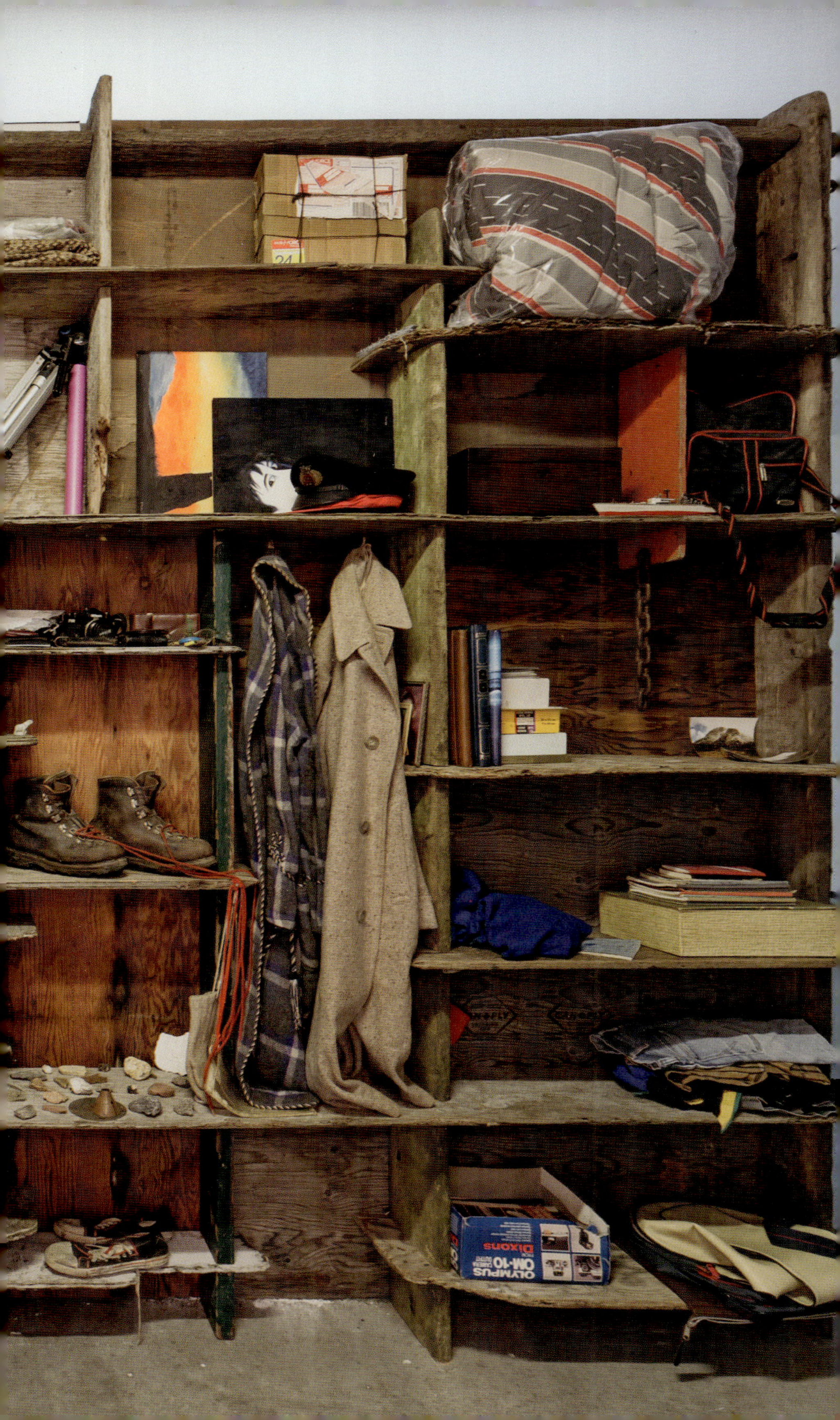
Dixons
OLYMPUS
OM-10

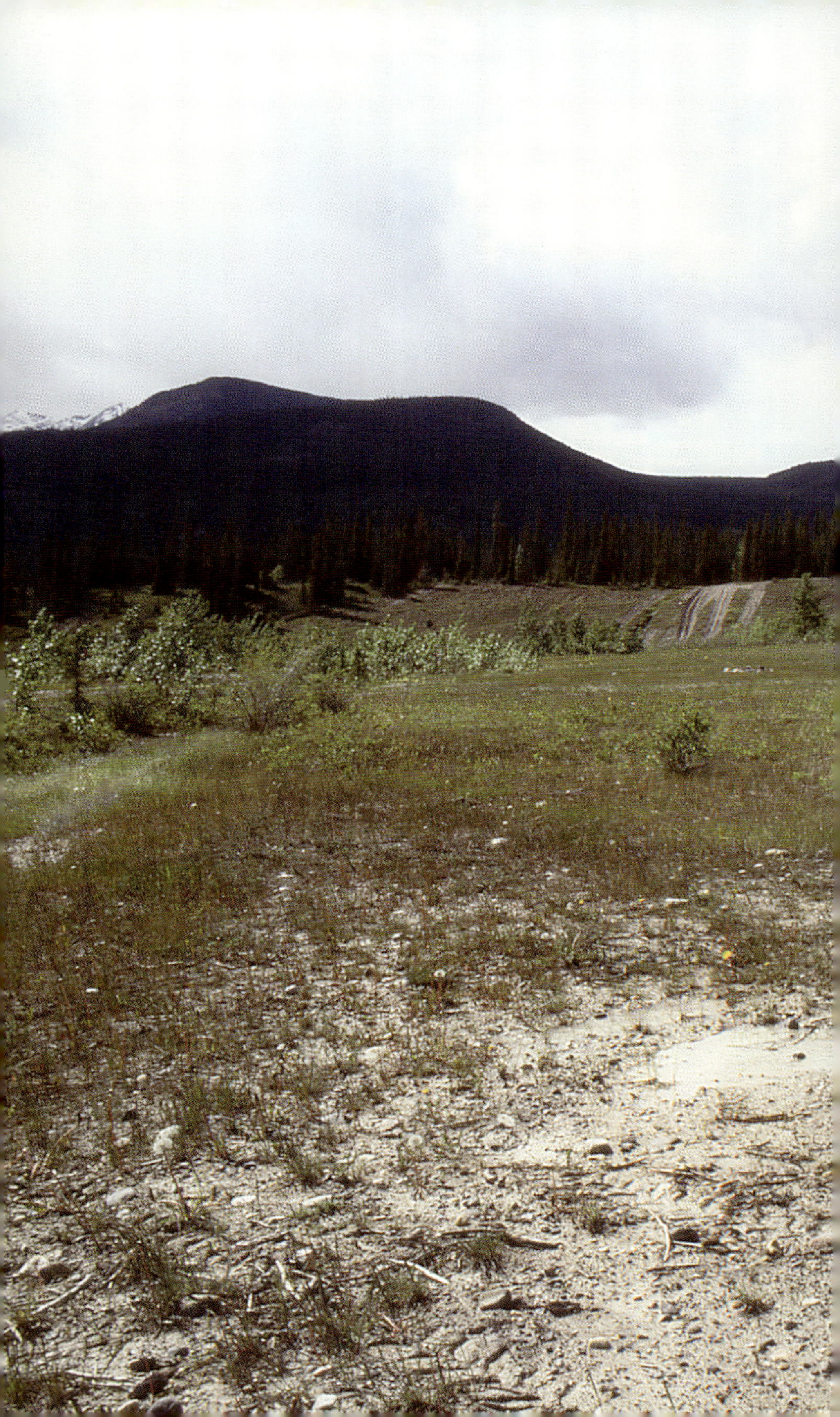

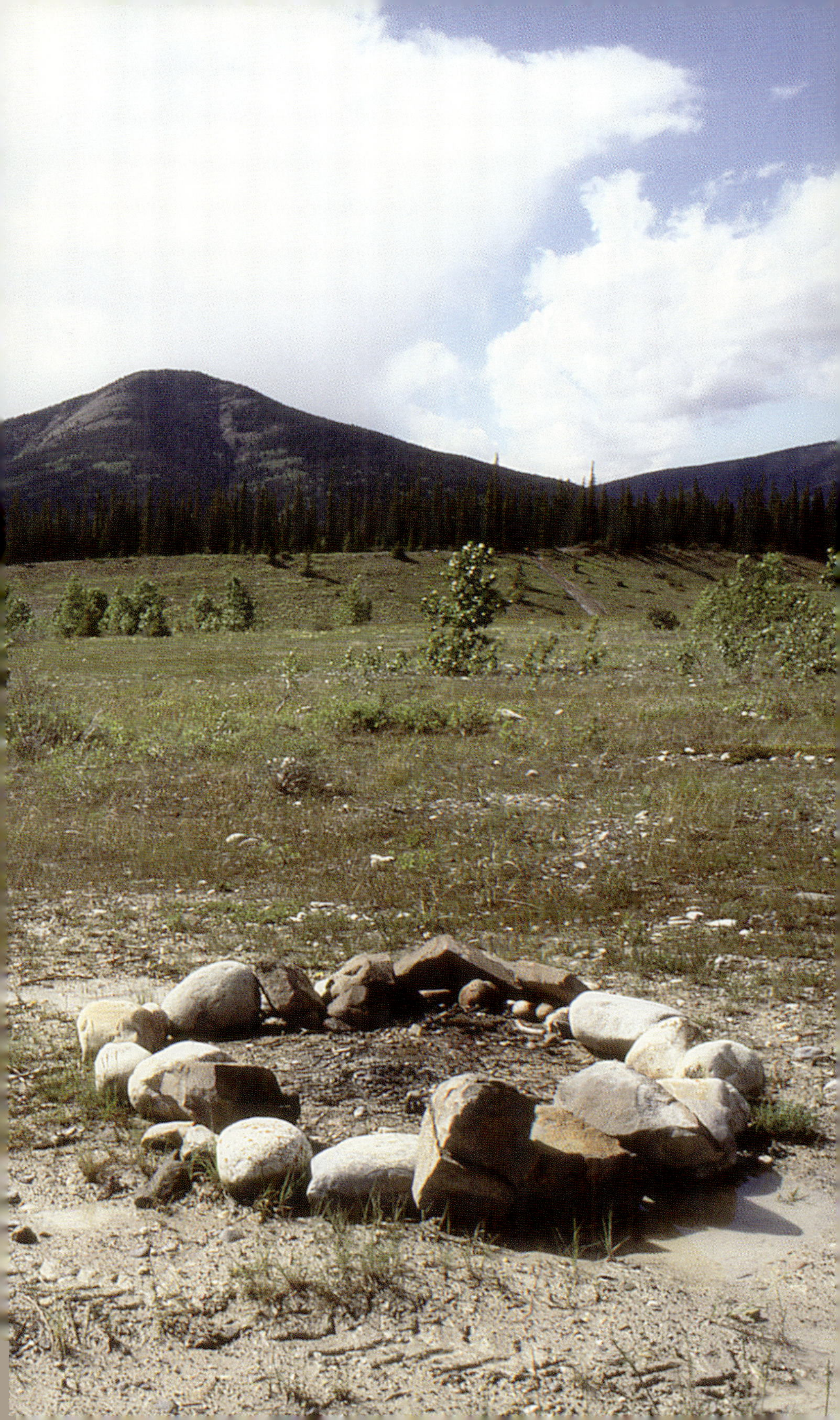

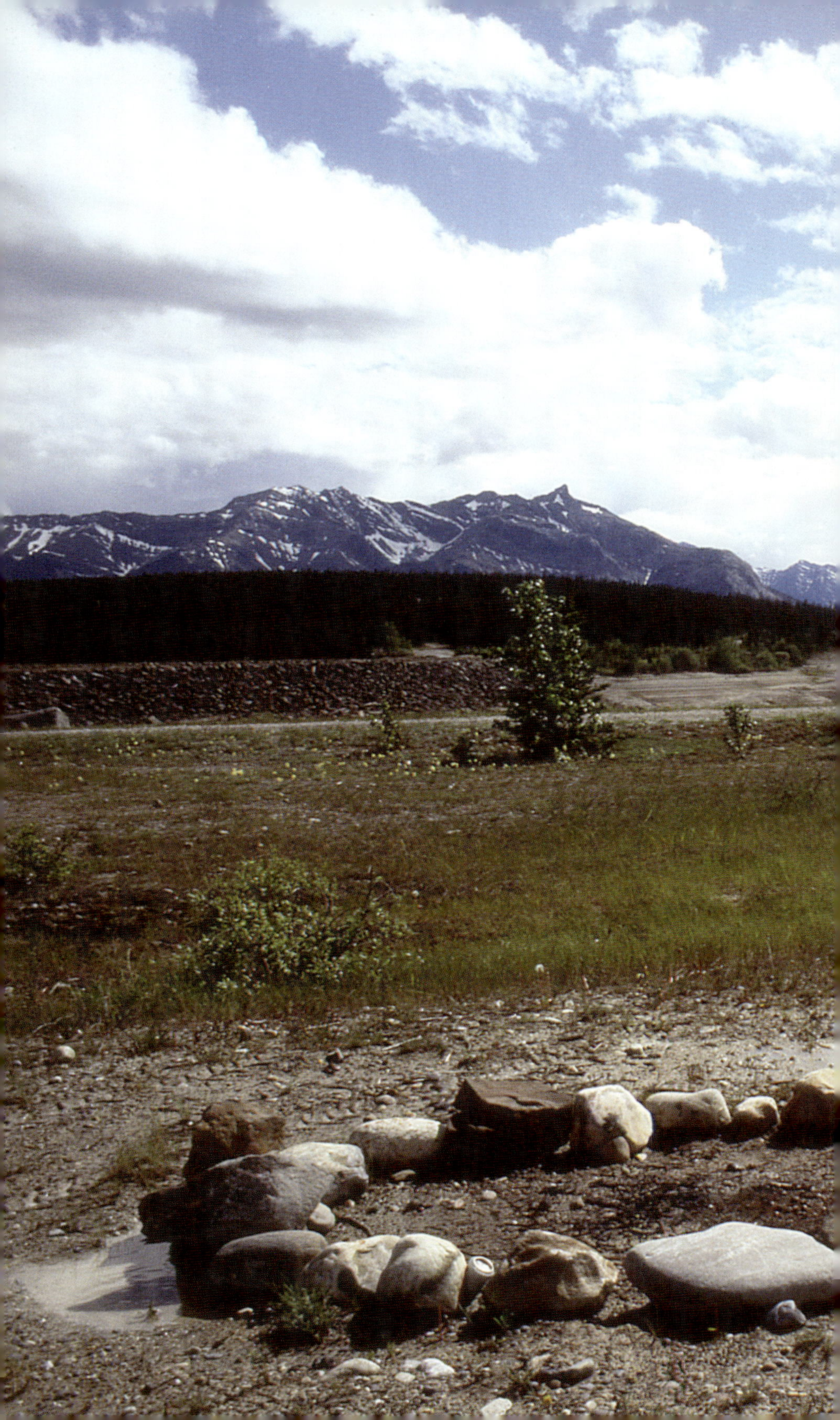

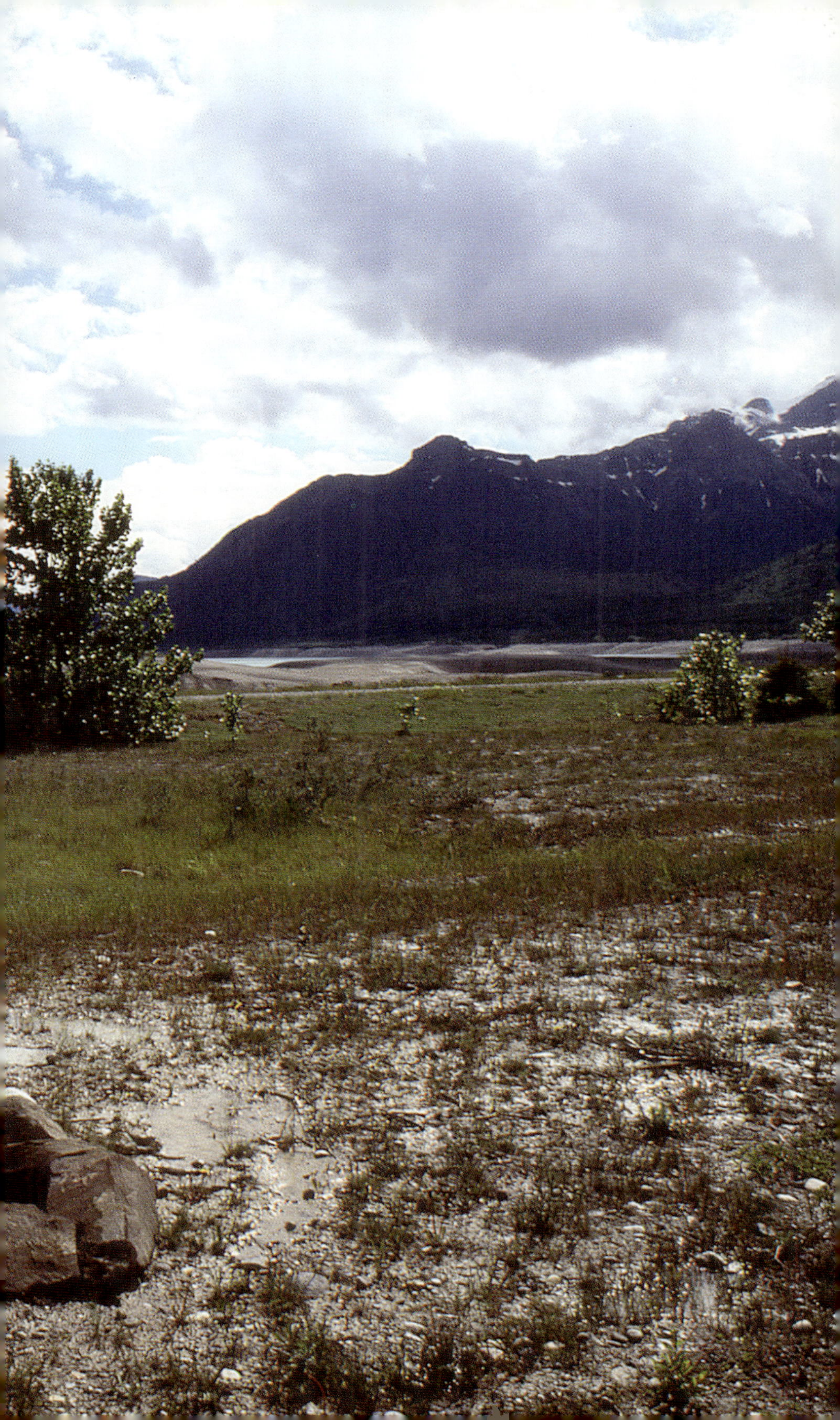

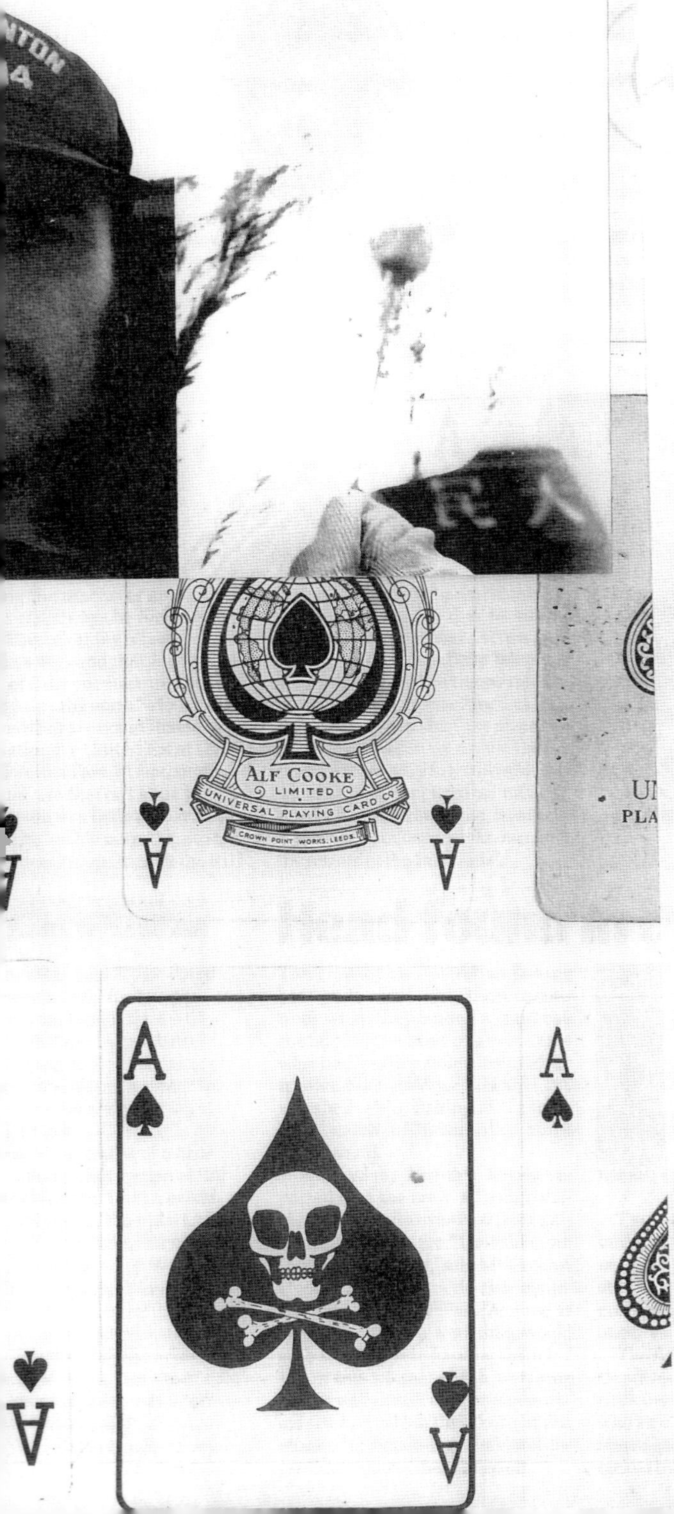

The Genie

Lanzhou, Gansu Pr
I see something, it re
but the circumstance

Xiahe
Cycling down from t
rocks. My mind rew
all takes a fraction of
back, turning it over
death.

Before action can be
face down; the deal'
The next second ro
another card, numb

The vultures circle,

Hezuochen
Leaving the comple
have to change stat
hand of five, six, m
the Ace of Spades.

Luqu
I've fucked up. I c
riding yaks down t
embroidered cases
outback, floorboar
has become my ha
pausing momenta
for god knows wh
console of a fruit
room violence adj
right, foregrounde

Darkness falls out

Langamusi
Two monasteries
and *The Tibetan*: i
the room opens
dialects. The toil
taking a shit is a
on the streets. L
card, face up, eq

I am getting pre
emulating the op

filed into the subconscious. Its existence is definite, and visual recollection are lost.

see a card face down amongst the gravel, earth and onscious awakening a dull sense of foreboding. This action later I'm thinking of dismounting and going he Ace of Spades, clichéd symbol of doom and

econd has elapsed and I'm looking at another card, re too good. I sink back into the saddle – relax. heels of the bike and I find myself looking down at : the Ace of Spades.

trate themselves, a creeping fear enters my psyche.

s behind I take the wrong bus, and end up here, and r the shoulder of a group of huddled Chinese. A s, the top one fully exposed and my point of focus, eet dodging traffic and hurry to the next terminus.

estination tonight, so have to stay here. Tibetans are hfare, rifles slung over shoulders in brightly ks like a prison commandant's house with a shack defecating. Still it's got a big TV in the room, so, as the bed clicking through the fifty or so channels, images or scenes: Chinese Americana, advertisements a sick game show where the TV became the front red within its pixelllated imagery, a video still of bar ily rendered interpretation of a hand of cards. To the pades.

lace as do two hotels imaginatively named *The Chinese* f political allegiance I go for the latter. A window from eeting area for locals and their respective languages and with low stalls, sporadically swilled out. A westerner here, therefore my choice of an evening is to urinate out relief, walking down the steep concrete steps I see a p and bottom: the Ace of Spades.

is point, the garbled voices swim in my head, my mind of the room. Fear of the unknown. Fear of the

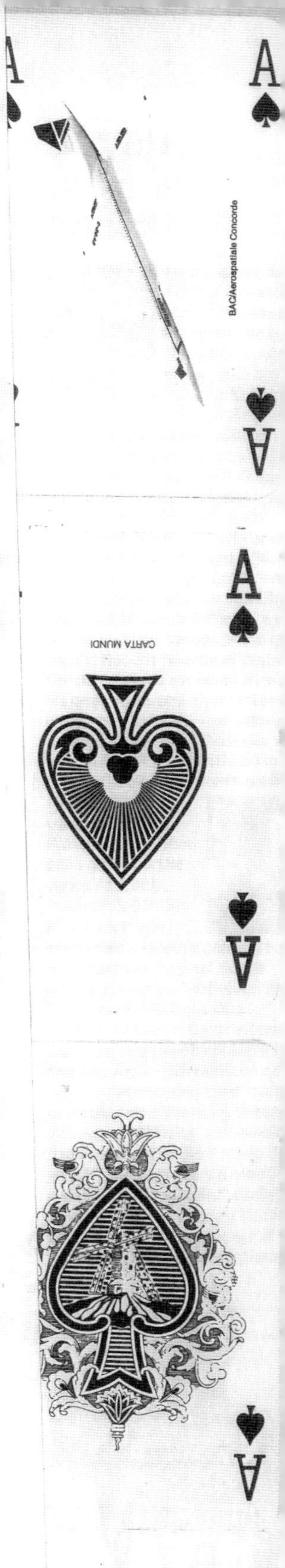

unseen. The blowing green curtain, a barrier only teasingly revealing
from the void on the other side.

I decide to kick the card, to see if it lands face down – my mind's res games now – face up. Try again, best of three, the game extends, fac

Zoigê to Songpan

I'm on the bus leaving this cowboy town. The seat in front is broken off my chest. We've an eight hour journey and it's raining really hard hills roll by in the misty rain, the rivers full to burst. Sporadically we the bus which slaloms through the axle deep mud into which the roa metamorphosized. Hours go by punctuated only by the occasional e tents. Sometimes the bus stops to let the inhabitants on or off.

He wore the usual mixture of traditional and modern. His black felt the long woollen coat trimmed with fur from the snow leopard, held leather belt from which hung a golden handled dagger. On his feet n boots in the style of the Wild West, the Cuban heels allowing a little mud. The bus was heavy with condensation and heat from bodies in

He found a seat half way up on the right. He removed his coat. Un jeans and a sweatshirt. He turned to face me. The sweatshirt bore a majority of his chest, the symbol of the Ace of Spades. He stared st turned and sat.

Out of the window I could see a flock of large black wading birds, th

Chengdu, Sechuan Province

I'm safe, back in civilized territory, the capital of the province. My h of the few international gay pick up points this side of China, as I ge my room asking for 'man from the west'. The moustache will have t

I ring home to check everyone's okay, no death or doom there, I rel streets three men are playing cards sat on small wooden stools. The single pile onto which each member places a card in turn. As I pass down…..the Ace of Spades.

Seven Aces, all Spades in as many days. I laugh, strangely comforta metropolis. Whatever it was has gone, I can sense it.

Postscript

Some weeks later back in London I developed some films from whi a black and white, was double exposed. I had taken half the film pr but failed to note down the exposures. Half of my images from Chi over documentation taken during the construction of 'Trading Stati show I made in 1995. Helping at that time was Erelend Wiilliamson and collaborator. These were to be the only images I have of him, a whilst climbing in Scotland in 1996. I had carried his undeveloped years until now, the re-exposure unleashing the genie from the ench

ıs

d it
ı
sh

lack

ain,
oad

ne

ie
e,

one
to

ınd

One,
d,
red

nd

hree

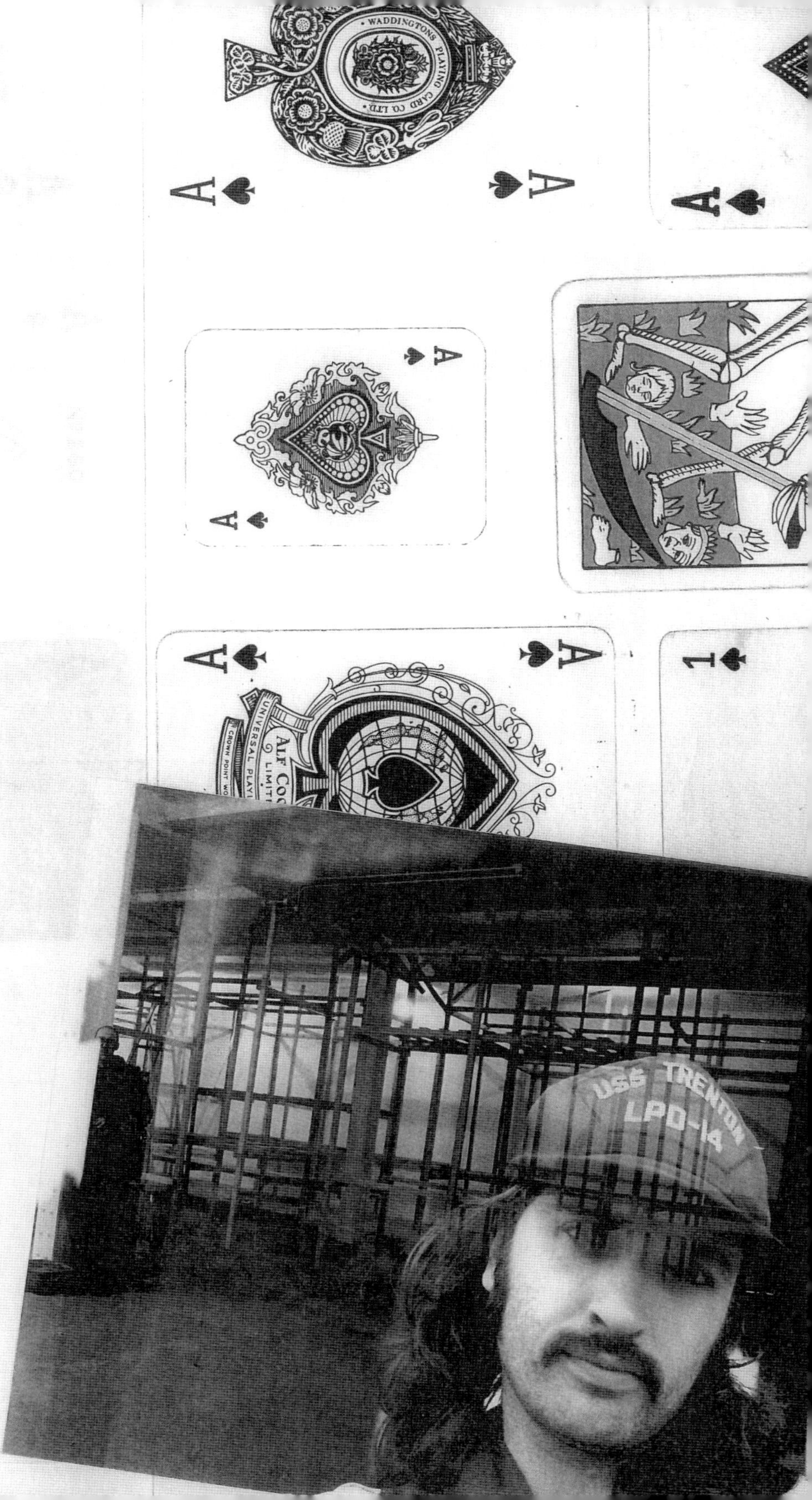

Encountering the Live

Julia Paoli

When the performance and conceptual artists of the 1960s picked up the camera and used it to document their work, they highlighted aspects of the medium that altered its history and asserted its complexity. At that time, artists with no interest in photography began employing it as a powerful means through which they might communicate and disseminate their practice. Performance artists in particular used photography as a way to transmit information; their work could exist outside of an ephemeral moment because the photograph—evidence of both the piece itself and an audience's interaction—might validate it. Much of performance art history follows this logic: whereby the event precedes and therefore authorises its documentation. Contemporary performance discourse has called for a rethinking of this argument; questioning the need for documentation in the space of an exhibition, expanding its limits beyond the boundaries of a photograph or a recording, and examining how a document, an object or an exhibition might reflect and enact live gestures. It is through this lens that I will read Mike Nelson's work *Double negative (The Genie)*, asking how Nelson's practice points to the performative as a tool for questioning the discourses that are indicative of contemporary performance art relating to an ephemeral moment or the afterlife of a live action. In so doing, this essay aims to expand the definition of performance art as well as address the viewer's experience in moving through Nelson's work.

Michaelangelo Antonioni's 1966 film *Blow Up* follows a fashion photographer searching for the truth behind a presumed murder he accidentally captured on film. Whilst developing photographs he had surreptitiously taken of a young couple in a deserted London park, the protagonist believes he has spotted something suspicious in the grainy imagery. He repeatedly enlarges the photos in order to analyse them more clearly, yet the quality of the prints are such that, rather than clarifying the situation, the images become increasingly indecipherable leaving the photographer no closer to the truth. It is this struggle for clarity in the image that link *Blow Up* to Nelson's most recent installation *Double negative (The Genie)*—a work comprised of seven full-sized and outdated photocopiers compositionally placed throughout the gallery, each surrounded by enlarged photocopies emanating from the respective machines they encircle. The installation's point of departure is an unrealised bookwork based on a series of seemingly coincidental occurrences that took place in 1998 while Nelson was travelling along the periphery of Tibet through the Gansu and Sichuan provinces of China.

The trip took place two years after the unexpected death of his friend and collaborator Erlend Williamson, who had fallen to his death in 1996 whilst climbing in the Scottish Highlands. During his travels, Nelson had sighted the ace of spades—the symbol of death within a deck of cards—seven times within as many days. His spectral sightings included observing the ace of spades playing card in a street game, and as lone cards, one on the steps of his hotel and another at the side of a mountain road. The playing card also appeared to him on a gambling channel on a hotel television, and emblazoned upon a nomad's sweatshirt, revealed from beneath a snow leopard trim cloak. In *Double negative (The Genie)* every day of Nelson's card sighting is represented by one of the seven photocopiers, and is accompanied by text from the artist's travel journal alongside enlarged copies of photographs that had been subjected to double exposure. Many of these self-portraits from his trip were unknowingly layered on top of images from the installation in 1996 of his first exhibition, *TRADING STATION ALPHA CMa* at Matt's Gallery, London. In the background assisting Nelson was Williamson. Nelson states "the last image I was to take of him [Williamson] before his death in (October) 1996, had remained undeveloped within this canister for three years, only to be re-exposed whilst I travelled this particular section. A genie, of sorts, unleashed from the magic lamp."[1] No longer straightforward documents of the artist's trip, the series of photographs became an incomplete and blotted record of his experience, filtered through the lingering presence of the tragedy of Williamson's death. The ghost-like re-appearance of his friend clouds Nelson's memory and interpretation of his journey through

1 Email conversation with the artist, 22 March 2014.

China. The photographs, coupled with the ace of spades' ominous imagery, create an eerie effect, documenting an uncanny coincidence or parapsychological occurrence.

Just as *Blow Up*'s protagonist finds that his photographs are unable to lead him to clarity, Nelson is unable to decipher reality in his images and the meaning behind his sightings of the ace of spades. There was an opportunity for Nelson to return to this story in 2001, when he was invited to produce a bookwork that would structure and present his journey using the personal collection of aces of spades that he accumulated in the years subsequent to his trip, a short text that provided an account of his sightings and the double-exposed images. The book never came to fruition and the publishing house disbanded without ever printing or returning the artist's material. All that remained in Nelson's possession were the photocopies of the layout that documented these original cards, and the negatives of the black and white film. As a result, the artist was left with a growing disbelief in the sightings. Now, almost 15 years later, Nelson revisits his trip through China by manifesting his experience in the remaining evidence to produce *Double negative (The Genie).*

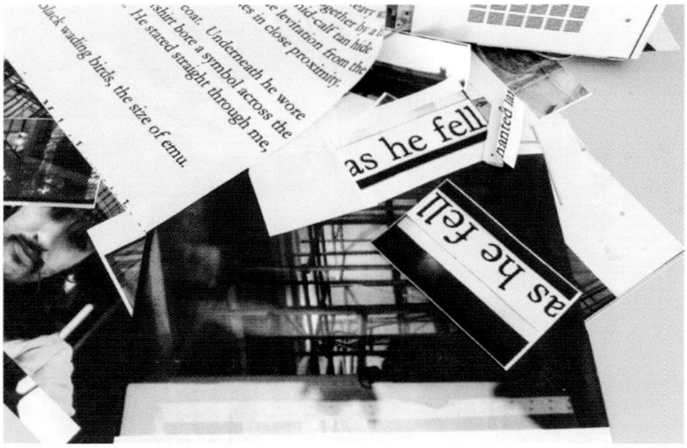

Upon entering the installation, the viewer has a sense of having arrived right after something has happened, missing the hurried and intensely driven action of an absent investigator, and is left with only the detritus of the search. The machines are sculpturally positioned throughout the gallery with their power lights flashing, indicating that they might be ready for use. Strewn around the base of the copiers and covering their tops are sheets of photocopied text and images of the material from Nelson's unrealised artist book. These elements are signs of life, showing that the machines have been in use and someone has been scanning and searching through the material. According to Nelson, "[t]he enlarged images and abstracted text are confused by the degradation and imperfections caused by the dated machines which emulates the confusion around the original tale. In a sense they are as a ghost in the proverbial afore mentioned machines."[2] The unseen investigator was examining the documents linked to Nelson's journey seeking something, but as to what that is, is uncertain. This feeling is common throughout Nelson's practice, such as the work *Quiver of Arrows*, 2010, where the audience is invited to explore the inside of five conjoined old aluminium trailers. While walking around the enclosed and linking structures, accompanied by the whirring sound of a fan, and the interference from an old television and radio set, there is a feeling you are always just behind someone, or you have entered just as someone has left. This feeling is also present in *I, IMPOSTOR*, 2011, which was presented at the 2011 Venice Biennale where Nelson used his previous work *Magazin: Büyük Valide Han*, 2003, as its point of departure. Originally installed in a seventeenth-century caravanserai in Istanbul, this piece was a darkroom constructed within, and in the style of its neighbours, filled with black and white images of the architecture that surrounded it, hung—as if to dry—from wires that criss-crossed its ceilings. For *I, IMPOSTOR*, Nelson relocated a replica of these darkrooms, built within a re-imagined vision of the caravanserai that had once enveloped it, and now exists in photographs hanging within the darkroom doppelganger. Moving through Nelson's interpretation or memory of the original space, the sense of an absent photographer who has since left the darkroom is inextricably bound to one's experience of the piece. In Nelson's *The Coral Reef*, 2000, the audience navigates through a maze of abandoned corridors and small rooms. All that remains from the previous occupants are an array of objects that feel increasingly menacing as the installation advances, and turns back in on itself. I consider the unseen occupants of Nelson's intricate spaces to be integral to his practice and can be understood vis-a-vis contemporary performance discourse.

Performance has long been regarded as a progressive art form that "values ephemeral action over the produced object".[3] Yet performance

2 Email conversation with the artist, 22 March 2014.

3 The art historian Sven Lütticken discusses the history of performance and its position as a progressive art form. See Sven Lütticken, "Progressive Striptease: Performance Ideology Past and Present", in *Secret Publicity: Essays on Contemporary Art*, trans Victor Joseph with Lütticken, Rotterdam: NAi Publishers and Fonds BKVB, 2005, pp 165–180.

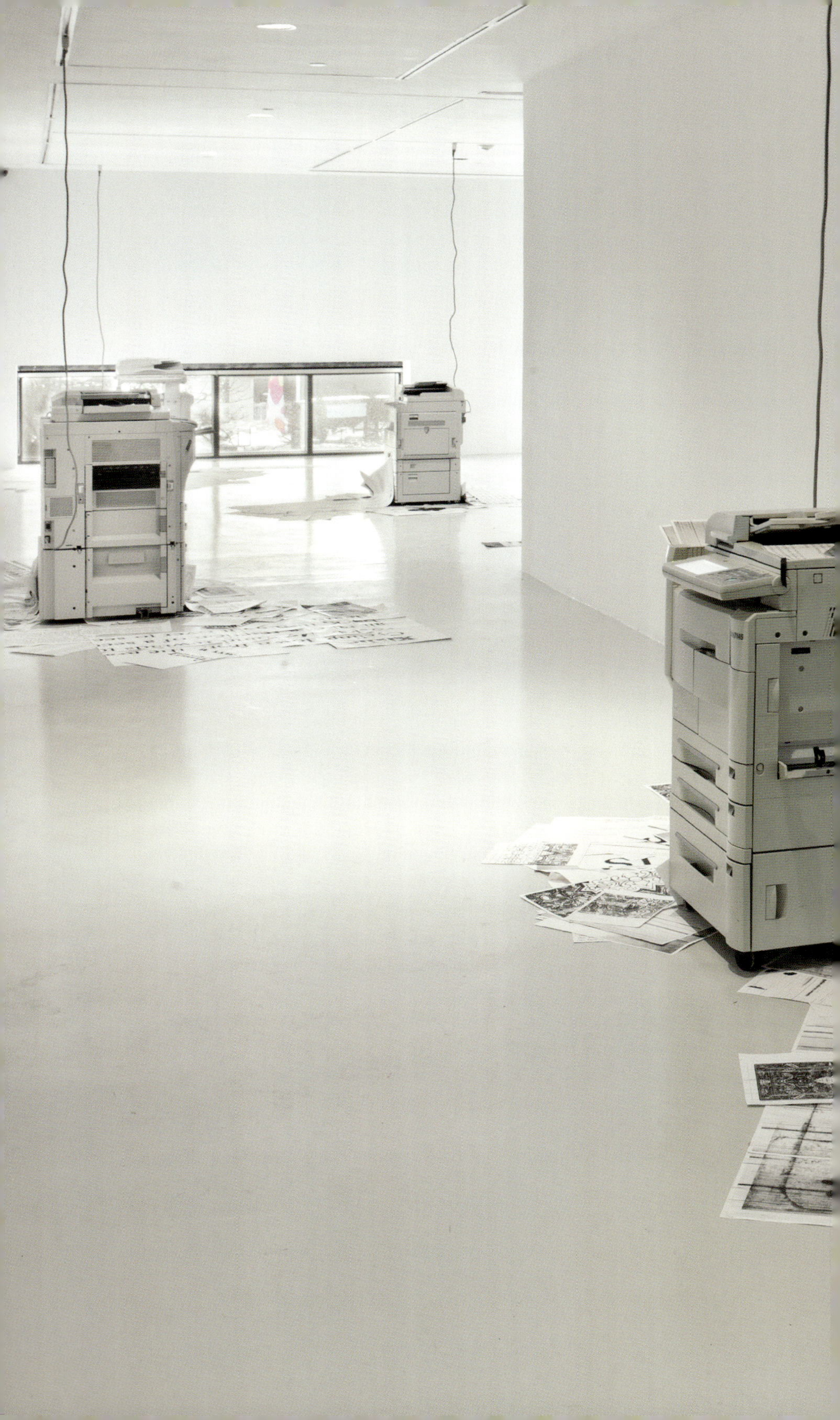

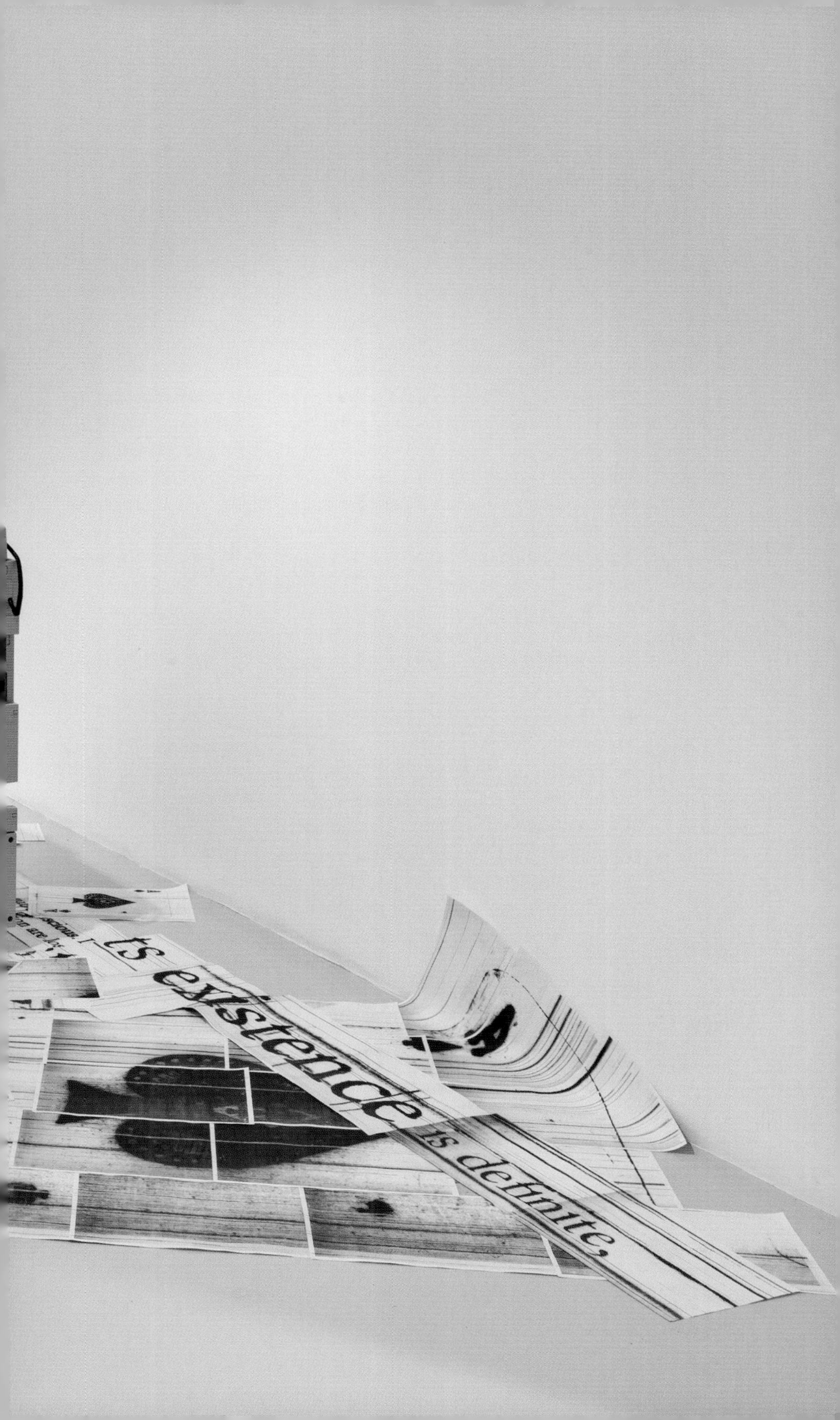
ts existence is definite,

in practice typically yields objects of some kind, whether they are recordings of the action through physical media, or installed relics after the action has taken place.[4] Both materials are documents thought to provide evidence of the work and testimony to the live event. More so, they enable those who did not witness the action the ability to linearly reconstruct it in their own mind. Thus the performance can survive in the memory of the direct viewer and as a reconstructed version for a later audience. But how might we think about performance and its subsequent documentation or residual installation without its witness? In looking at Nelson's work through the lens of contemporary performance we will achieve a greater understanding of the artist's process and our experience engaging with his work. Doing so prompts a series of other questions: how might a private action lend itself to a rethinking of the stakes found in performance work and challenge the conventions of what an audience is to experience?[5] How might we consider and write in a manner that accounts for the performative which does not include a live event or a document of a specific action? What are the stakes in reading Nelson's work as such?

These queries might become clear when juxtaposed with a straightforward definition of performance as it has been understood through art history. The art historian Richard Bauman offers a well-sourced definition:

> Briefly stated, I understand performance as a mode of communicative display, in which the performer signals to an audience, in effect, 'hey look at me! I'm on! Watch how skilfully and effectively I express myself.' That is to say, performance rests on an assumption of responsibility to an audience for a display of communicative virtuosity. [...] The collaborative participation of an audience, it is important to emphasise, is an integral component of performance as an interactional accomplishment.[6]

4 Philip Auslander writes about how performance documentation alters the reading of a live work. See Philip Auslander, "The Performativity of Performance Documentation", *PAJ: A Journal of Performance and Art* 84, 2006, pp 1–10. See Philip Auslander, "Toward a Hermeneutics of Performance Art Documentation", *Kunsten A Falle: Lessons in the Art of Falling*, ed Jonas Ekeborg, Norway, Preus Museum, Horten, 2009, pp 93–95.

5 I am speaking of dominant typified performance work that grows out of a 1960s and 1970s tradition: work that expects the presence of the artist in a live event which is experienced directly by an audience. The implication of the artist's body is emphasised in the work. The artists in particular who exemplify and are attributed to this moment include Marina Abramović, Vito Acconci, Chris Burden, Yves Klein, Gina Pane and Carolee Schneemann. Their work may or may not have initially taken place in front of an audience but the action required enacting the artist's body and was then documented so it might be subsequently experienced. The live performance and its relationship to documentation has been discussed extensively. See Amelia Jones, *Body Art: Performing the Subject*, Minneapolis: University of Minnesota Press, 1998; Kathy O'Dell, "Toward a Theory of Performance Art: An Investigation of Its Sites", PhD dissertation, City University of New York, 1992; Peggy Phelan, *Unmarked: The Politics of Performance*, New York: Routledge, 1993.

6 Bauman, Richard, *A World of Others' Words: Cross-Cultural Perspectives on Intertexuality*, Malden: Blackwell, 2004, p 9.

Bauman's emphasis on the framing of an event as a performance and the concept of responsibility in relationship to an audience is a useful counterpoint when reading Nelson's *Double negative (The Genie)* insofar as there was no audience present for the artist's mining of his narrative

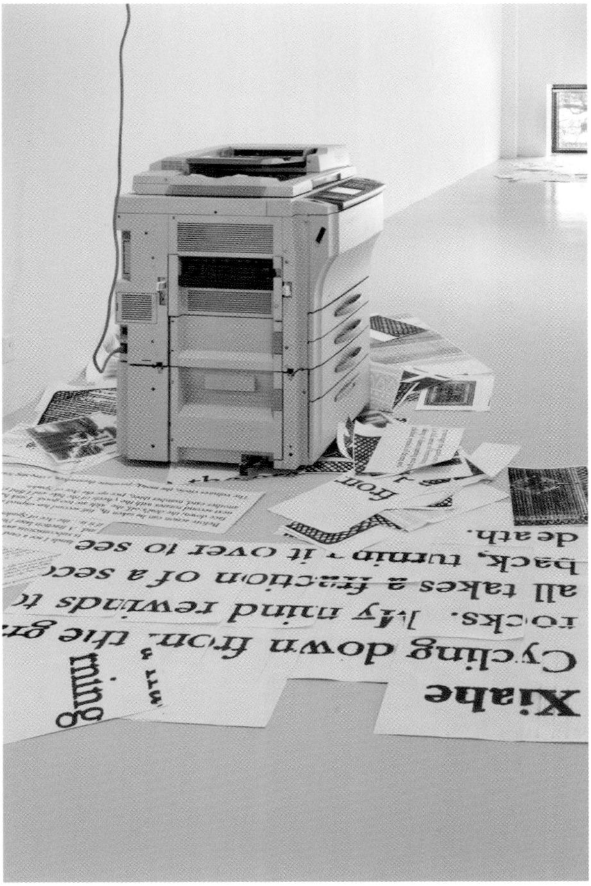

nor did he frame his action as performance. It is solely through the detritus of Nelson's search: the relics or photocopied documents—and nothing else—that an audience might understand that someone was actively sorting through the displayed remnants. Furthermore, without the presence of a performing body, the public moving through the installation is essential in reading Nelson's work. Counter to Bauman, Professor Philip Auslander suggests that it is no longer necessary for an audience to have witnessed the live, and posits that artists documenting their performance might render

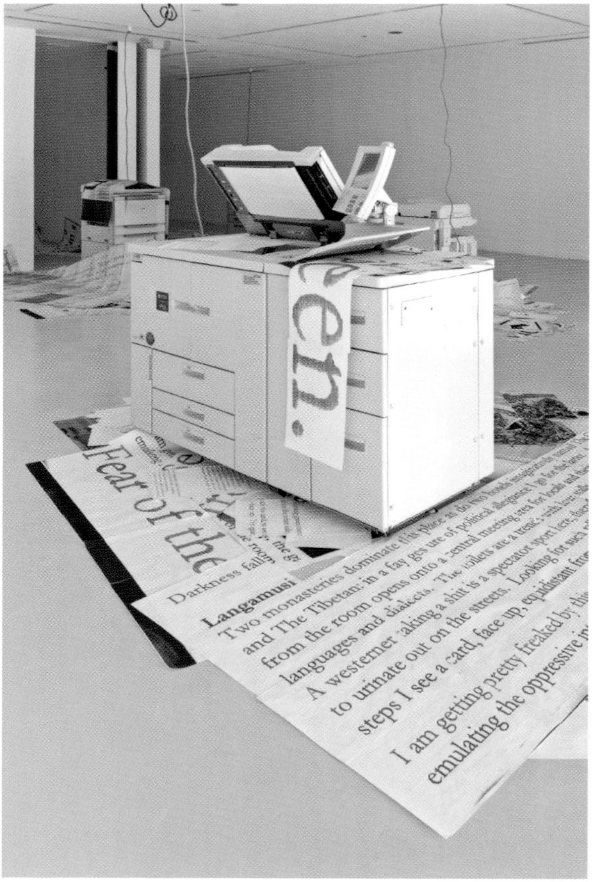

the initial audience null.[7] Auslander calls into question the relevance and importance of whether the event actually occurred: "It may well be that our sense of the presence, power, and authenticity of these pieces derives not from treating the document as an indexical access point to a past event but

7 Auslander, "The Performativity of Performance Documentation", pp 1–10.

from perceiving the document itself as a performance that directly reflects the artist's aesthetic project or sensibility for which we are the present audience."[8] In this respect, the viewer is integral. Artist and writer Aaron Williamson positions the public as an active body whose role in performance

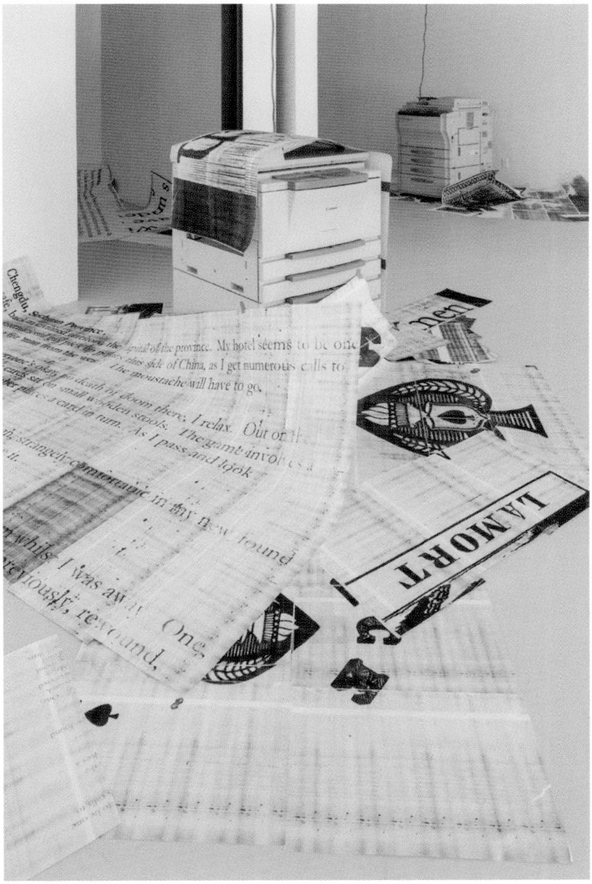

is essential. In order to do so, he suggests that an artist "incorporate literally unconscious participation into a performance; that is, to make unwitting members of the public 'perform' in some way, or even to make them and their responses the subject of the work".[9] Following the arguments put

8 Auslander, "The Performativity of Performance Documentation", p 8.
9 Williamson, Aaron, "The Unconscious Performance", in *Art, Lies, and Videotapes*, Liverpool, 2003.

Luqu
I've fucked up.
embroidered ca
outback, floorb
has become my
pausing momen

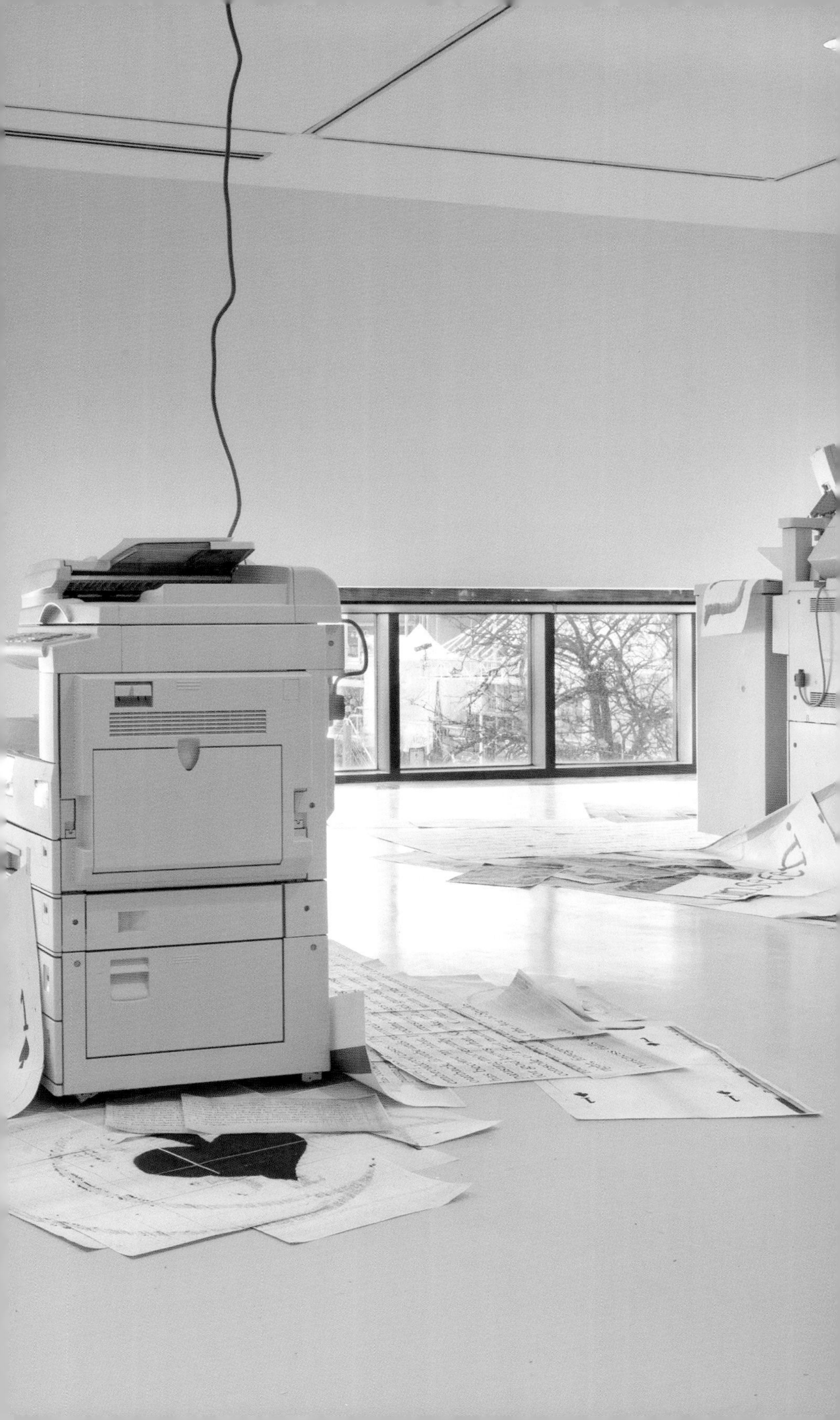

forth by Auslander and Williamson, it seems that the crucial relationship in thinking through a work as performance is that between the document and the audience. In the case of Nelson's work, because we cannot know that the performance took place—which is to say there is no performing body nor direct recording of the artist's action—constructing a narrative while moving through Nelson's installations, or to speak Auslander's language, his documents, assumes that when an audience is present the performance is taking place.

The viewer moving through Nelson's work is confronted by several ghosts: the unseen investigator whose action we missed and Erlend Williamson, a ghost in Nelson's travel story and a grainy figure in the photos by each machine. While Nelson doesn't consider a specific individual or character in his work, his installations call this consideration to the fore. If there is always a ghost, always someone who came through before us, then there is always action that occurred in the space. The pivotal action is that of the viewer, whose unconscious narrative construction is central in Nelson's practice. In this respect, the contemporary discourse surrounding performance has challenged the medium to alter the way we communicate, relate to and identify with the works positioned as such. Nelson's work seems to call for a rethinking of the limits and expectations of the medium and prompts a series of questions regarding the categorising of performance itself. Further, this redefined understanding of what can be categorised as performance art impacts the way we might experience Nelson's work by levelling both artistic process and audience experience.

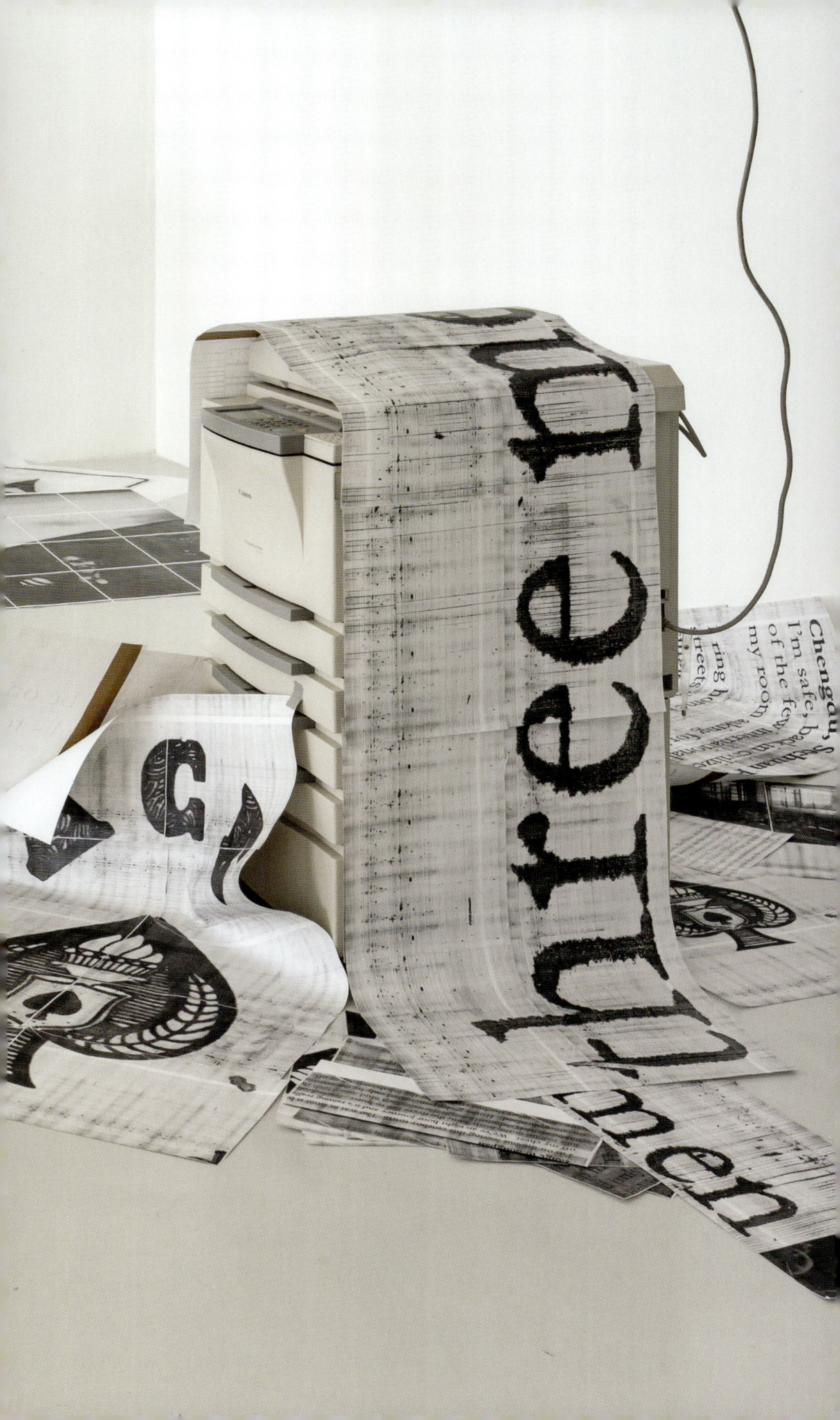
I'm safe,
of the few
my room

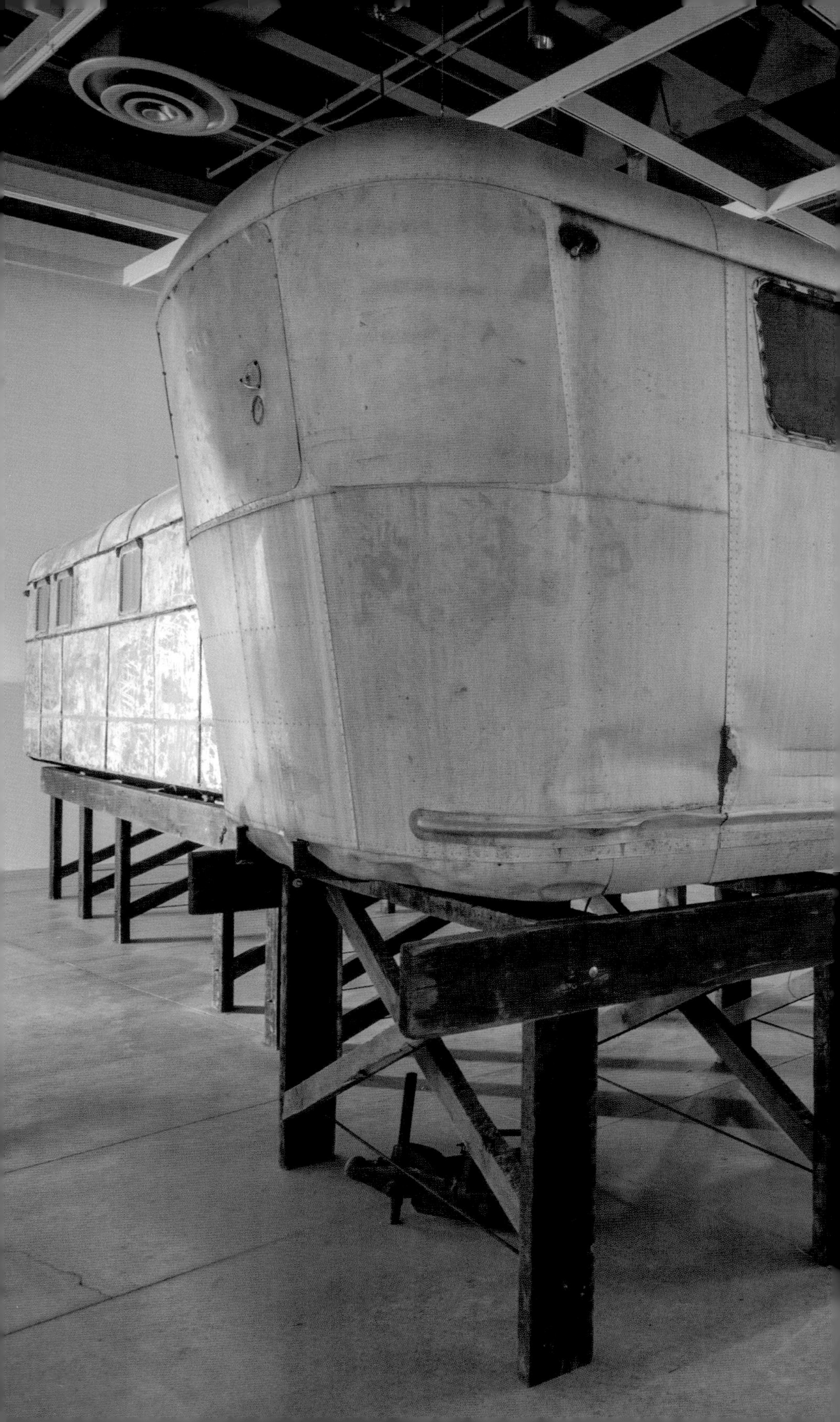

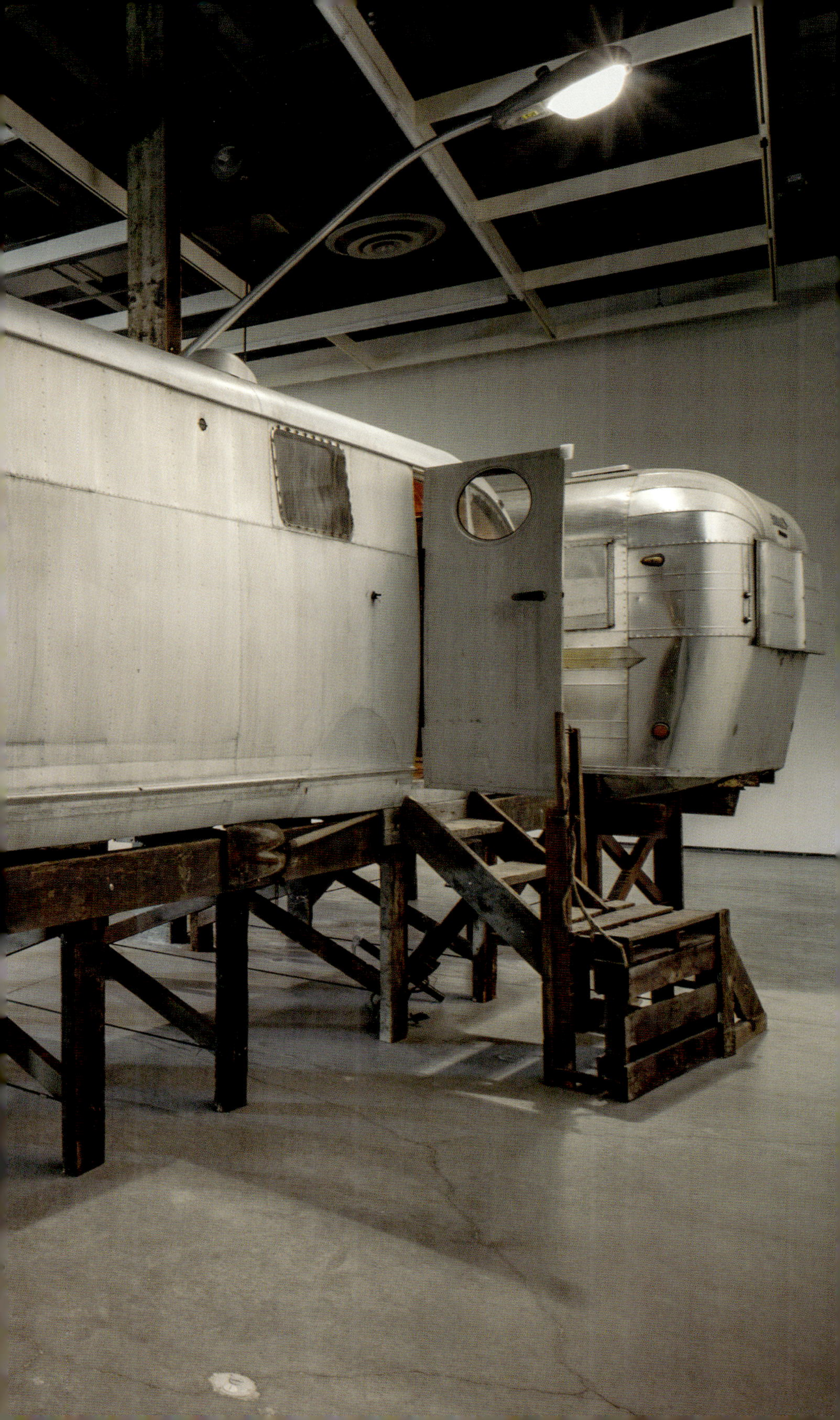

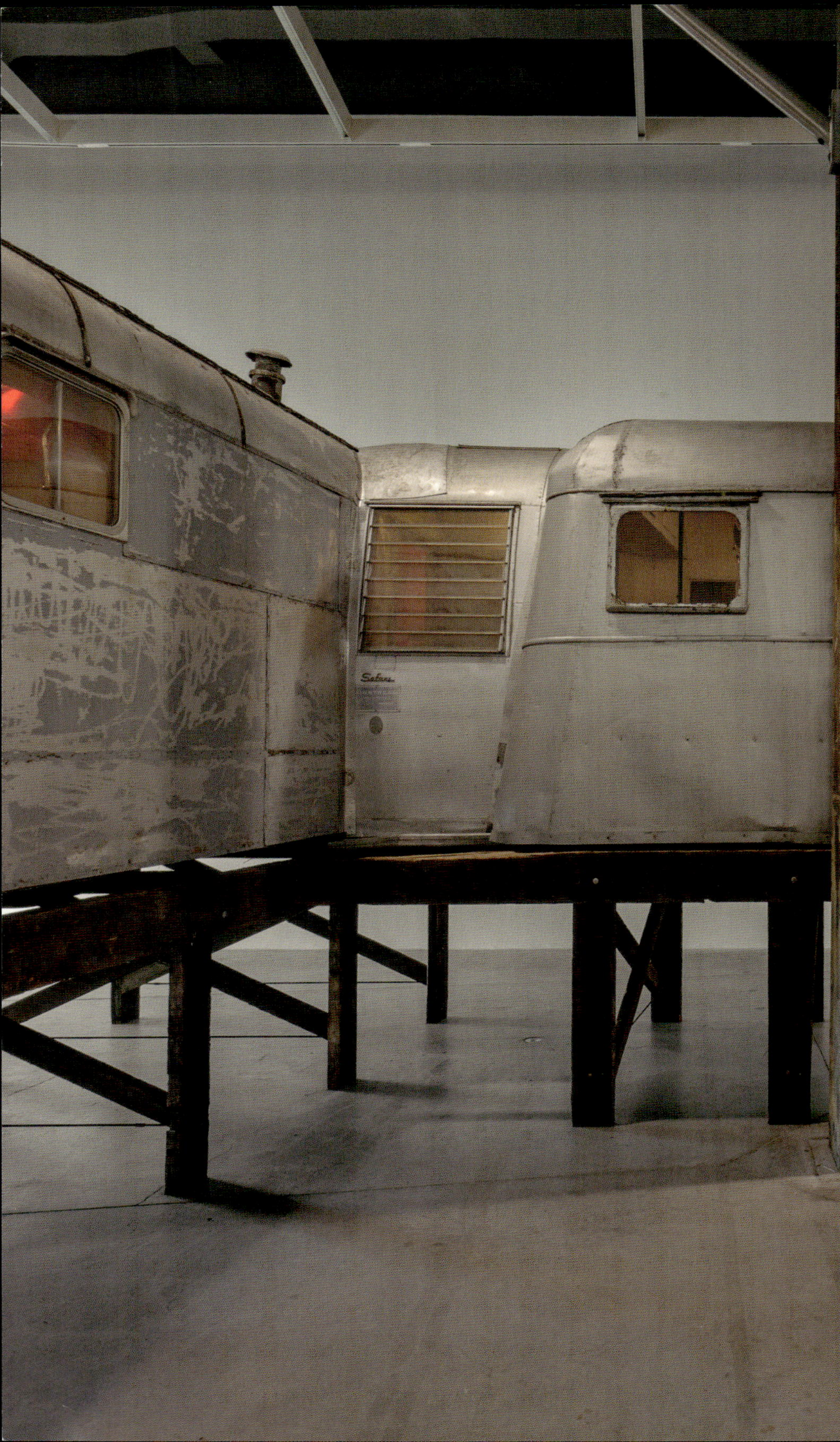

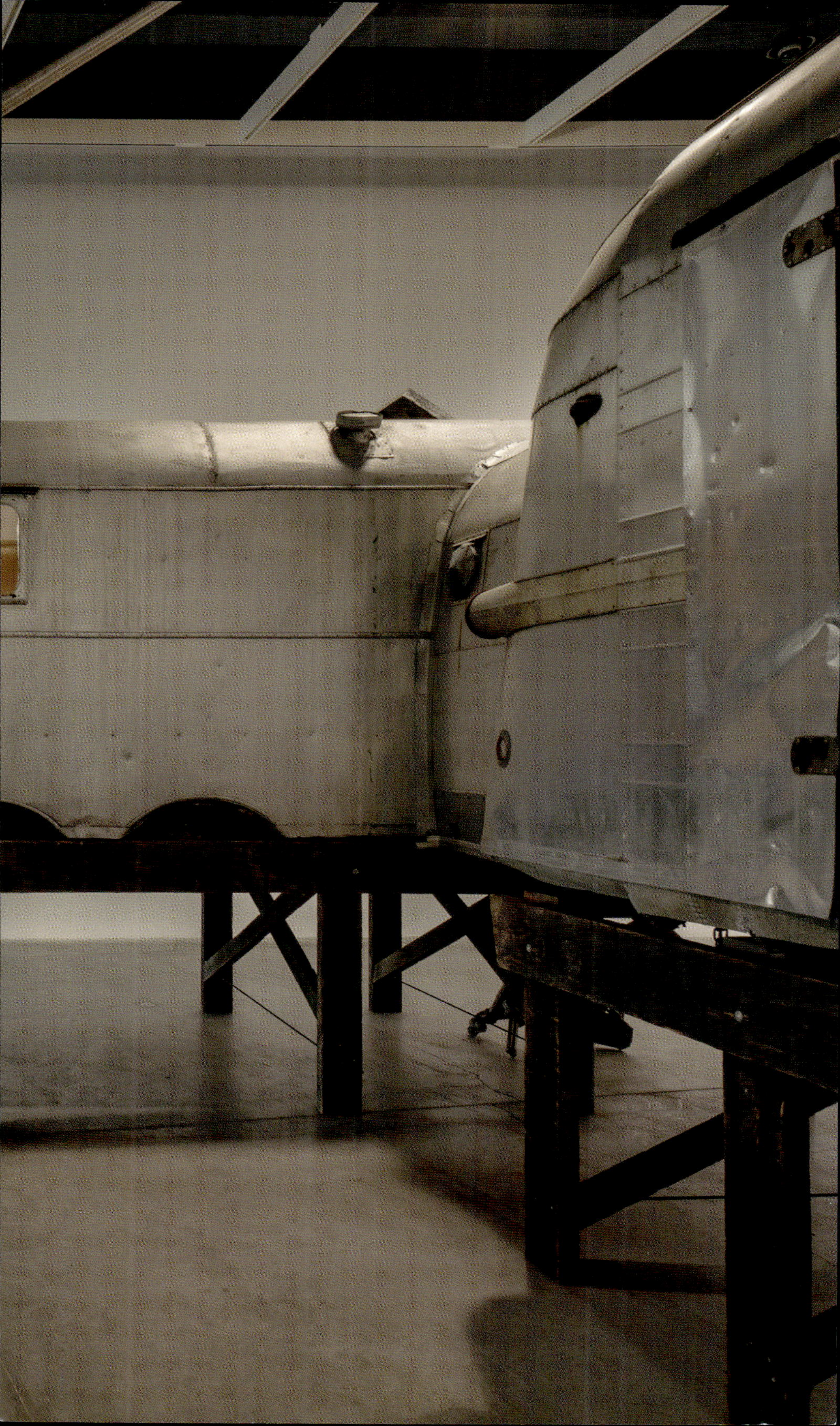

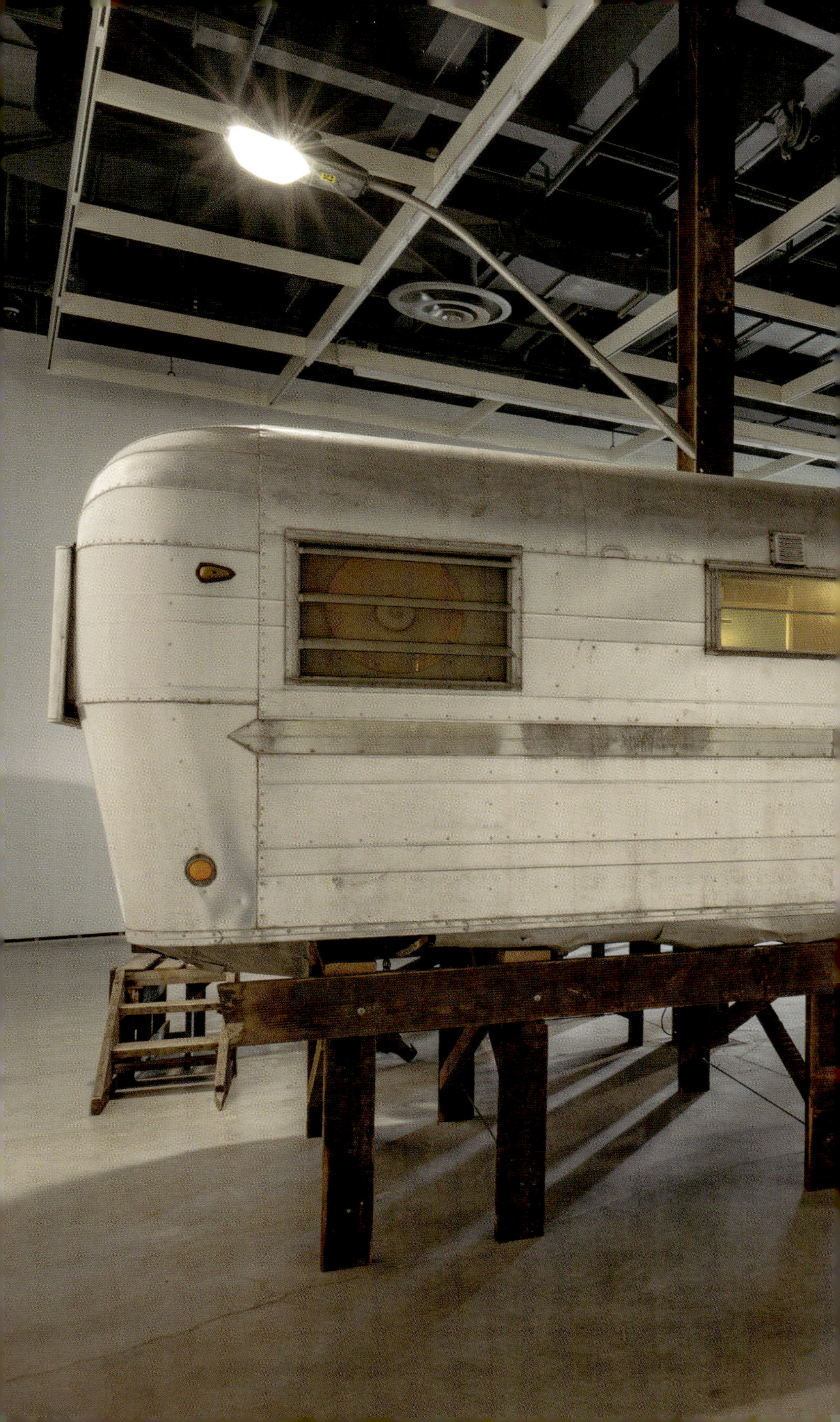

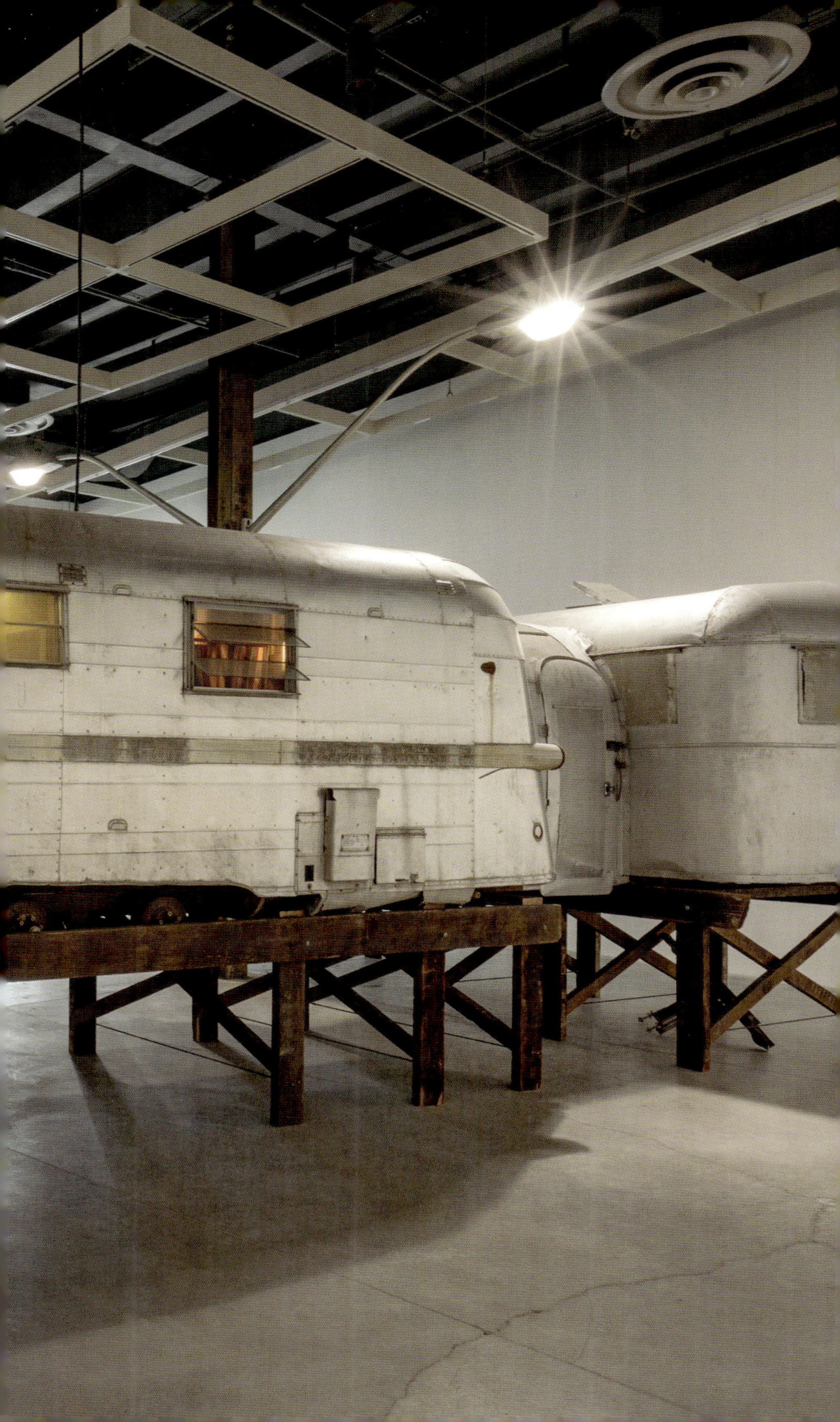

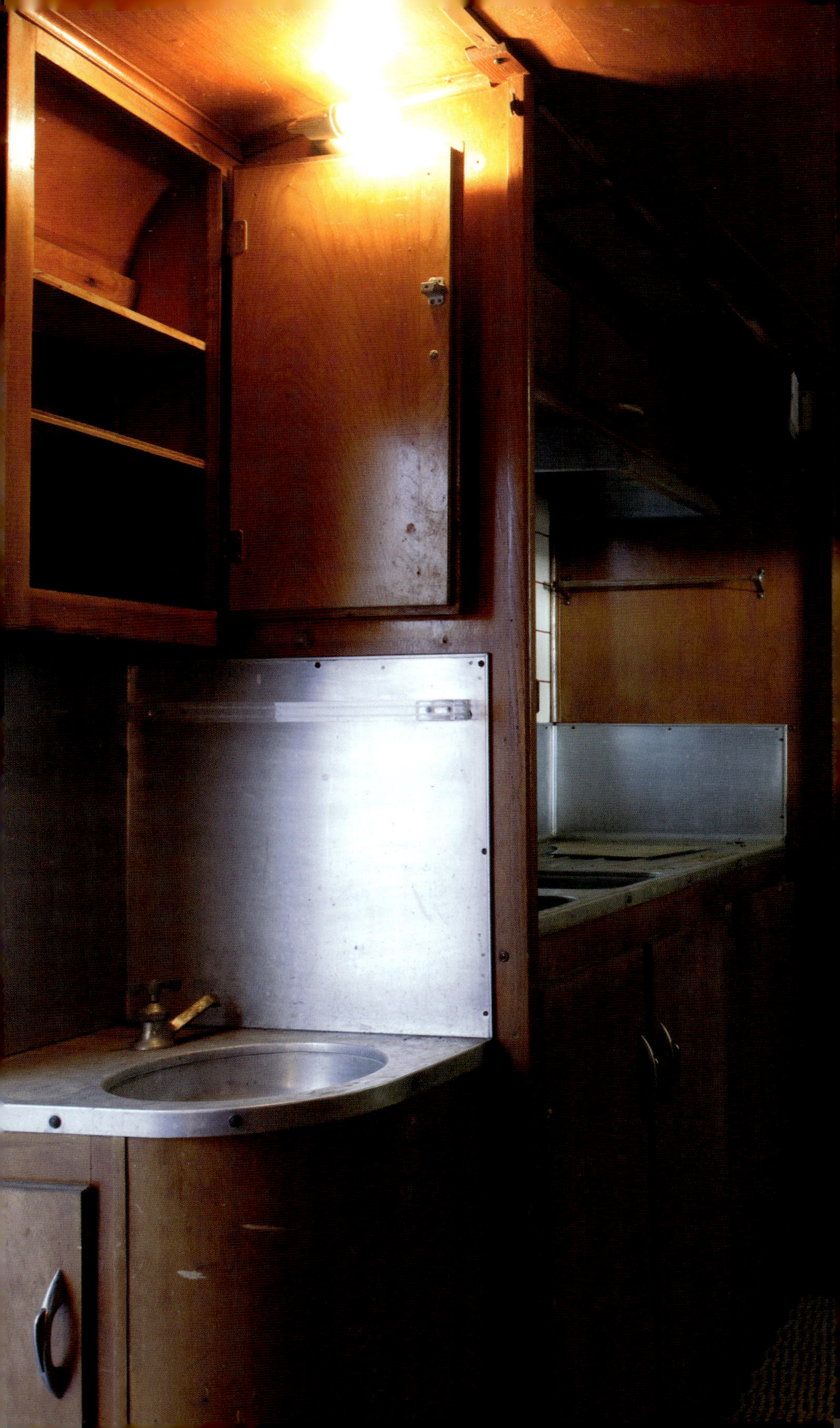

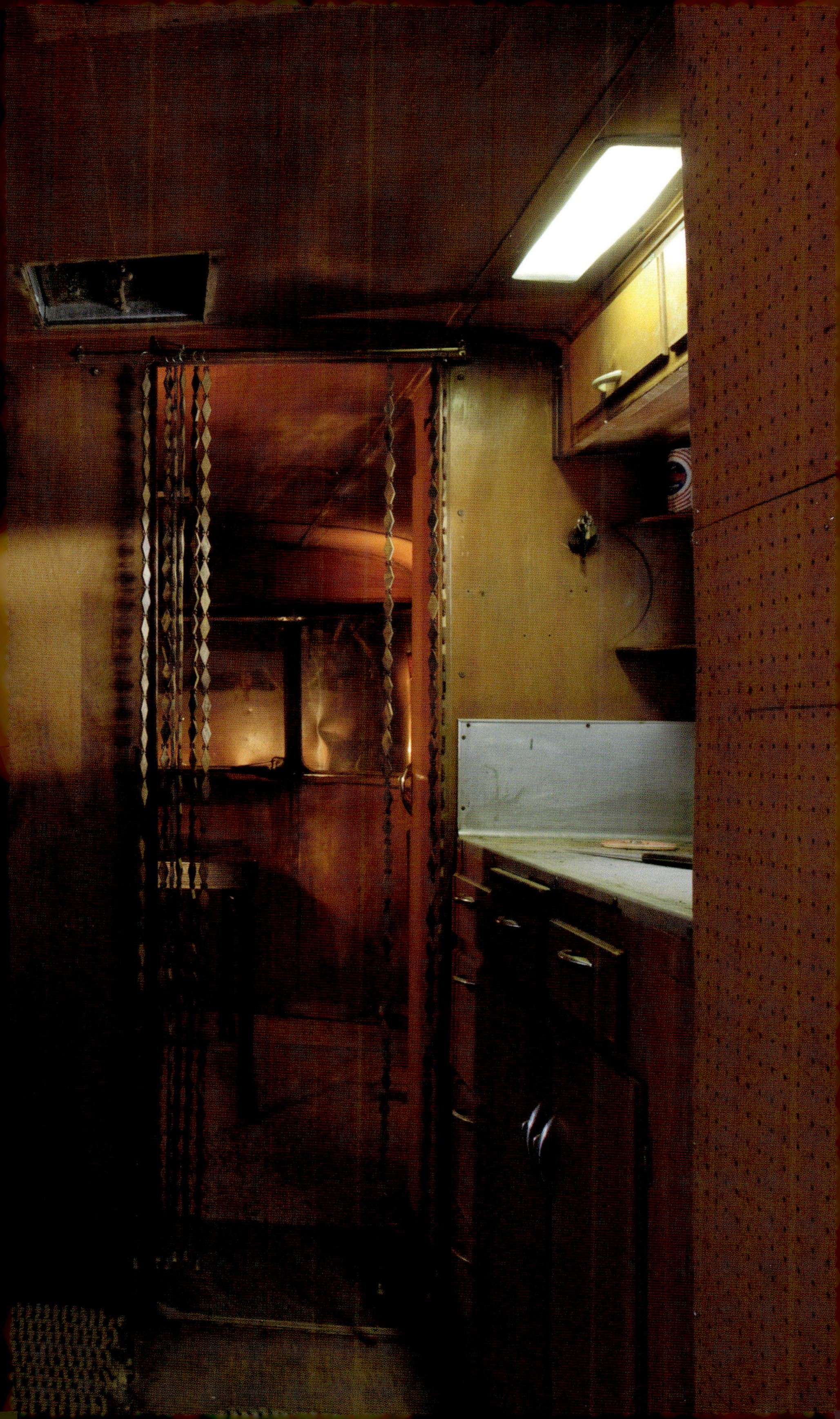

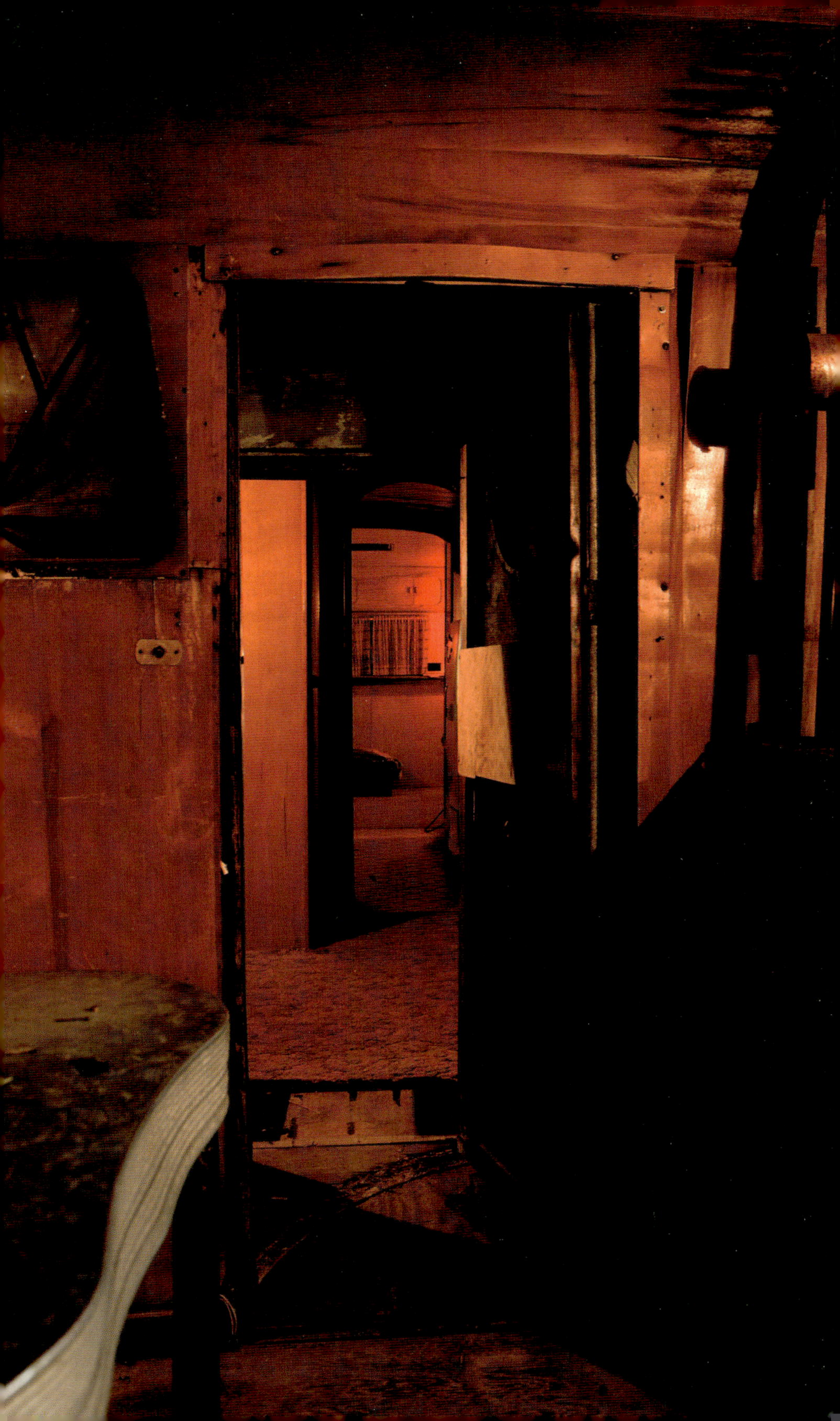

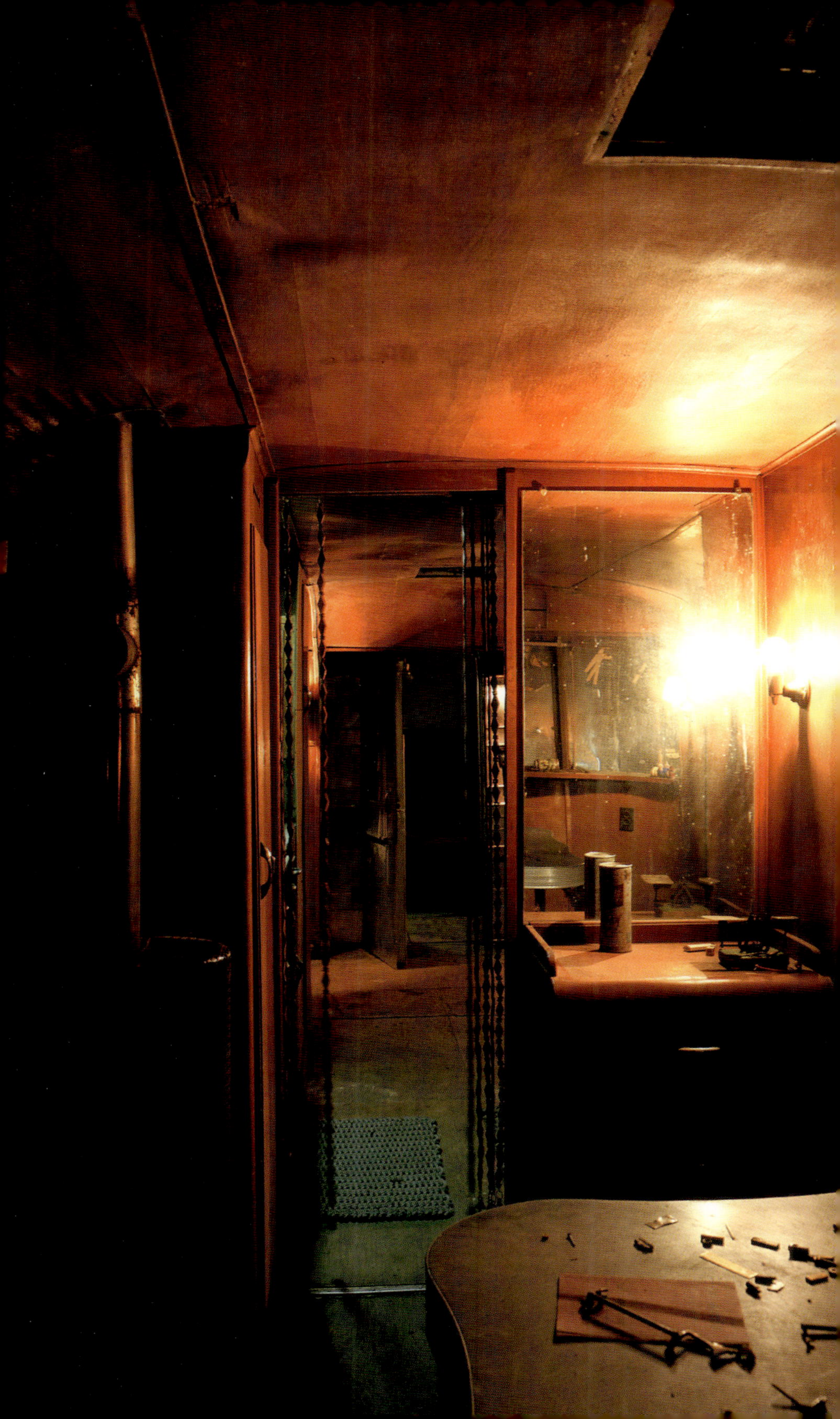

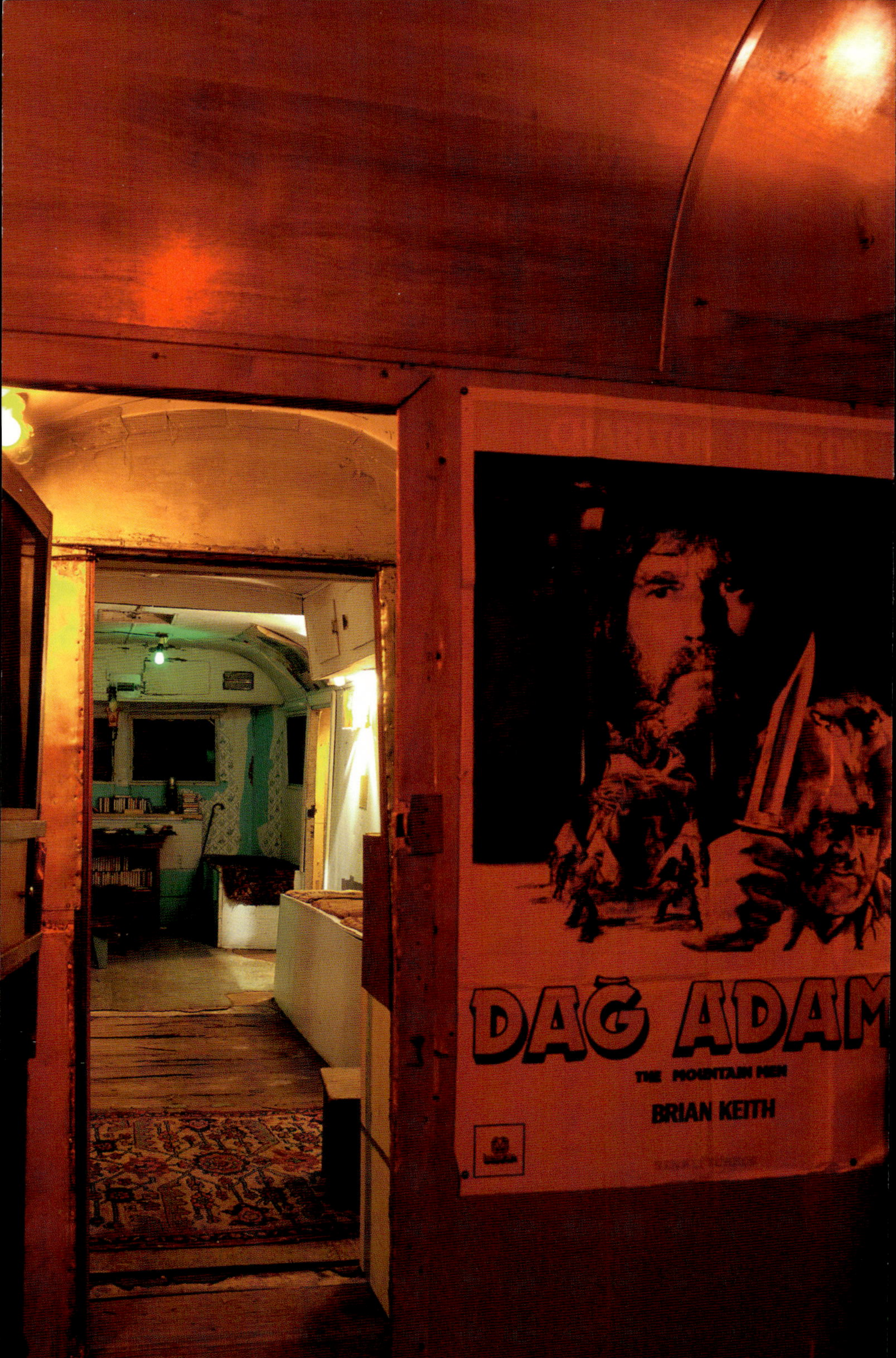
DAĞ ADAM
THE MOUNTAIN MEN
BRIAN KEITH

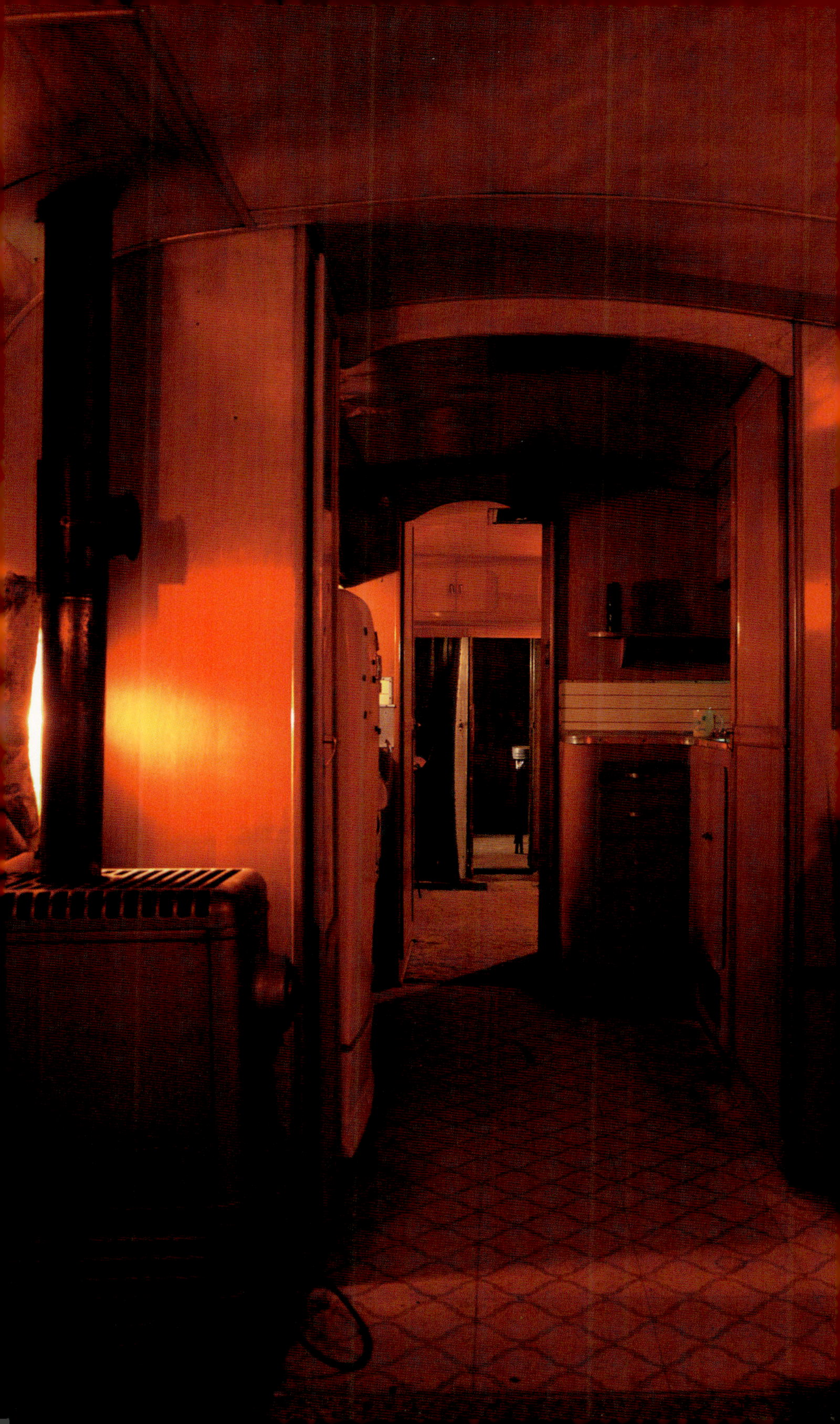

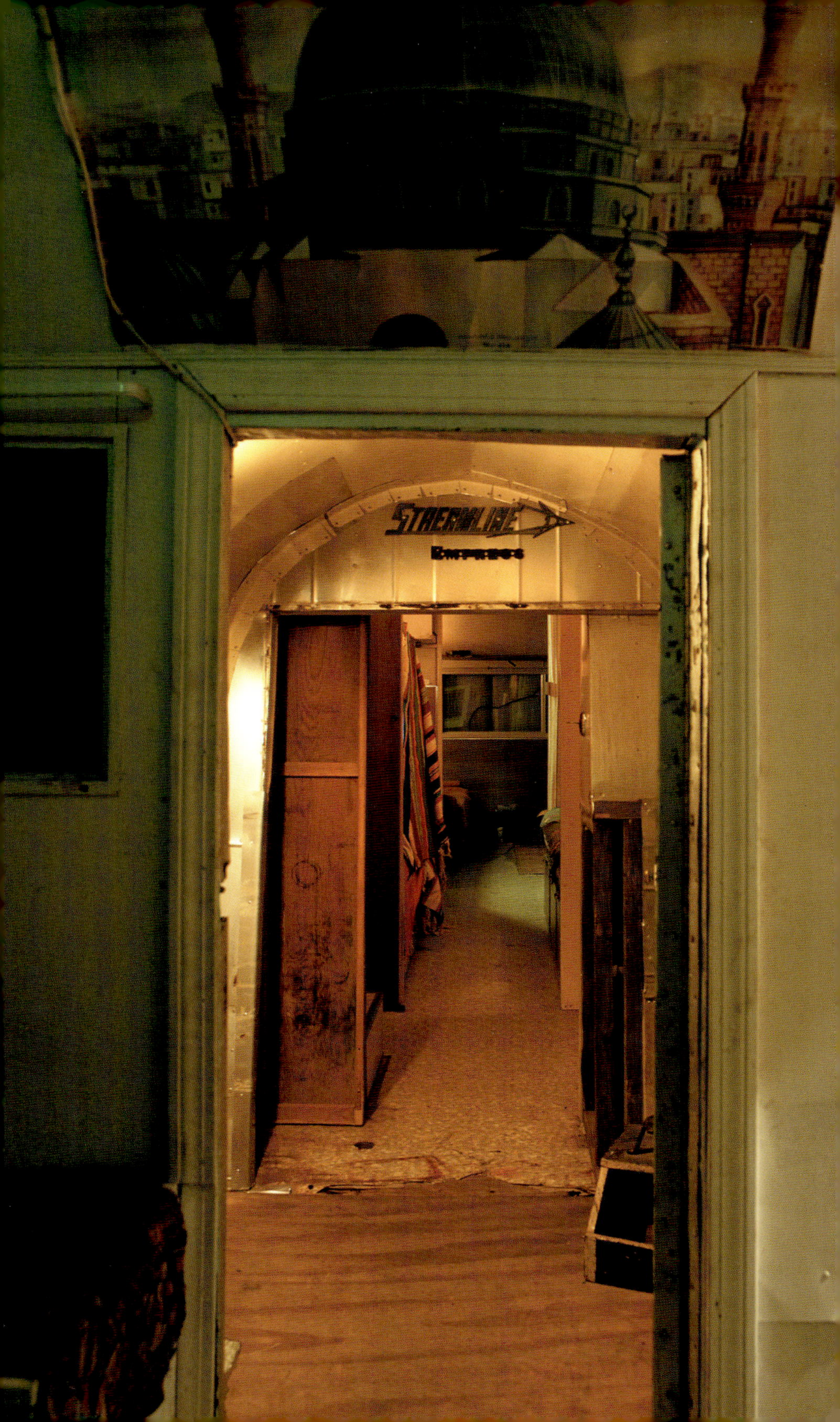
STREAMLINE

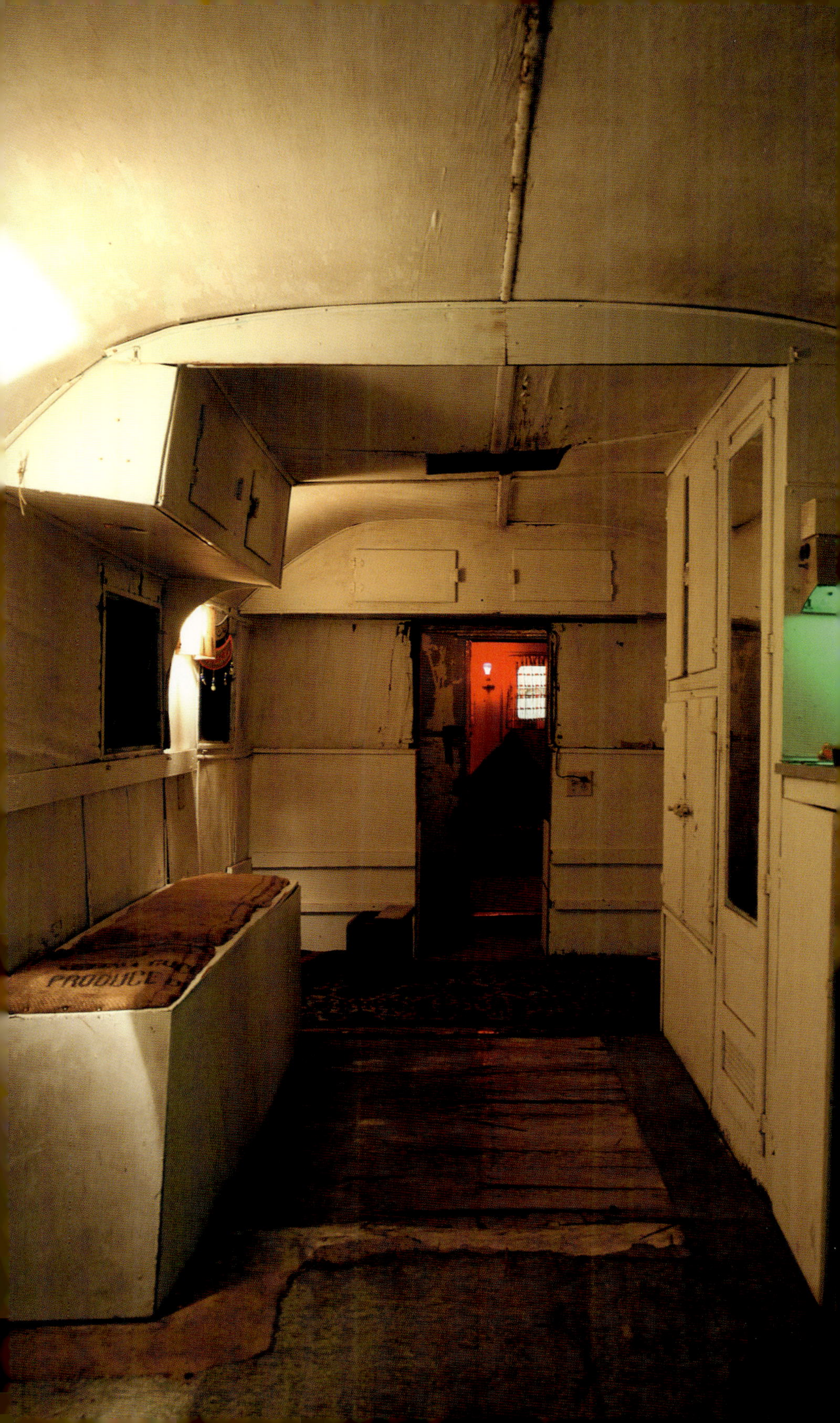
PRODUCE

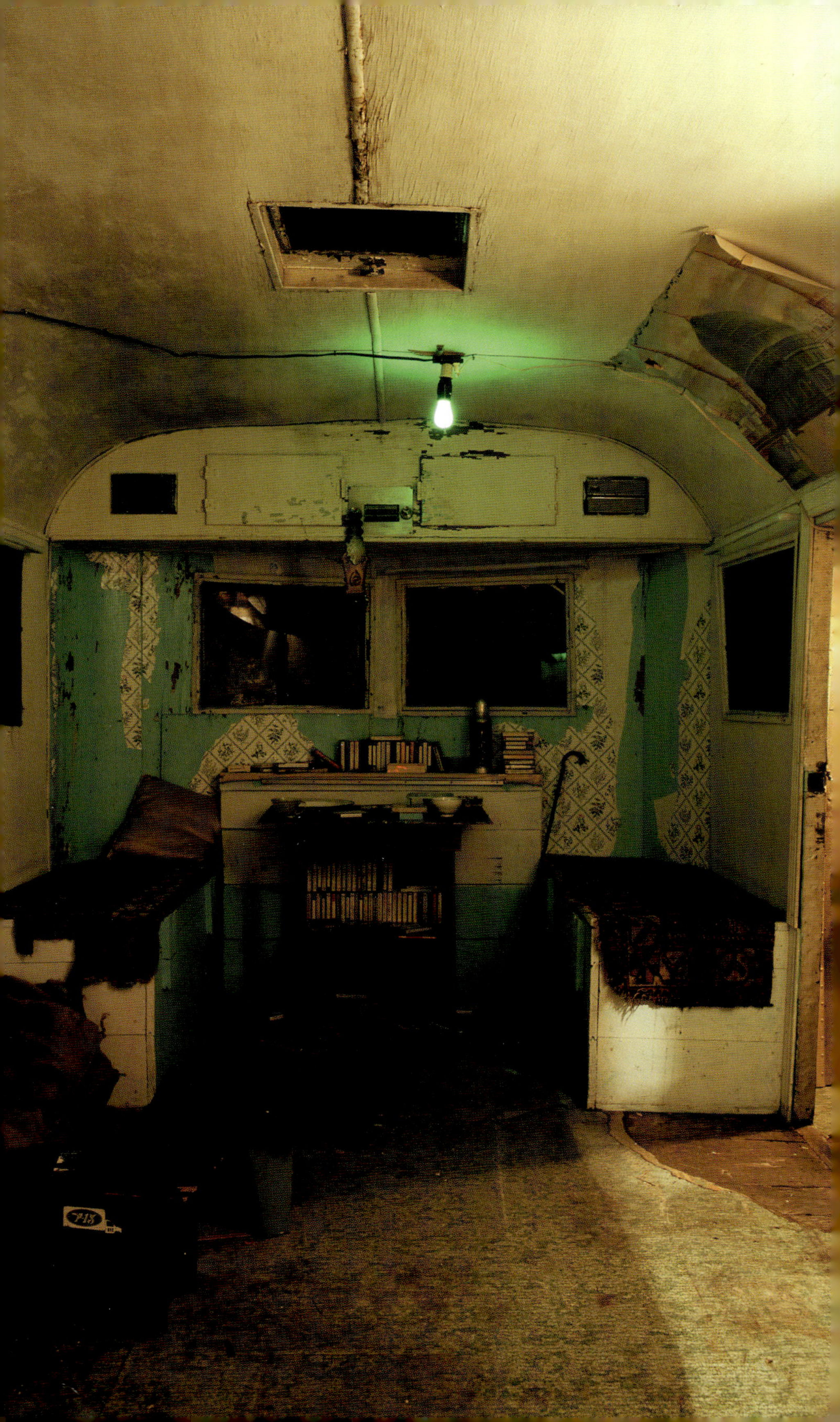

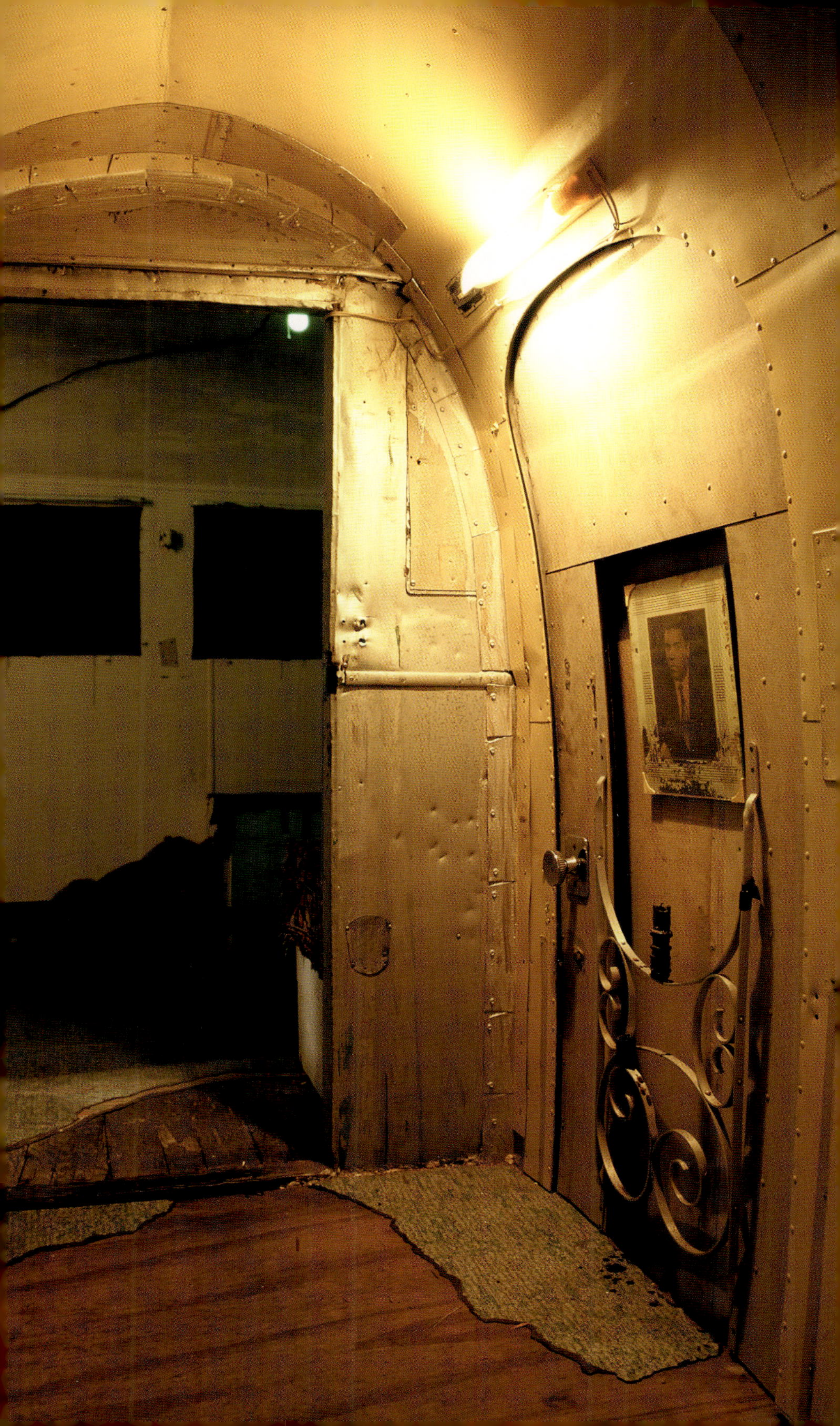

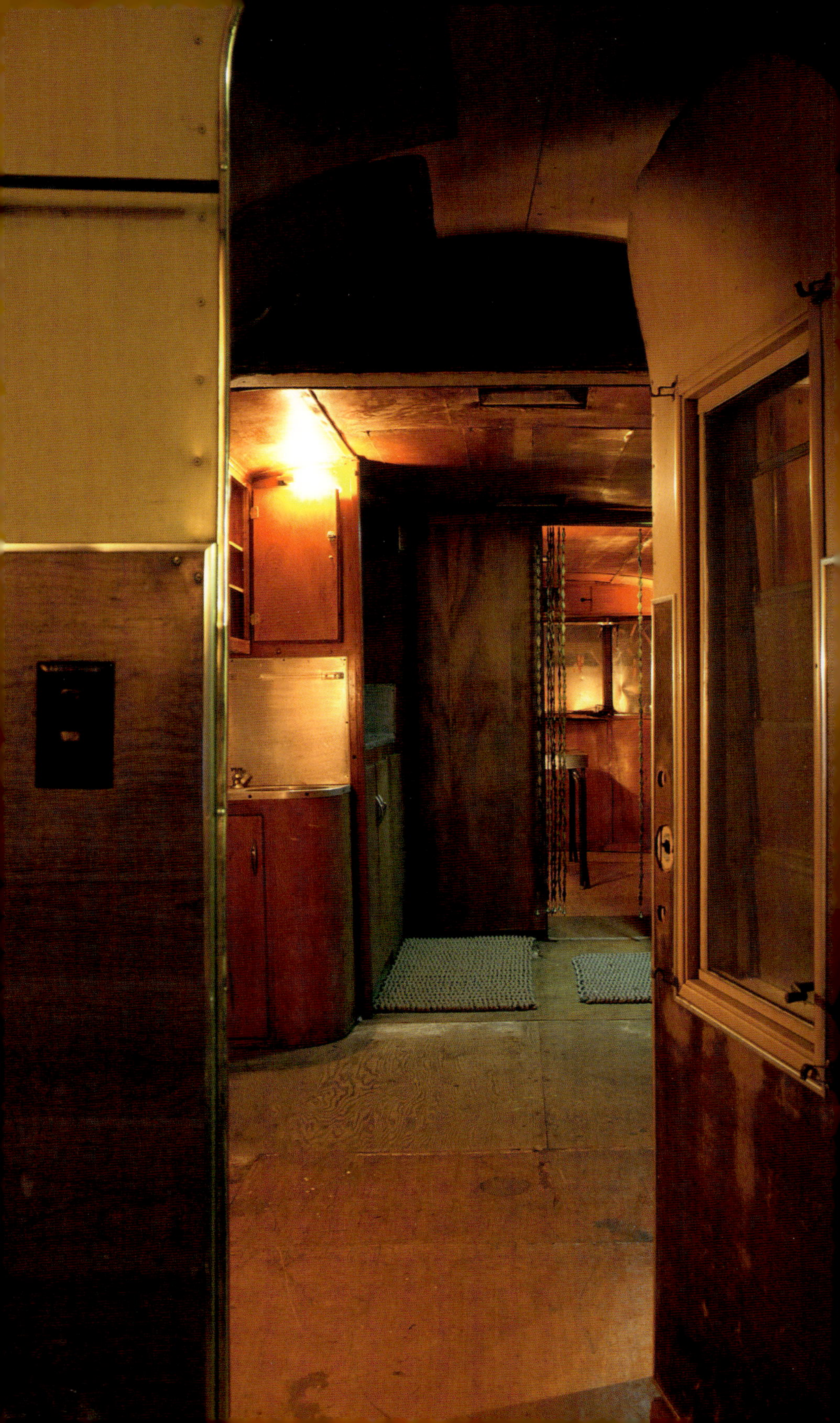

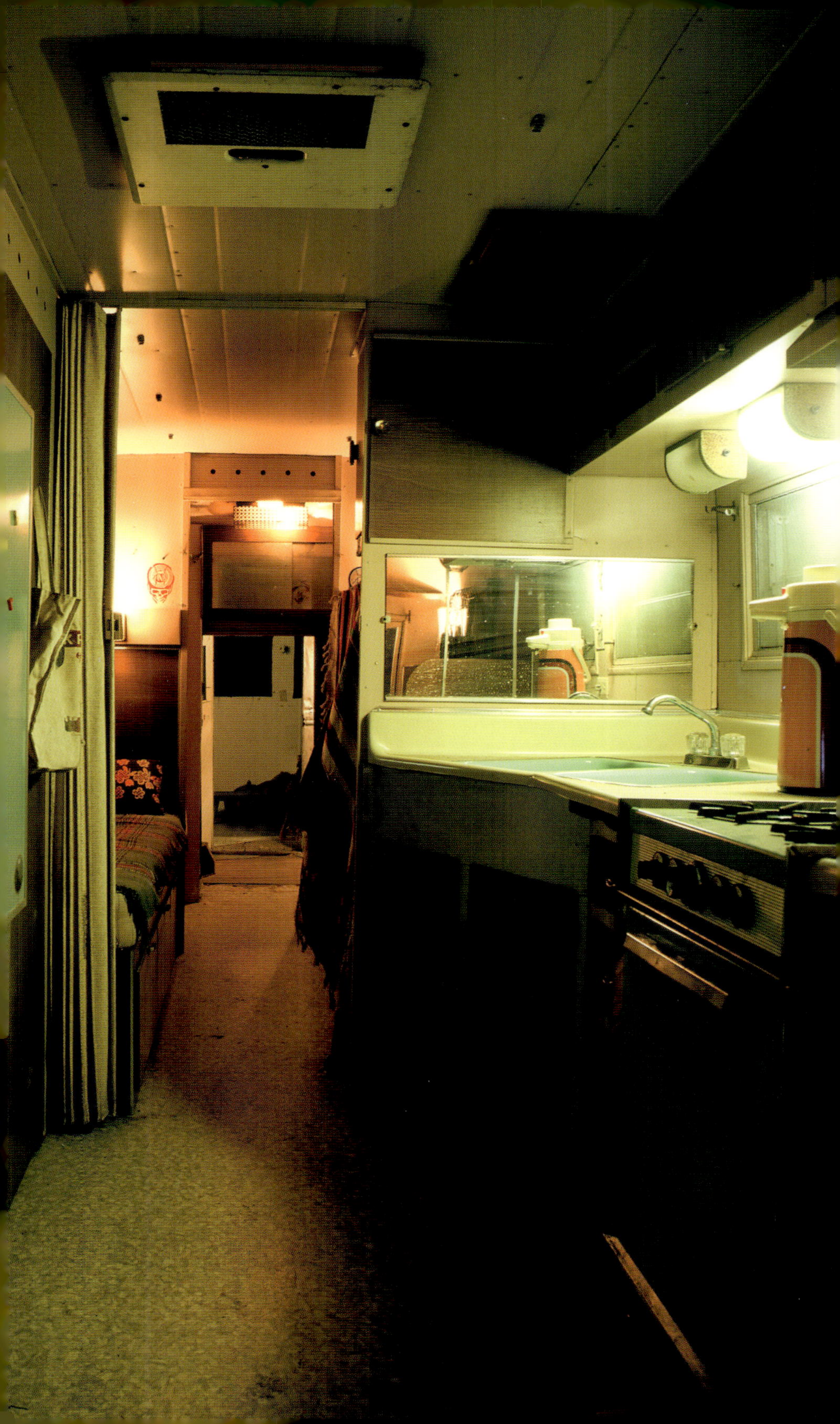

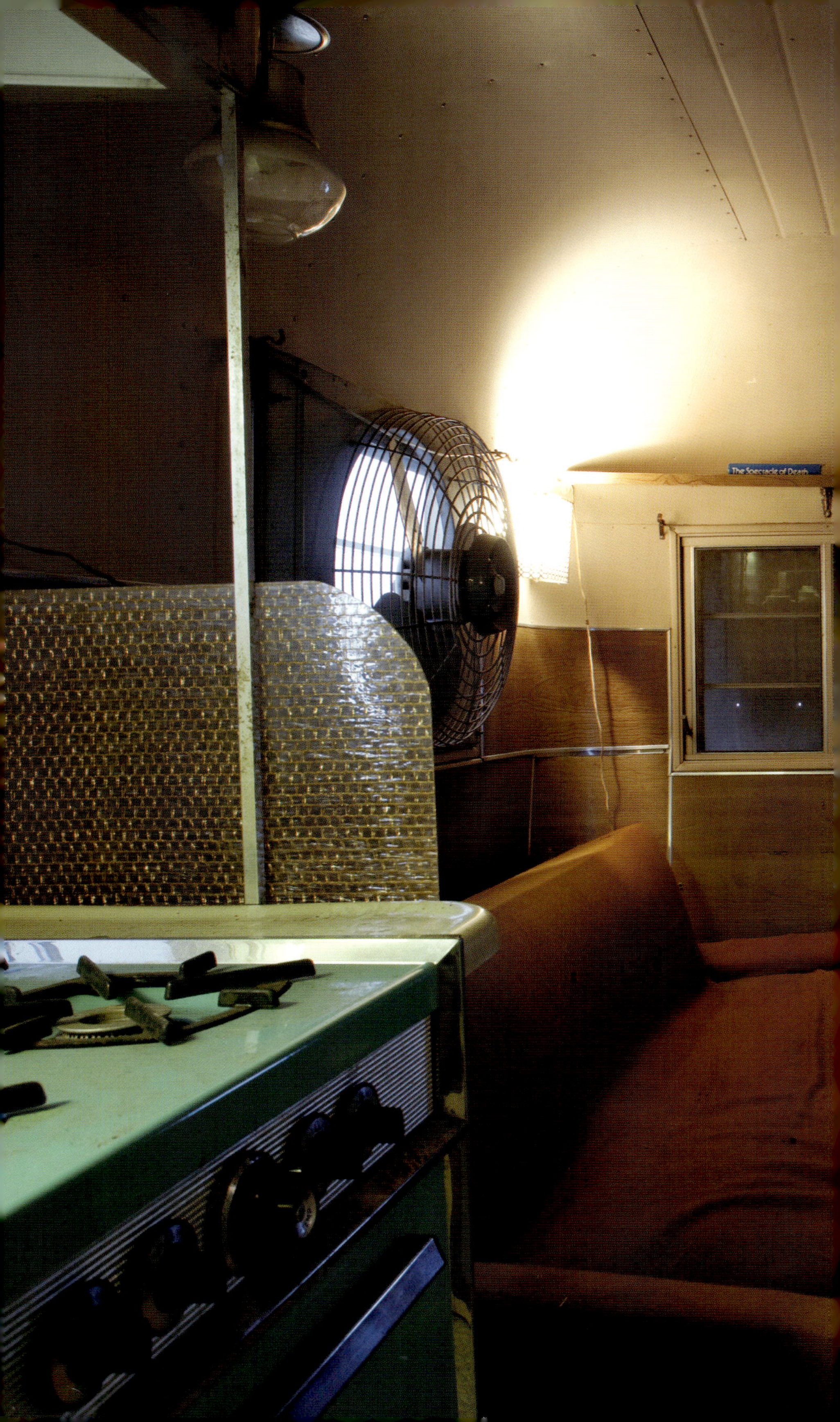

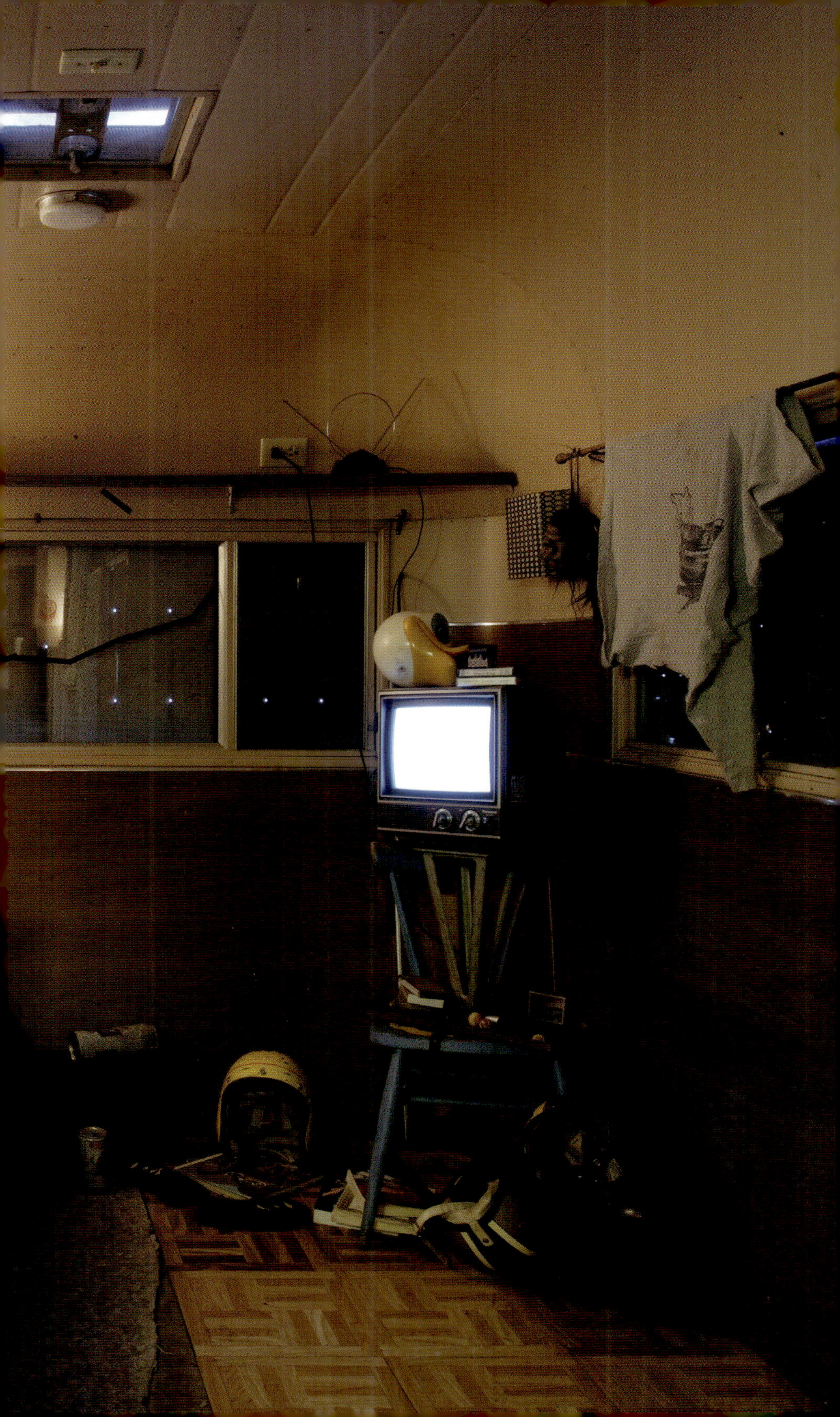

Lionheart, Master of Reality

(Featuring The Amnesiacs)

Jaki Irvine

They're driving through London in a red pickup truck, looking for the M1 motorway, heading North. A cigarette hangs from his bottom lip. Her elbow rests on the rolled down window, fingers up tapping the roof.

> For fuck sake... sorry... this car...
> ... I just can't pull out...

Finally, the last of London's sprawl shrinks behind them and she's asking him something about Helgoland.

> ... Helligoland... yeah, a big lump of red rock in the middle of the sea... after the Second World War the British decided to blow it up... just pack the whole thing full of explosives and blow it up. It was the largest nonnuclear explosion to that date I think... tails of smoke ten thousand feet high... but when the dust kind of settled the island existed as it always did, just with a few new geological features...

Meanwhile in a gallery in Bremen, bits of masticated wood and paper and shit pellets litter the bottom of a large cage. The bits of newspapers that remain legible are full of hope in a future that has receded into the past. *1969: Prince Charles becomes Prince of Wales, heir Incumbent to the British throne... Men walk on the Moon...* dreams of progress and development... of Britain... and the Western world.

More animal and human debris is housed in nearby cages: a rubbish sack stamped "Helgoland '97"; a telephone directory; sheepshit; bits of red rock stored in a Cuban cigar box... all heralding from the same wasted island.

> ... Helligoland, now little-more than a cheap duty-free for day-trippers.

And the red pickup turns off the motorway, as the conversation turns towards Lionheart.

> Lionheart: the heroic twelfth-century king of England, the first true British imperialist... to cross the seas, to fight the Arab or the African or the Muslim... for the good of Christianity... for the good of country... for the good, of territory... Lionheart... whose name is replete with ideas of conquests in foreign parts; of exoticism and mystification... and the golden lion takes its place—heraldic symbol of a majestic nation.

In Bremen, an armless figure stands on top of a cage. Toy arrows stick out of the body that is little more than a pair of waxed overalls on a wooden armature. Its dishevelled lion's head is thrown back in a pantomime of pain. *Lionheart*.

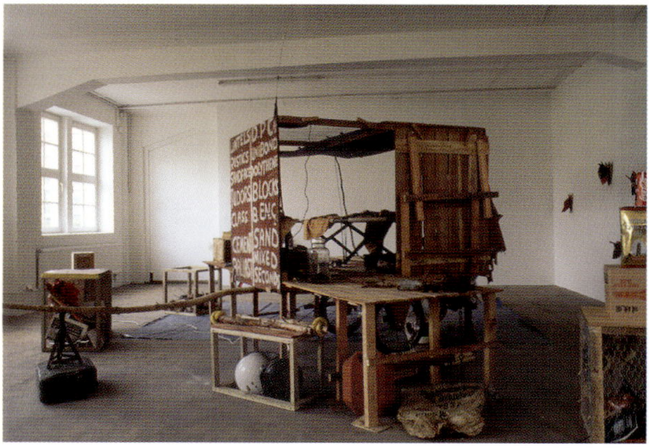

Lionheart, 1997
Galerie Im Kunstlerhaus, Bremen, Germany
Front view—the trapper's cart

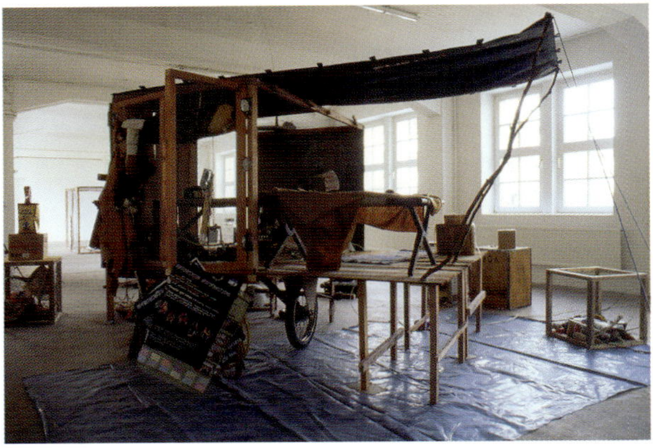

The overalls bear that quintessentially British trademark "Barbour", its embroidered logo hinting at the pretensions of a class for whom hunting and fishing are a sport.

Lionheart—the hunter and trapper turned scarecrow, mocked by its own waxed overalls... pierced by the arrows of 'Red Indians' and the implicitly childish ignorance of other cultures and histories which these arrows point to.

"We've come to a point at the end of the empire, a kind of deadend point—we're as low as we've ever got in the last thousand years." He slams the door of the pickup and sets off in search of a bite to eat. "Y'know, this may all look very picturesque, but it can be a pretty rough place...."

Back in the gallery, a makeshift trapper's camp has been cobbled together out of bits of wood and rope and tyres. Inside the trailer there's a homemade dartboard, drawn up in chalk on the back of an old board. The darts sticking out of it bear union-jacks and golden lions on their flights. A small table sports carved lion's feet.

Charred wood, like the remains of an oversized campfire, rests on the floor in a parodic memorial to itself.

Nearby, on a small prayer rug, a bundle of *National Geographic*s tied together with string rest on a cardboard box.

There's no invitation to undo the knots, to find out a bit more that might enable one to learn something new about the countries and cultures charted so diligently for so many years in the pages of these magazines. It's somehow too late for that, at least for the present—right now they

ABOVE *Lionheart*, 1997
Galerie Im Kunstlerhaus, Bremen, Germany
Rear view—sleeping quarters (social housing banner canopy)

OPPOSITE *Lionheart*, 1997
Galerie Im Kunstlerhaus, Bremen, Germany
Barbour-clad lion atop cage, with Landrover parts, crate lid

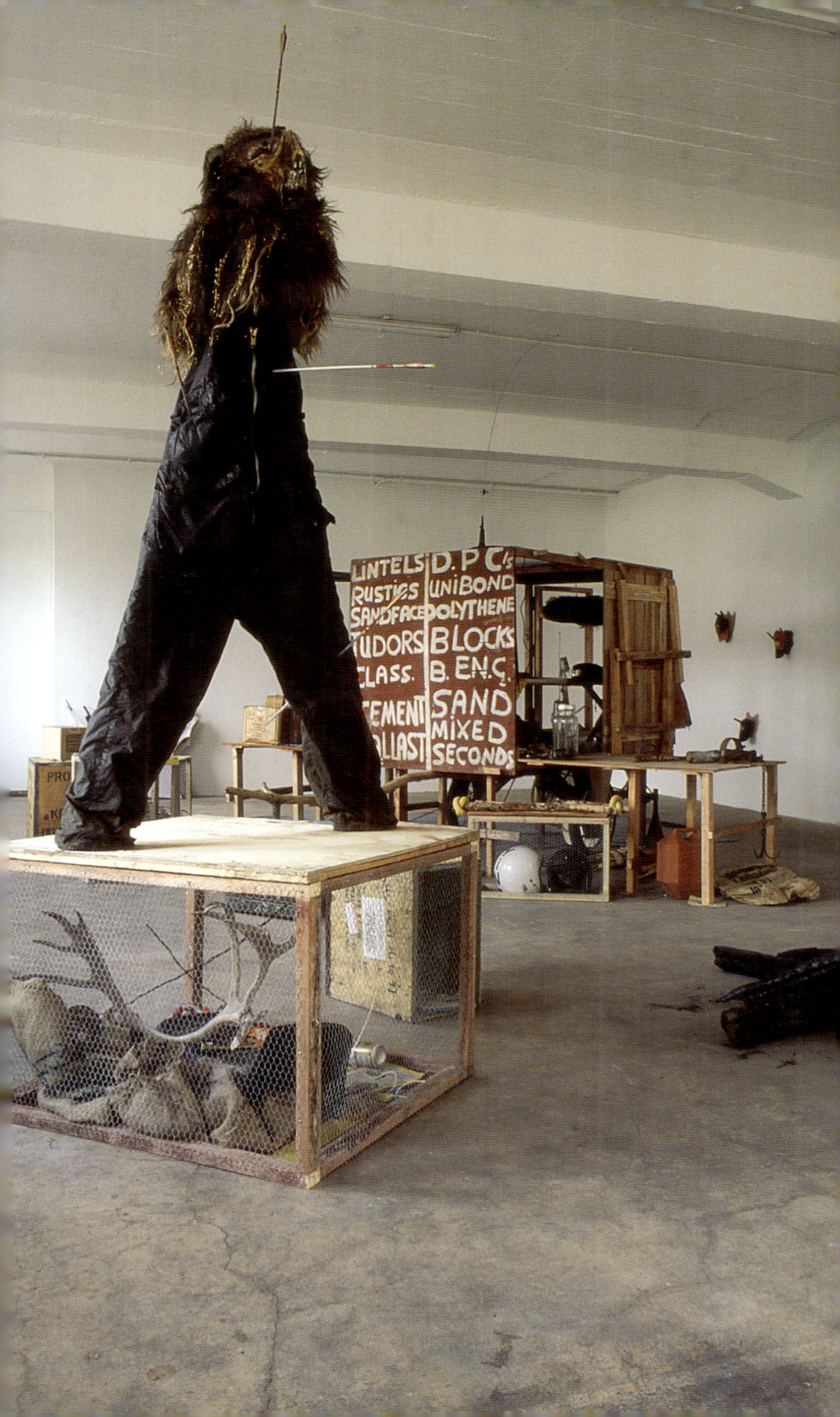
LINTELS
RUSTICS
SANDFACE
TUDORS
CLASS.
D.P.C's
UNIBOND
POLYTHENE
BLOCKS
SAND
MIXED
SECONDS

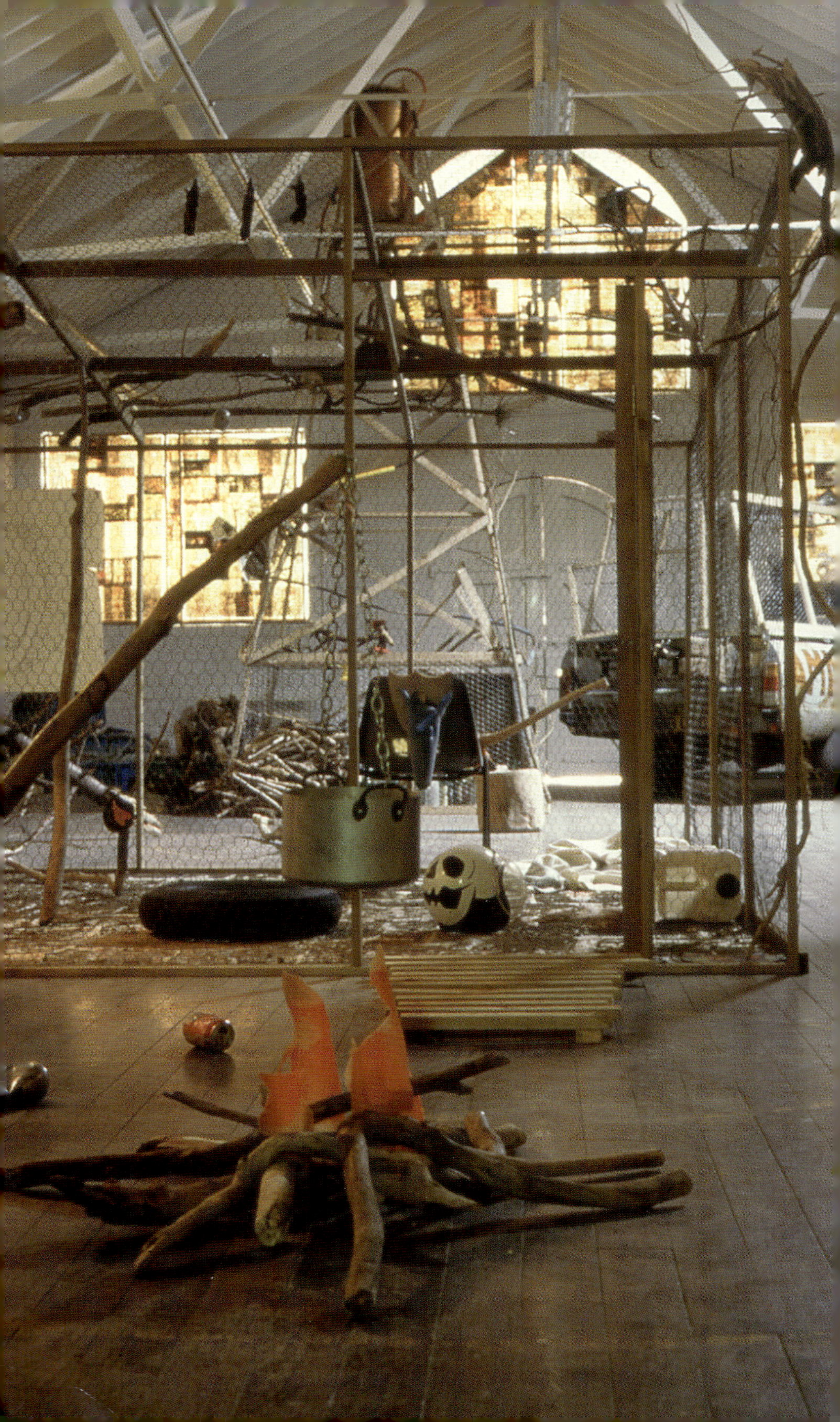

themselves are the things to be looked at, not as ciphers of knowledge, but as signs of the arrogance perhaps of presuming to make one culture available to another as something to be vicariously explored or perused. And for those who are not already conversant in Arabic or Muslim, the prayer rug and writings turn back towards themselves, indifferent to the demands of those who might claim to want to know more. If they still hold out a possibility of reading, then it is in a hermetic self-referential language, where they become signs of themselves, as things lived with and familiar but fundamentally unknown and unknowable to a gaze that has for centuries sought to dominate.

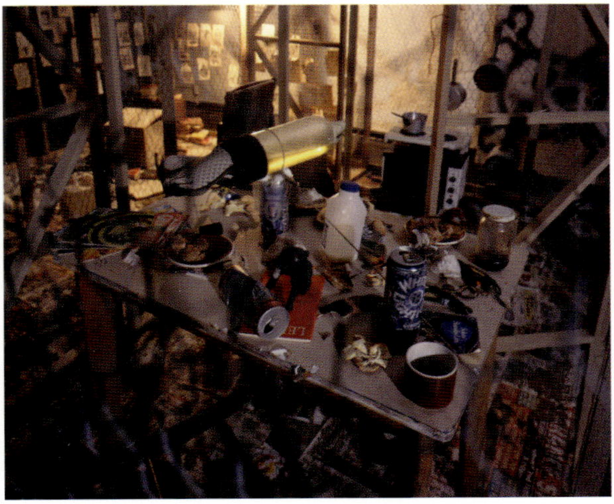

Other bundles of magazines, an American football, a toolbox, fuel cans clutter the floor, testifying to their far-flung origins and to the nomadic eclecticism of their owner. And slowly, the discarded objects begin to betray the identity of that owner. The skins, cages, traps, darts, beer cans, books—all make insinuations about an English drifter whose livelihood is based on gleaning discarded objects from the streets and markets of London, moving from one section of the city to another through Asian, Turkish, Afro-Carribean, Irish communities... sifting through things whose origins and functions were once known and cared about... things that were made specifically to perform precise functions in certain circumstances...

CPPOSITE *Master of Reality*, 1997
Berwick Gymnasium Gallery, Berwick-upon-Tweed, Northumberland UK
Southern view from centre. Amnesiac beach fire with skull helmet

ABOVE *Master of Reality*, 1997
Berwick Gymnasium Gallery, Berwick-upon-Tweed, Northumberland UK
Table view with shark, solaris, and white lightning

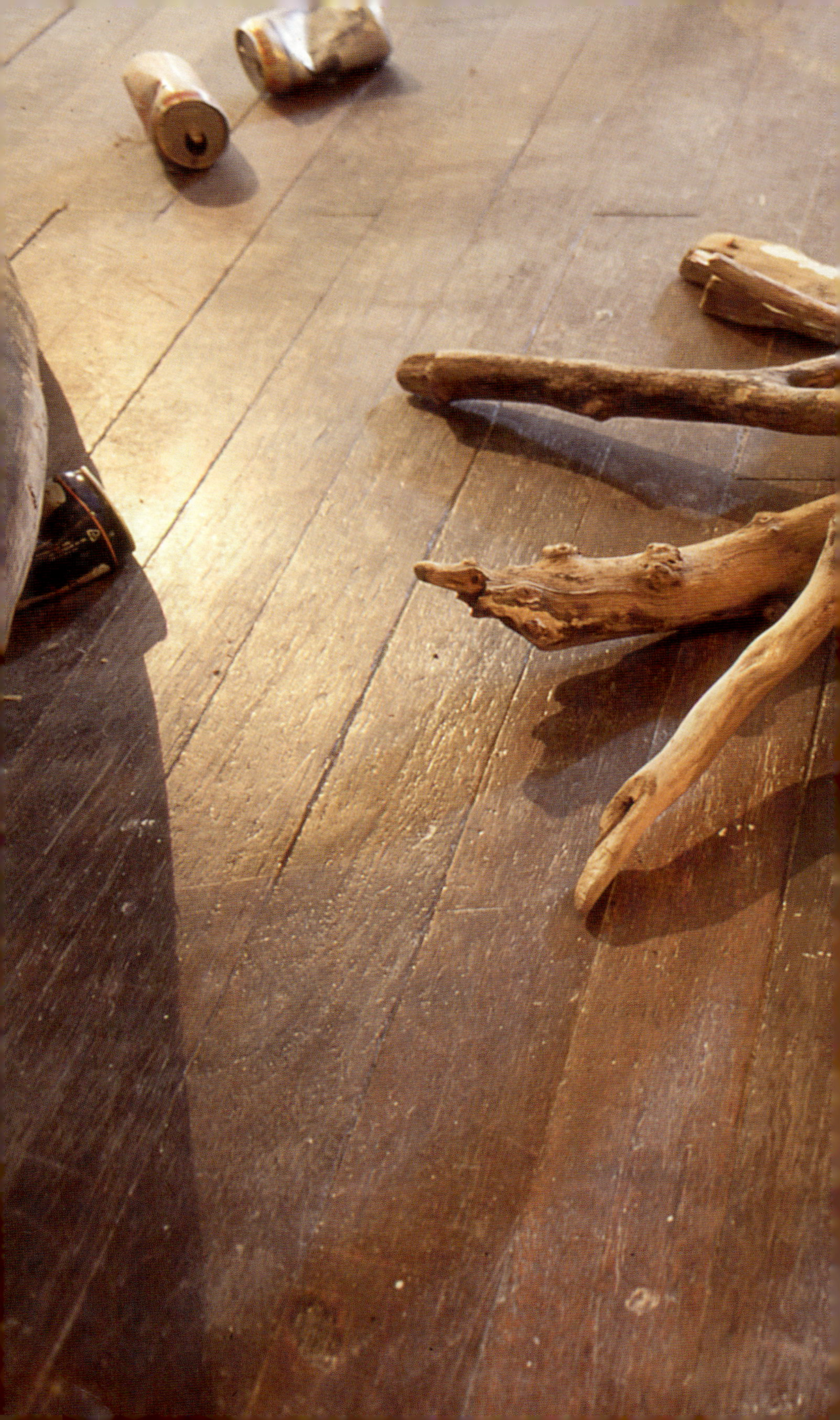

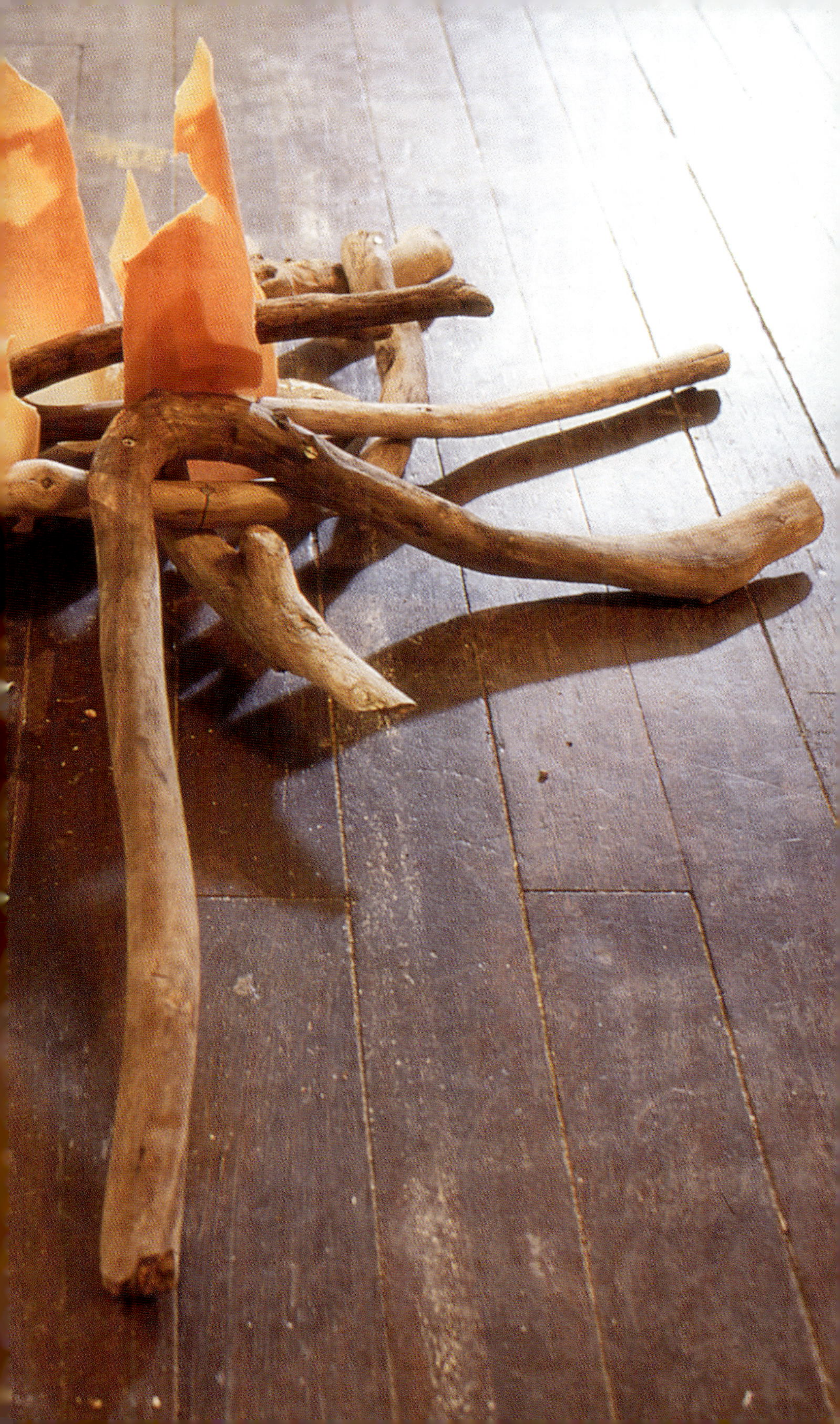

that now, dislocated from their beginnings have turned into so much junk... to be peddled by the growing numbers of poor white British trash.

And the fleamarkets of Britain are awash with secondhand goods and junk... as if the rubble of those countries once colonised had washed up on its shores, burying the possibility of forgetting what this kingdom would gladly disown.

Scrawled in white paint on the rickety walls of the trailer: ... **LINTELS... BLOCKS... SAND... CEMENT...**

In the absence of the actual materials they were once employed to advertise, the words shift and change until they begin to ask vague questions that have something to do with the possibility of building something new, out of necessity.

... **TUDORS... GLASS... POLYTHENE...**

Beer cans... a rusting animal trap... a kerosene lamp hangs on a hook above an old-fashioned wood and canvas fold-up camp bed. Its yellow blanket has the air of having been only recently cast off. A black felt hat sits beside it on the bed awaiting its owner's return.

Trophies fashioned out of baseball caps adorn the gallery walls, absurdly recalling dreams of big-game hunting and the contemporary landscape of rubbish through which our hero wanders, a landscape of hybridization where things can assume a preciousness and lose it at the drop of a hat.

The red pick-up is crossing over a long narrow bridge heading into the Northern English coastal town of Berwick-upon-Tweed. It pulls up at an old army training centre and the two people get out and go into the gallery at the back. A cluster of fishing weights has been rigged up on a pulley system so that the door closes behind them as soon as they have entered. The windows have been blocked out with screens of chicken-wire and newspapers and the smell of animal feed and bone meal hangs heavy in the air.

At the end of the long hall that serves as a gallery, a pale blue pick-up sits rusting. The cage built onto its back is held shut with the bone of some unknown animal. The word AMNESIACS is emblazoned on its sides in vinyl woodgrain. Its doors have been left open and the radio still crackles, picking up the space between the officially occupied airwaves. Something like an old homemade whiskey still, made out of a copper water tank, and a collection of piping stands nearby, the rickety structure of its high wooden armature reminiscent of the old water-mills that are dotted around the landscape in this end of the country.

PREVIOUS PAGES *Master of Reality*, 1997
Berwick Gymnasium Gallery, Berwick-upon-Tweed, Northumberland UK
Twisty cone flames

OPPOSITE *Master of Reality*, 1997
Berwick Gymnasium Gallery, Berwick-upon-Tweed, Northumberland UK
Drawing affixed to mesh dwelling interior

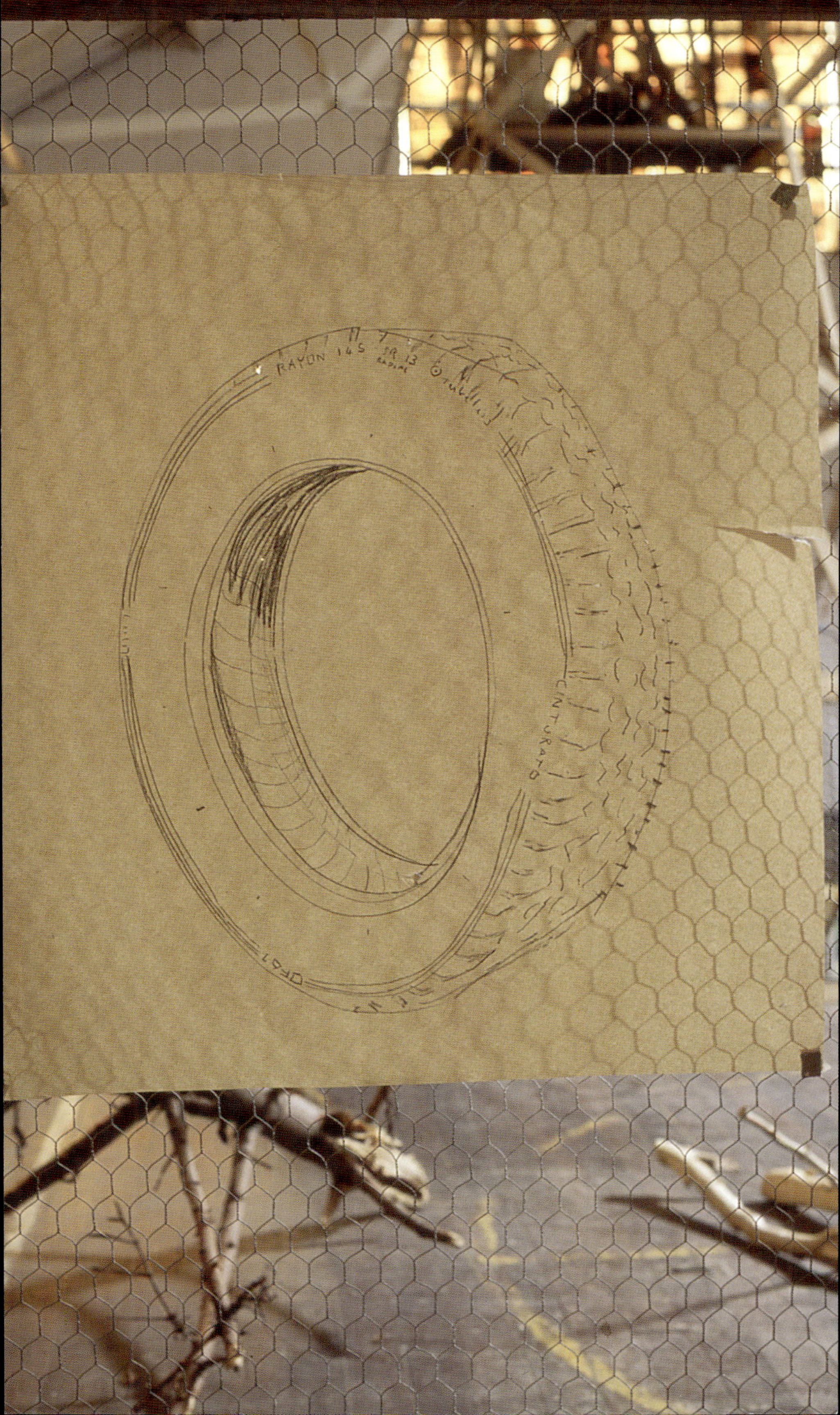
RAYON 145 SR 13
CINTURATO

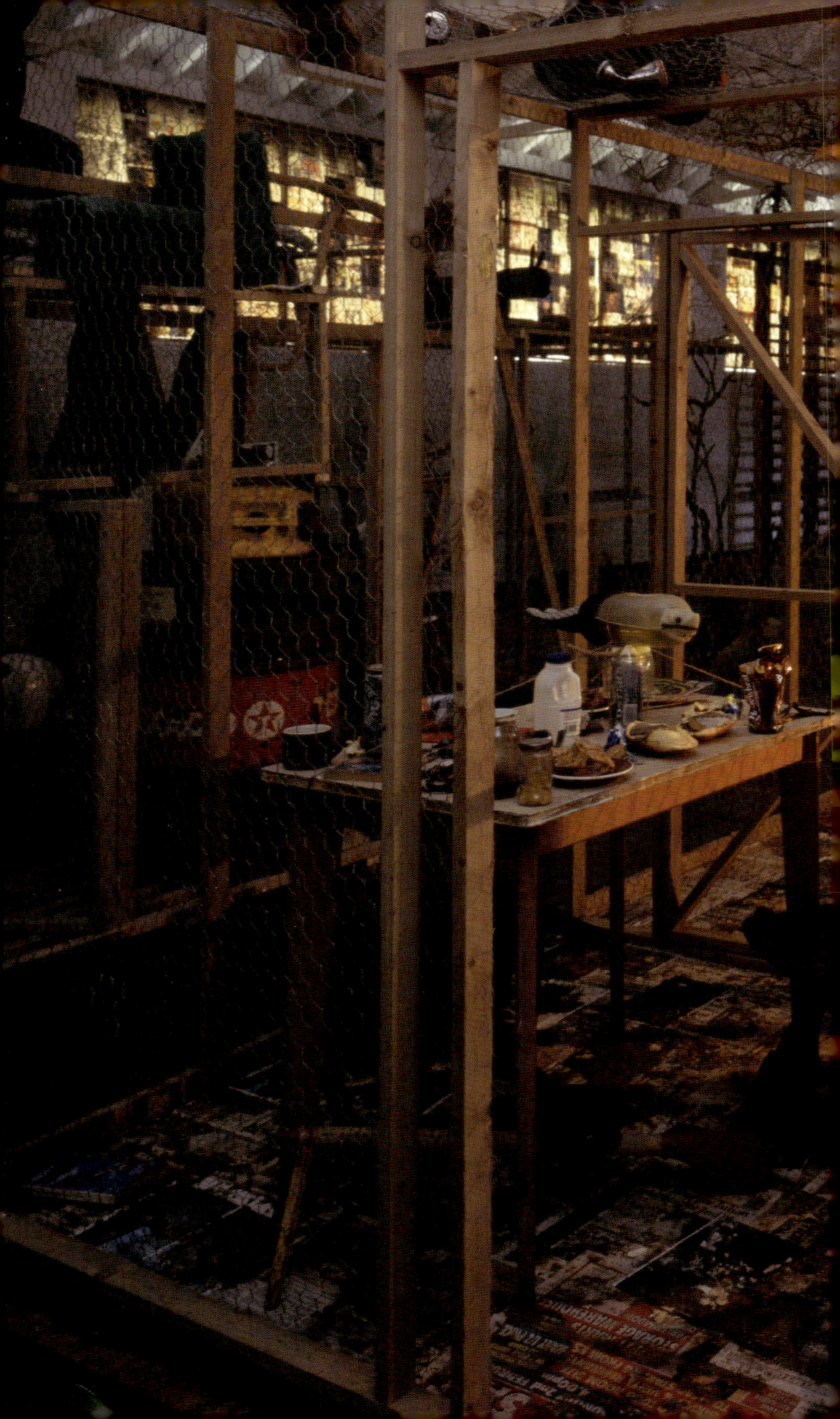

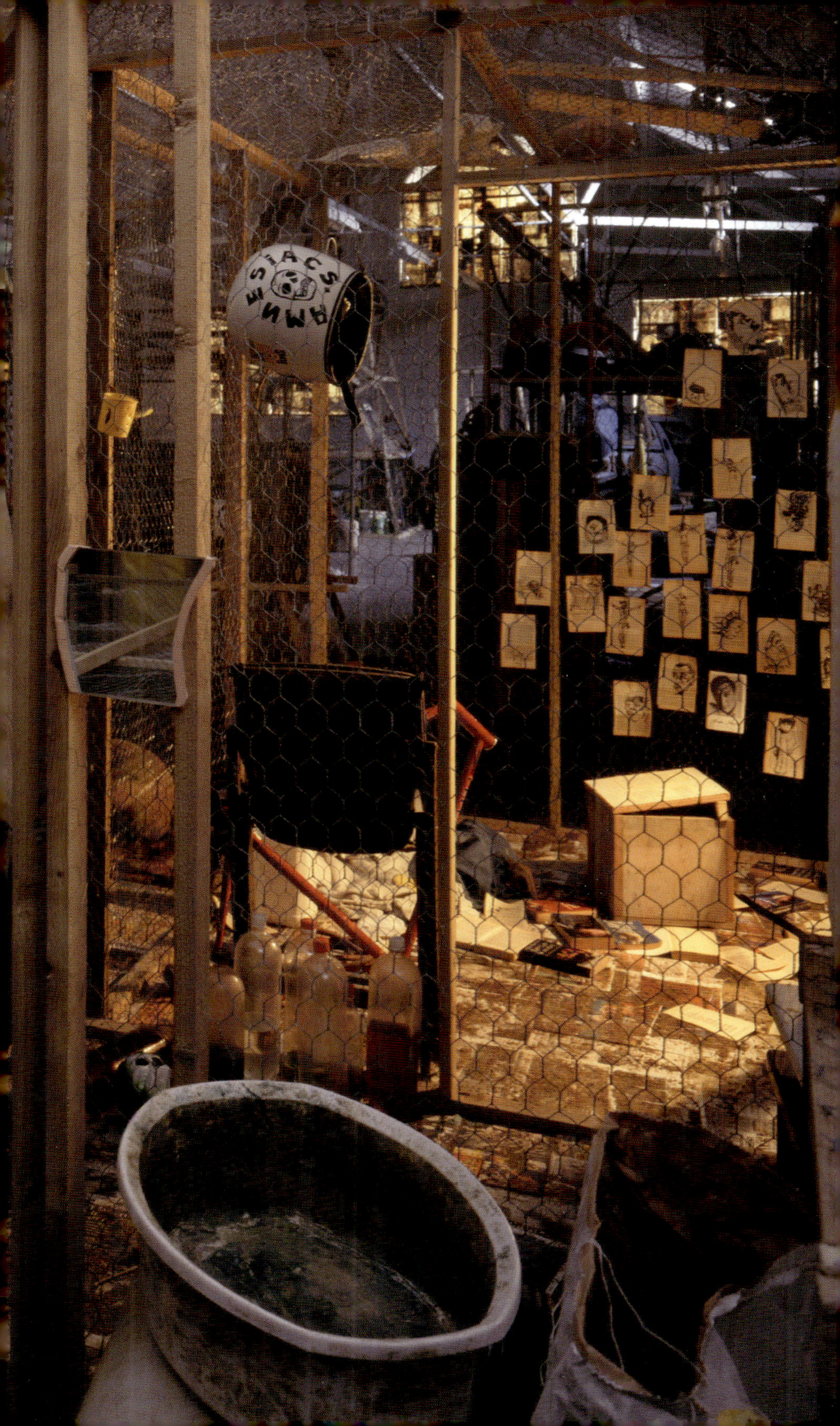

The rest of the space is filled with cages of all shapes and sizes as if in memory of a trade in exotic animals.

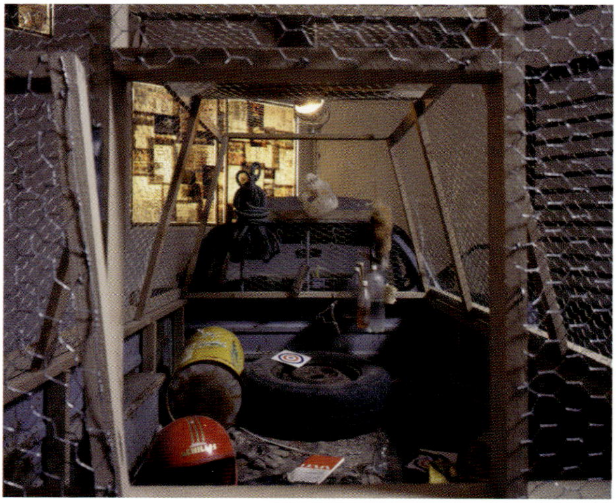

A small plastic lion stands in one of the chicken-wire cages that is big enough—if not strong enough—to hold a real lion. At first the apparent flimsiness of chicken-wire contradicts the idea that this cage could have been made with a lion in mind until it slowly becomes clear that this cage and the others around it have been made not for real animals, but for the idea of them—and as such they are perfectly adequate for the task.

A driftwood snake occupies a stripped tree with eyes fashioned out of a split golfball. In a cartoon-like gesture it ticks out a long red plastic tongue. On a table in another cage a toy chimpanzee, its baby moulded onto its back, stands on a book written by Lenin about Karl Marx's teachings. Plastic bottles, an old glove and a plastic mask have been tied together: a shark. It sits foolishly amongst the rubbish on a tabletop. A moose-like creature, its head a beaten-up traffic cone, stands on wooden trellis legs near an idea of a campfire.

PREVIOUS PAGES *Master of Reality*, 1997
Berwick Gymnasium Gallery, Berwick-upon-Tweed, Northumberland UK
Dwelling

ABOVE *Master of Reality*, 1997
Berwick Gymnasium Gallery, Berwick-upon-Tweed, Northumberland UK
To the rural poor

OPPOSITE *The Amnesiacs*, 1997
Galleri Campbells Occasionally, Copenhagen, Denmark
Pluto, an emblematic vision of fratricide

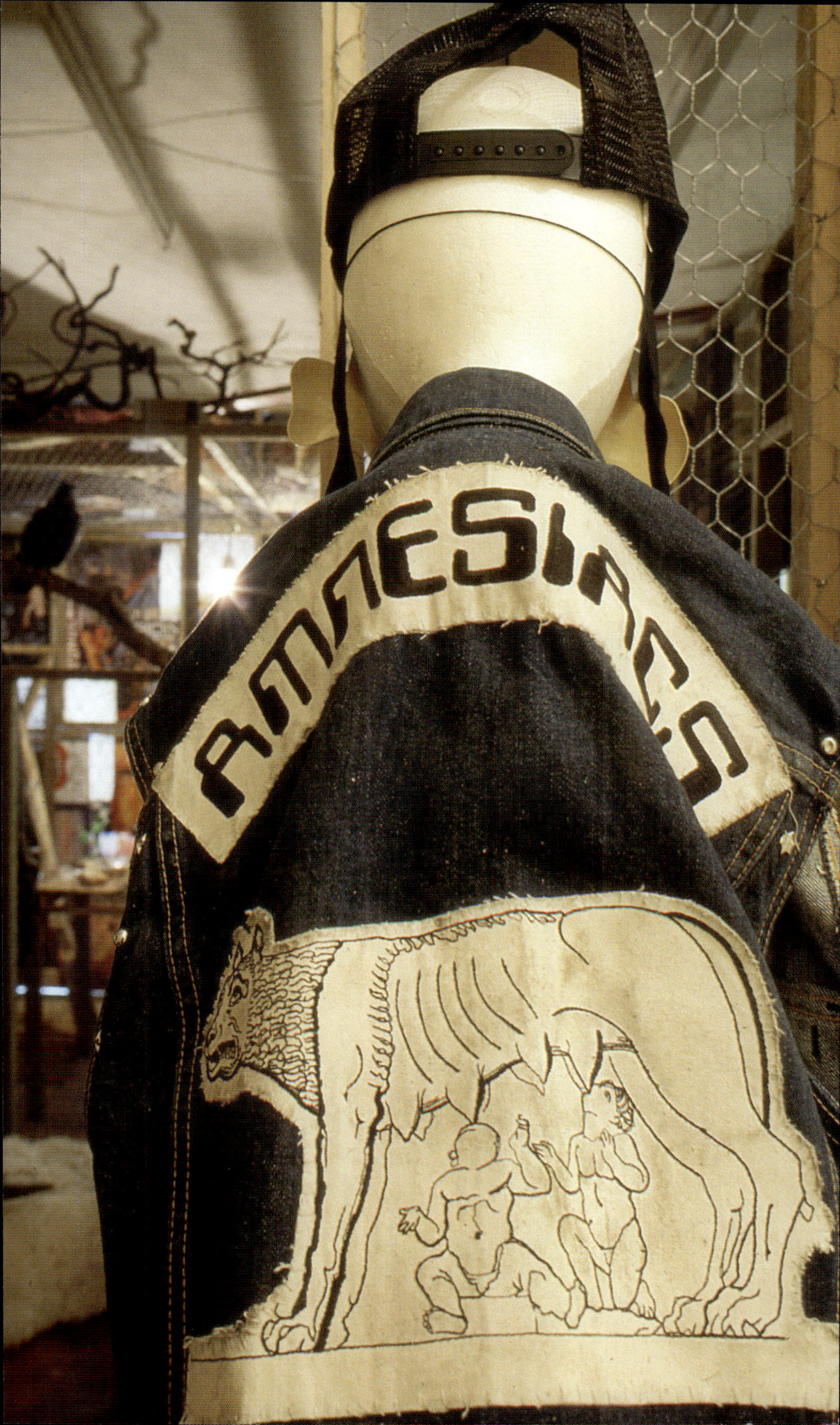

And the two people wandering through the warren of cages slowly become aware that the various enclosures, having been made specifically for this purpose, are physically occupied by the absence of the real animals. In that sense the animals, insofar as they have ever existed as anything other than an abstract and slightly corny idea, are there, in those cages.

But another scent is discernible here and the sense of following the meandering activities of someone who is trying to remember something is impossible to miss. It hovers about the bones and feathers of dried-up seabirds, the dried-out moles and seal-skin strung up on hooks and poles.

The place is full of things—discarded, left-over—logos, labels, bits of comics... that beckon to be made sense of, to be meaningful, until

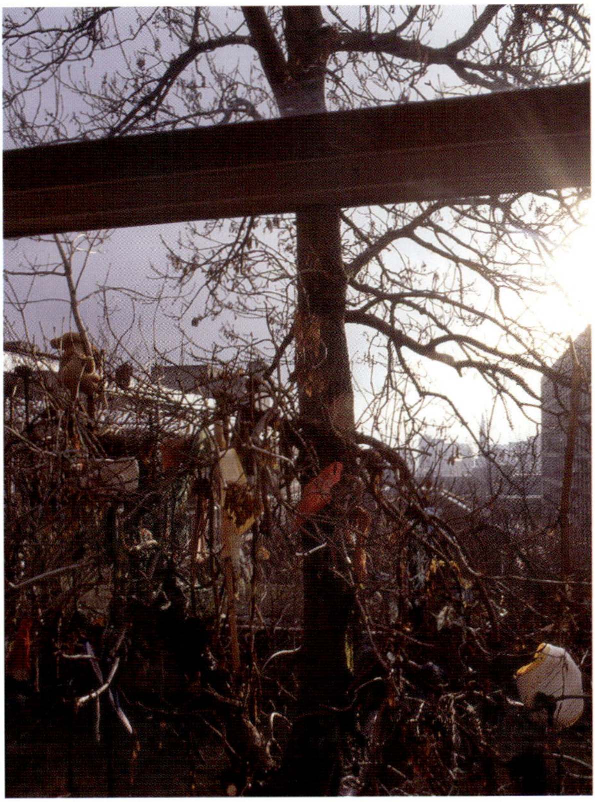

Untitled, 1996
Garnet Hill, Glasgow, Scotland
Drowned tree

they gradually reveal a despair in the very idea of being meaningful.... "For what? For whom? ... As if this could change anything, as if anything we could ever say could stop things from being as they are, could alter the fundamental indifference of the world to us and our inability to find a way to contemplate it, to believe it."

Someone has been trying to frighten themselves with the idea of death as if somehow this will make it more real, more tangible, maybe bring it closer.

Pages of Dennis Wheatley's tales of the occult and witchcraft have been drawn on in black ink. They decorate the walls of one of the cages. The red eyes in a plastic green and white skull flash on and off until the battery runs out. A plastic skull mask hangs in the cage of the pick-up.

Crash helmets have been left around the place, as if some bikers gang had been using the place as a den.

> Yeah that's right... the biker without a bike... too much danger in that... but he enjoys the idea of the danger.

The helmets bear logos and stickers... **Achilles... Extinction Beckons...**

Many of the helmets have a hallowe'en-type skull on their backs. **The Amnesiacs.**

A biker gang without bikes, without bodies.

Everywhere is marked by an overwhelming sense of absence and the impossibility of thinking about it except in the corniest of terms – the harum-scarum language of occult fiction that seeks to send a shiver up the spine, the skulls and dried-out bodies that have turned into so many things to thrill or scare as they waggle a grinning uncomprehending finger towards the idea of death.

But *The Amnesiacs* know something's missing.

'So where are we now?', she asks.

'Em, I don't actually know.'

Then she's thinking about how things would not have been the same had there been, for example, just a series of photographs here.

OVERLEAF *Untitled*, 1996
Garnet Hill, Glasgow, Scotland
Drowned tree

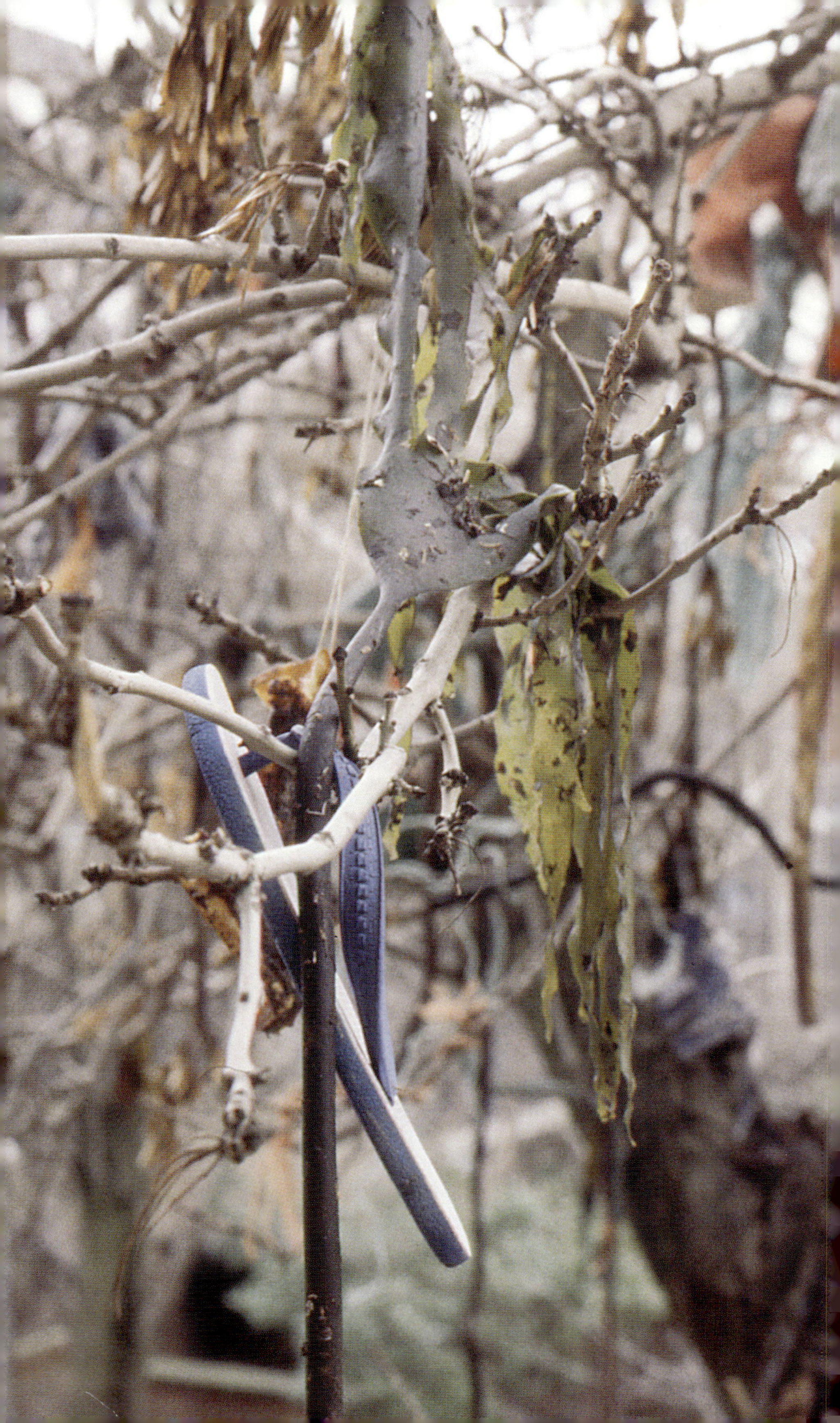

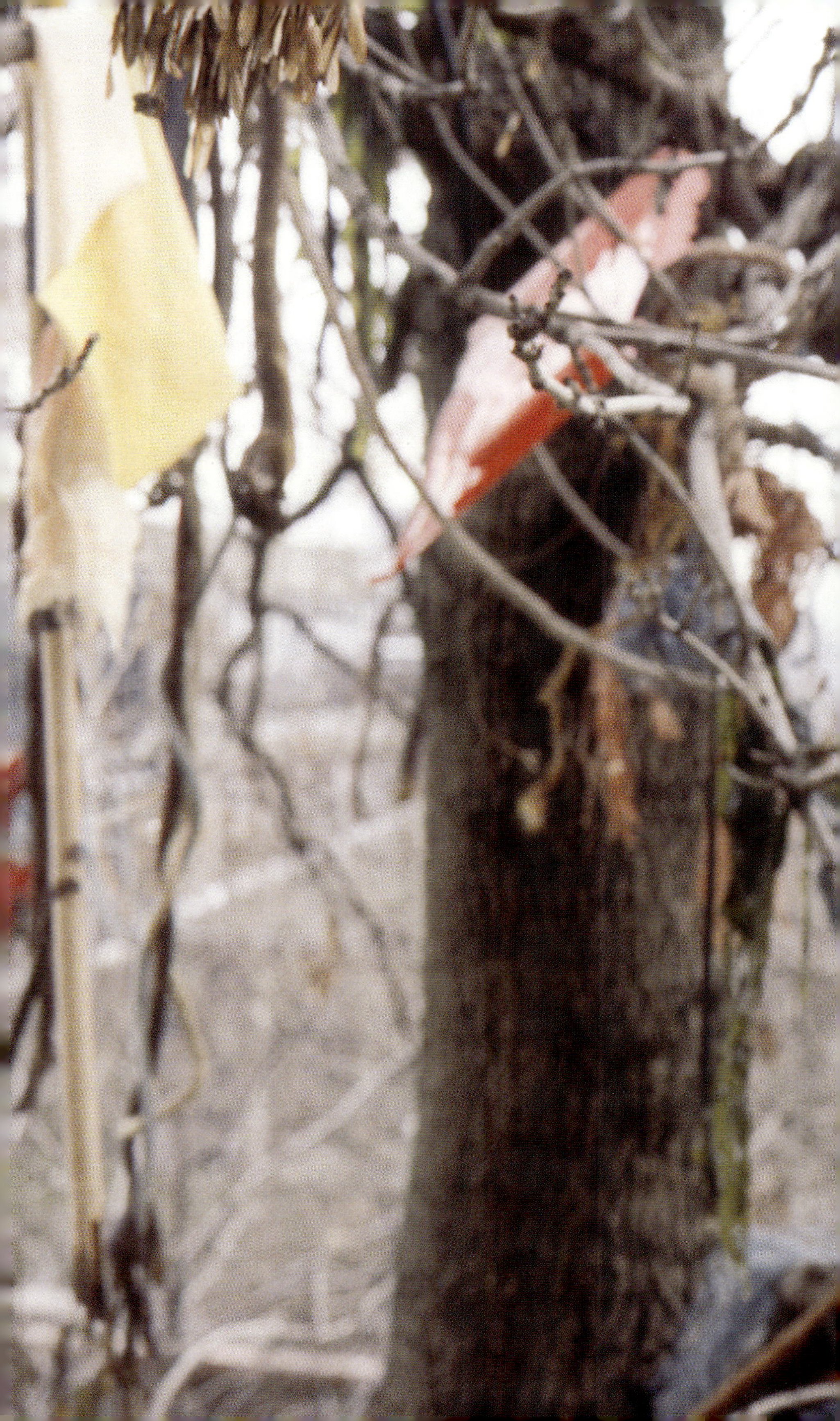

Maybe because I would, with an image, already have accepted the fact of the loss of the thing photographed—of the thing itself—whereas with an object I expect its full presence when it is there... and suddenly I've stumbled into the realm of loss, despite the physical presence of the things here and I'm struggling with that, partly because, like death itself, I know its possible, I know it's the condition of my existence in fact, that I will become a memory of myself, someone else's anecdote... but it's so difficult to accept... like the indifference of things in a world that can and will continue to exist without me... continue to signify and not signify, indifferent to whether I get it or not... and I experience it as something I have deliberately forgotten and have to struggle with every time I come into contact with it again... something that I have to forget in order to live... but how can you manage to sustain your forgetfulness of something that dogs your footsteps like a fictional monster?

The man is heading towards the door. He's been thinking about the death of his friend. He is gone and with that, something has been lost and it can't and won't be made sense of, there's no sense to be made of it, no knowledge that will change it.

Oh fucking hell, like, what does it all matter in the end?

Yeah ... and then it has to matter so we go back to have another look at it.

Something catches her eye—a comic-book lying in a small cage: **This is for the Big E idol.** 'That's funny', he says, 'I don't actually remember this at all.' She stops reading and looks at him.

So you're banging your head off the wall and need a crash helmet to do it.

Yeah, its a kind of quandary.

OPPOSITE *The Amnesiacs*, 1997
Galleri Campbells Occasionally, Copenhagen, Denmark
Pistol, pumpkin, prince

OVERLEAF *The Amnesiacs*, 1997
Galleri Campbells Occasionally, Copenhagen, Denmark
Snake head forks, chopper, with pan and horns

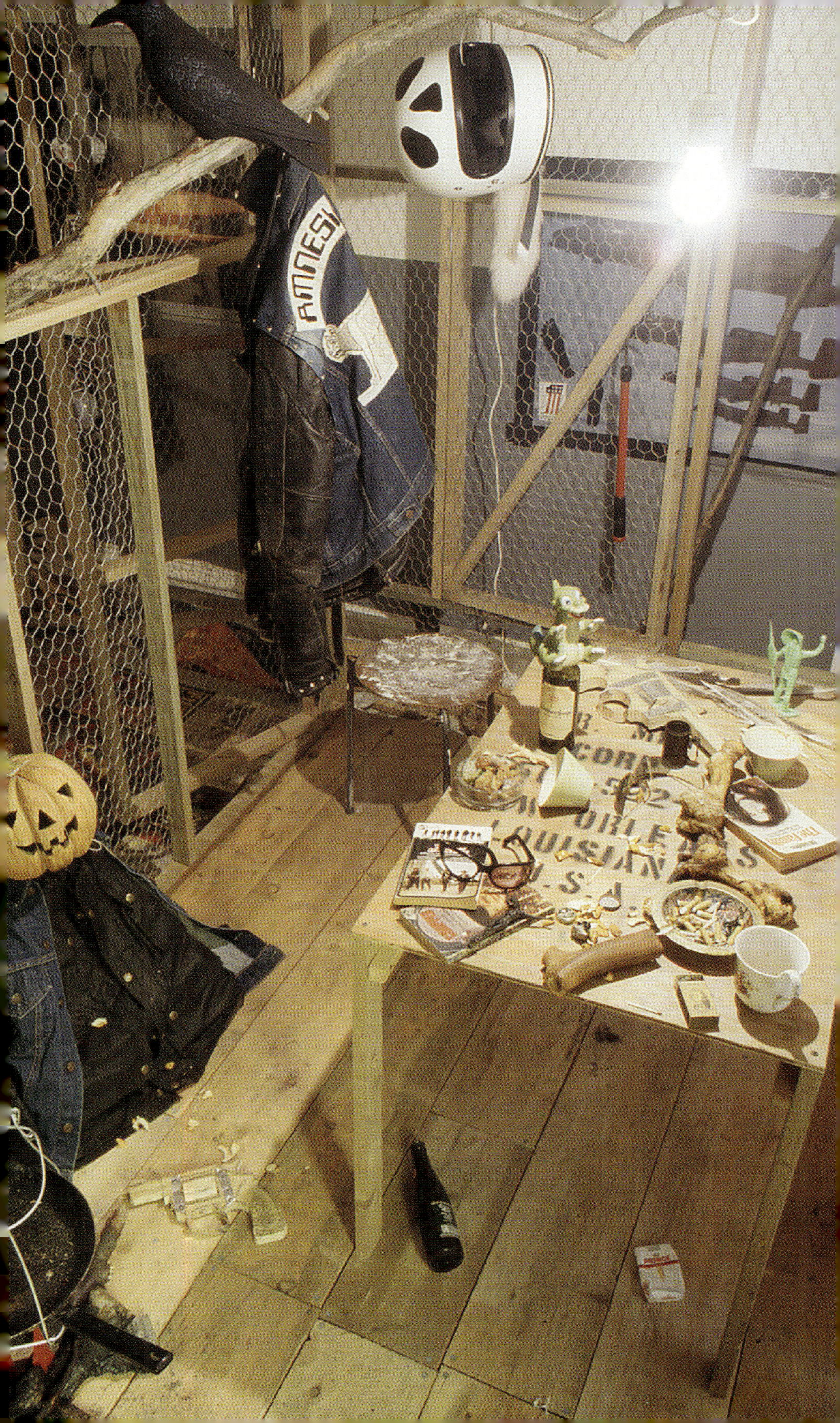

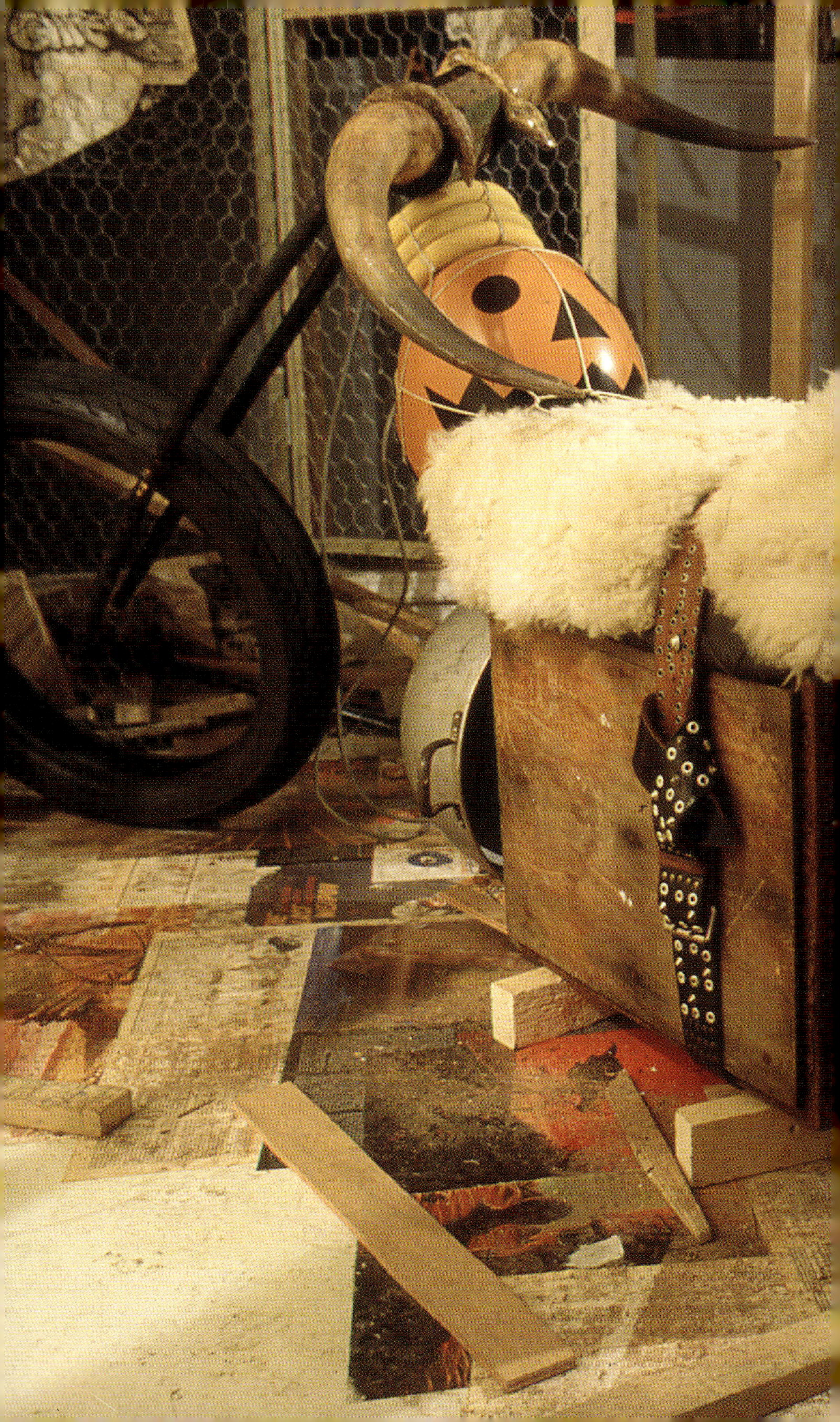

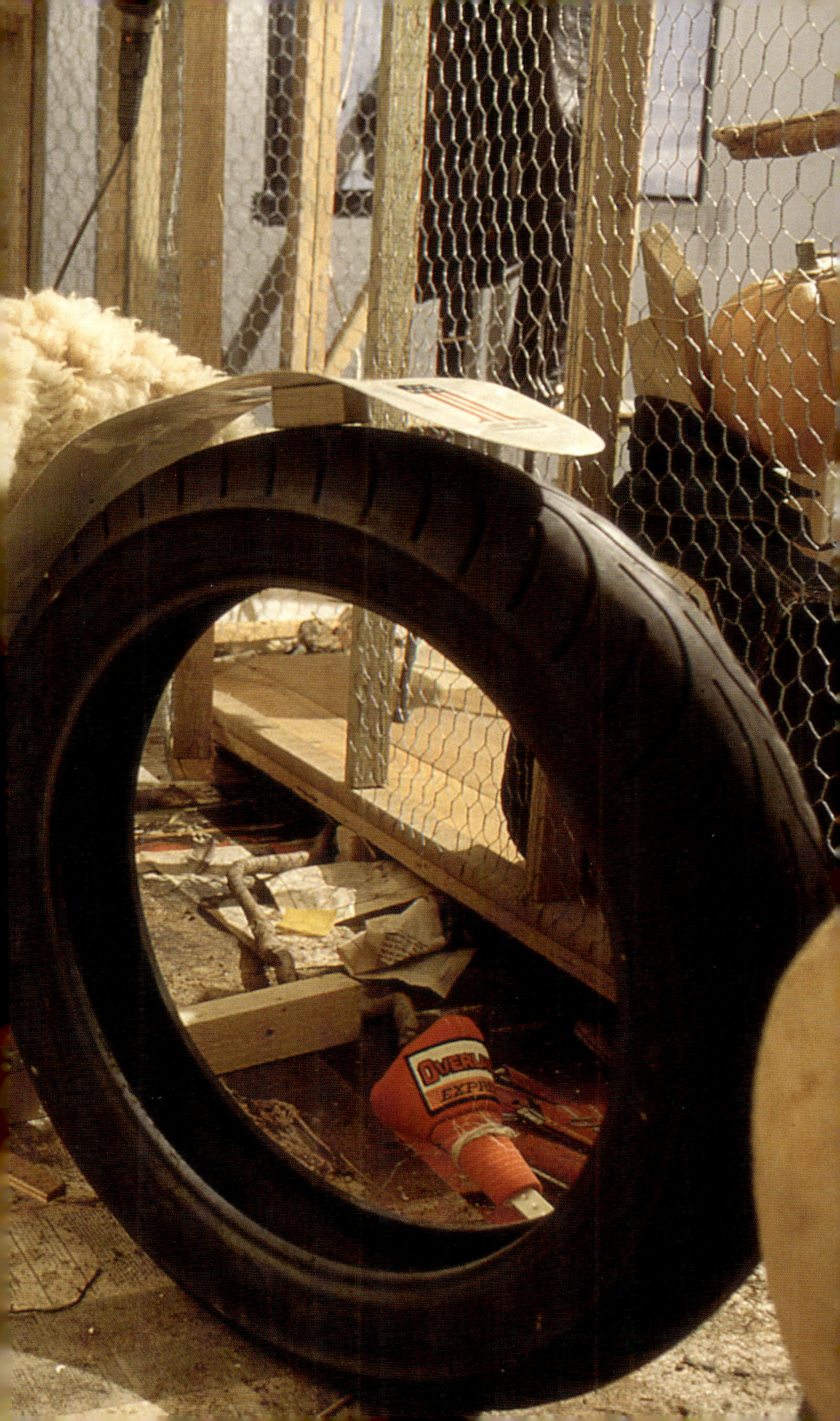

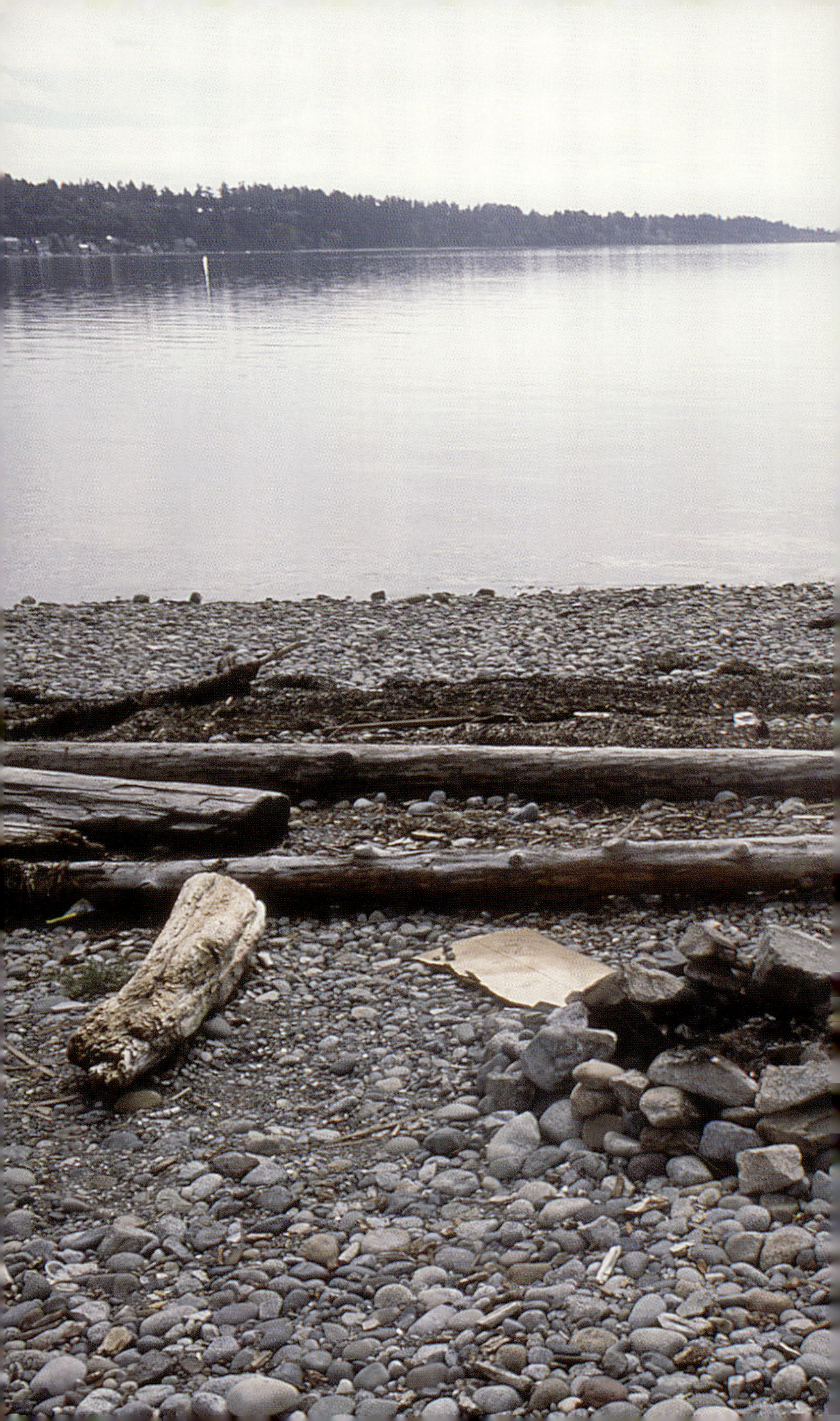

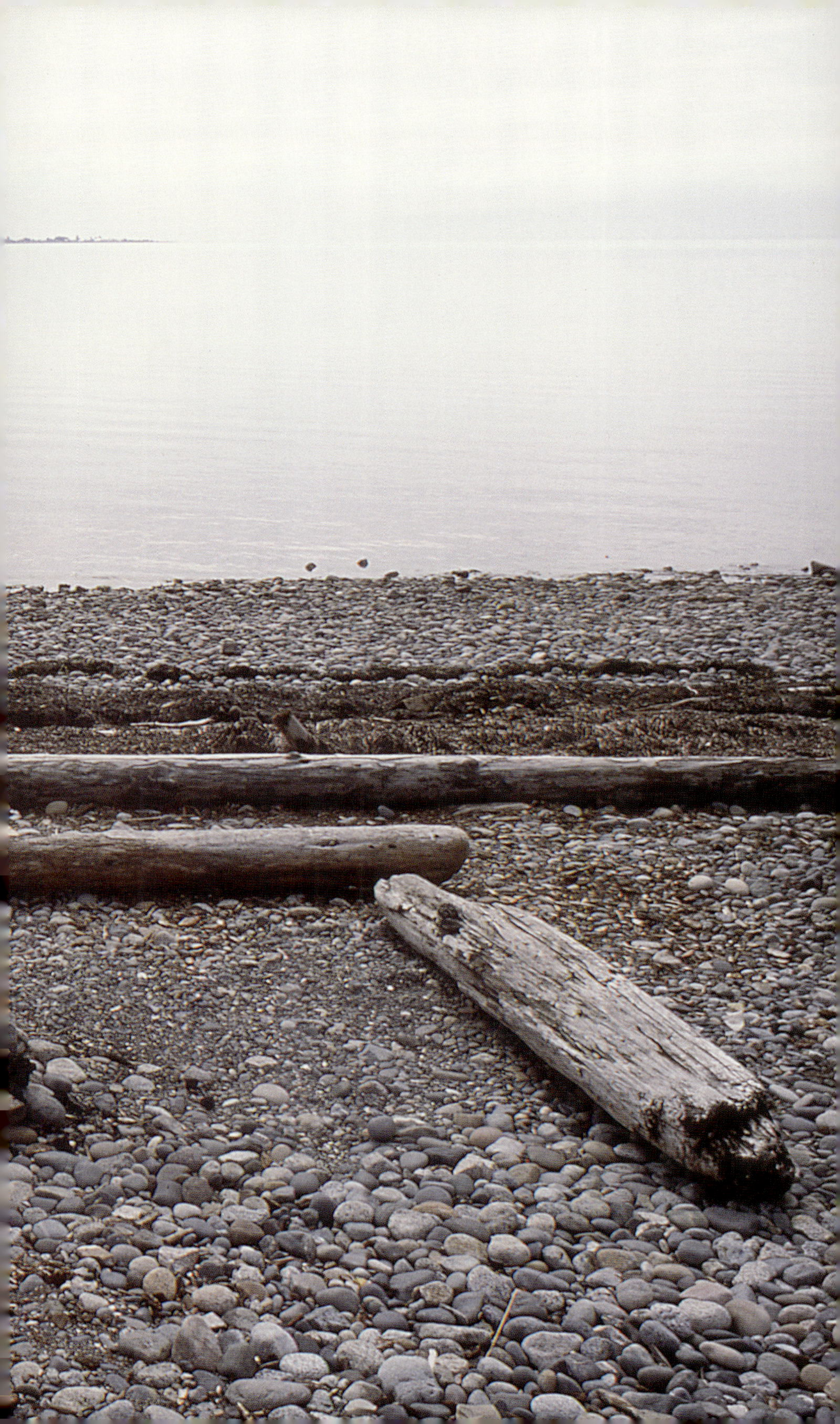

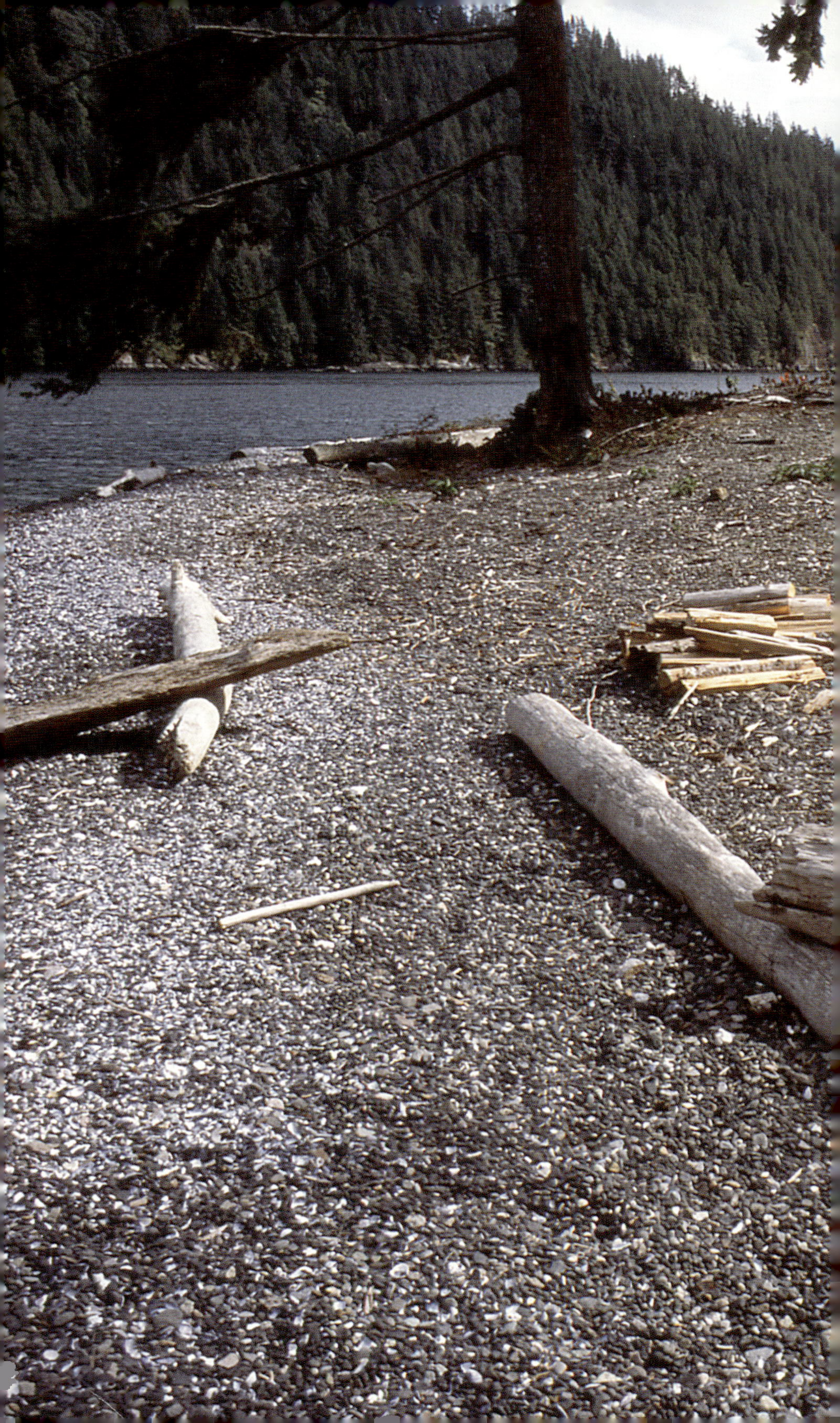

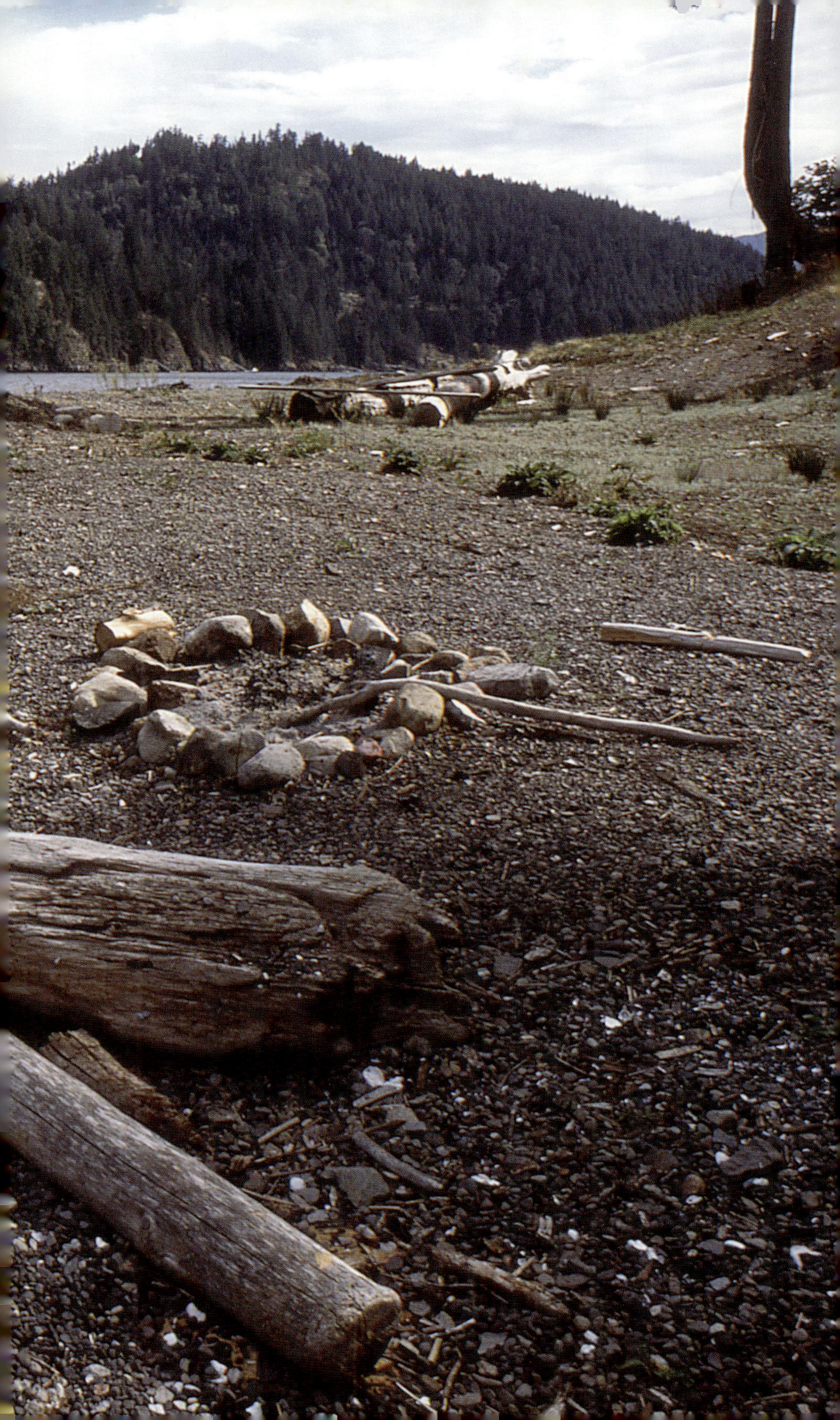

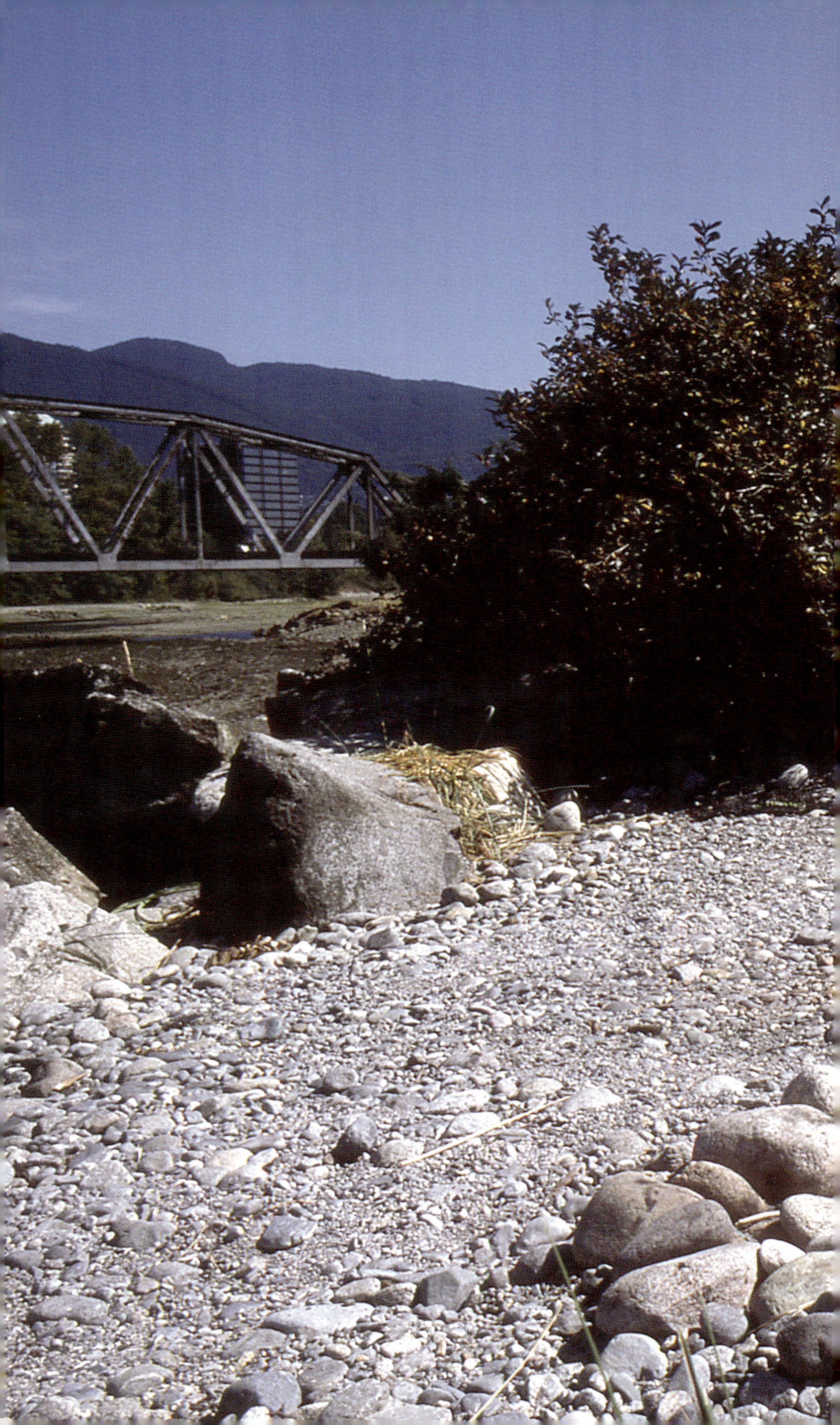

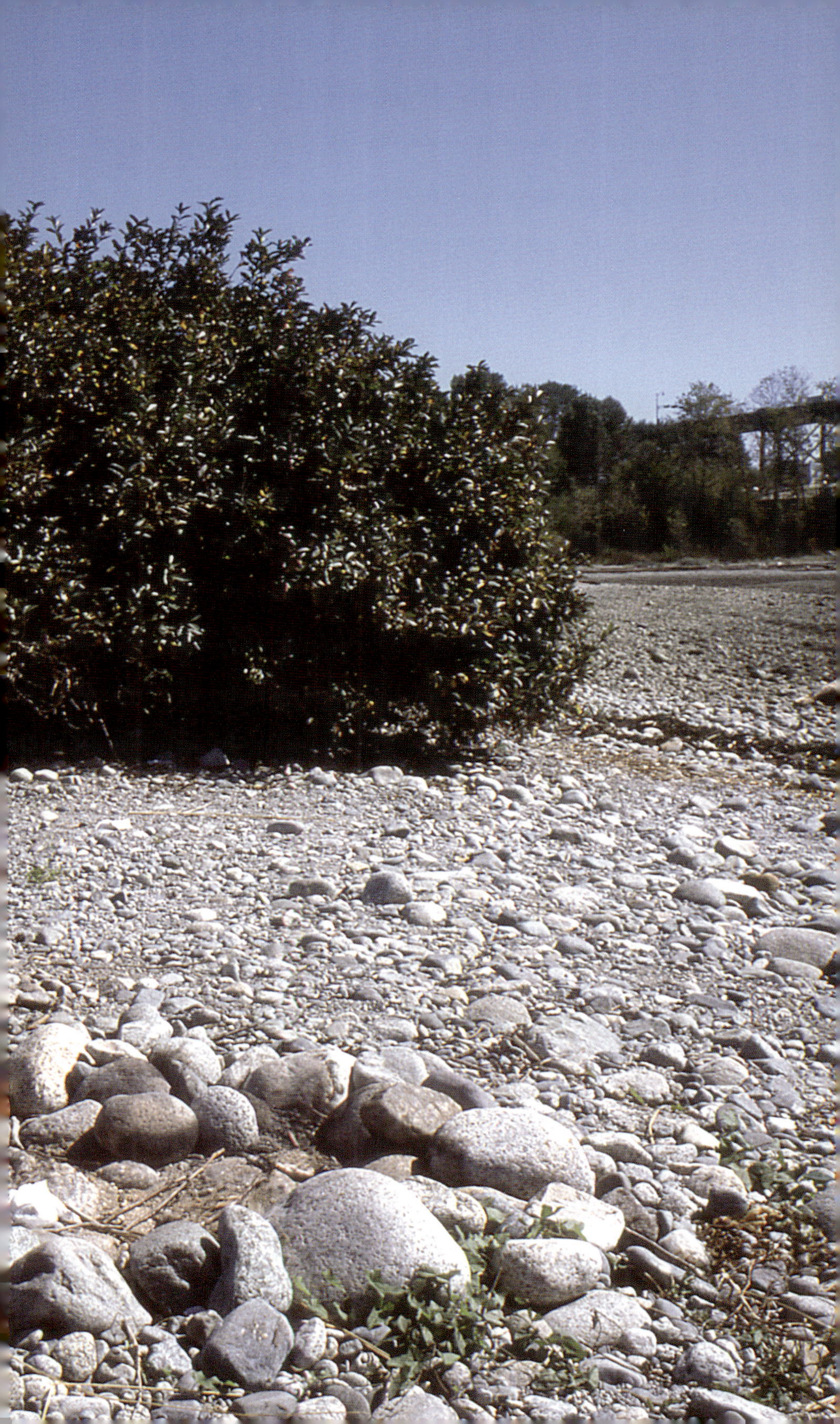

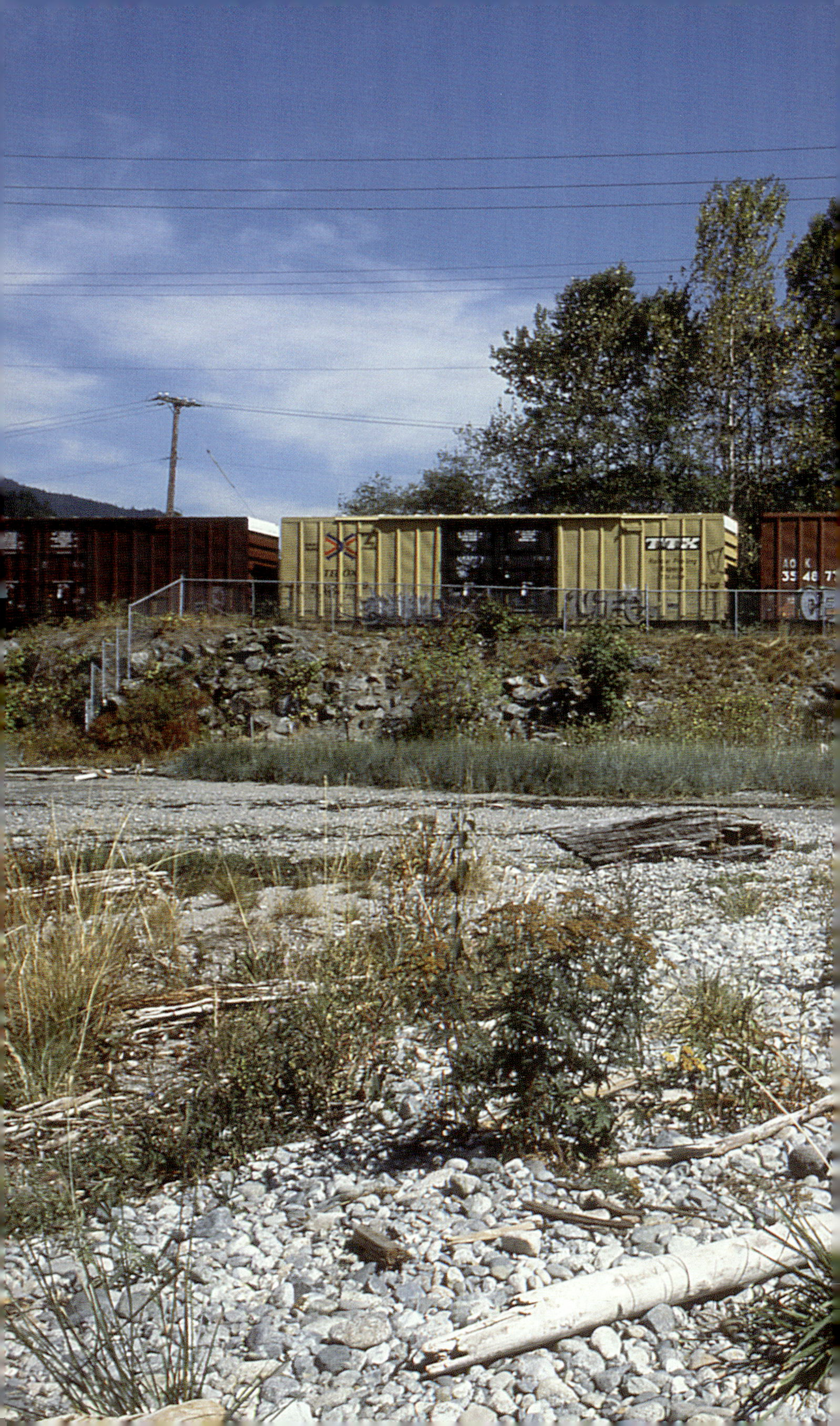
TTX

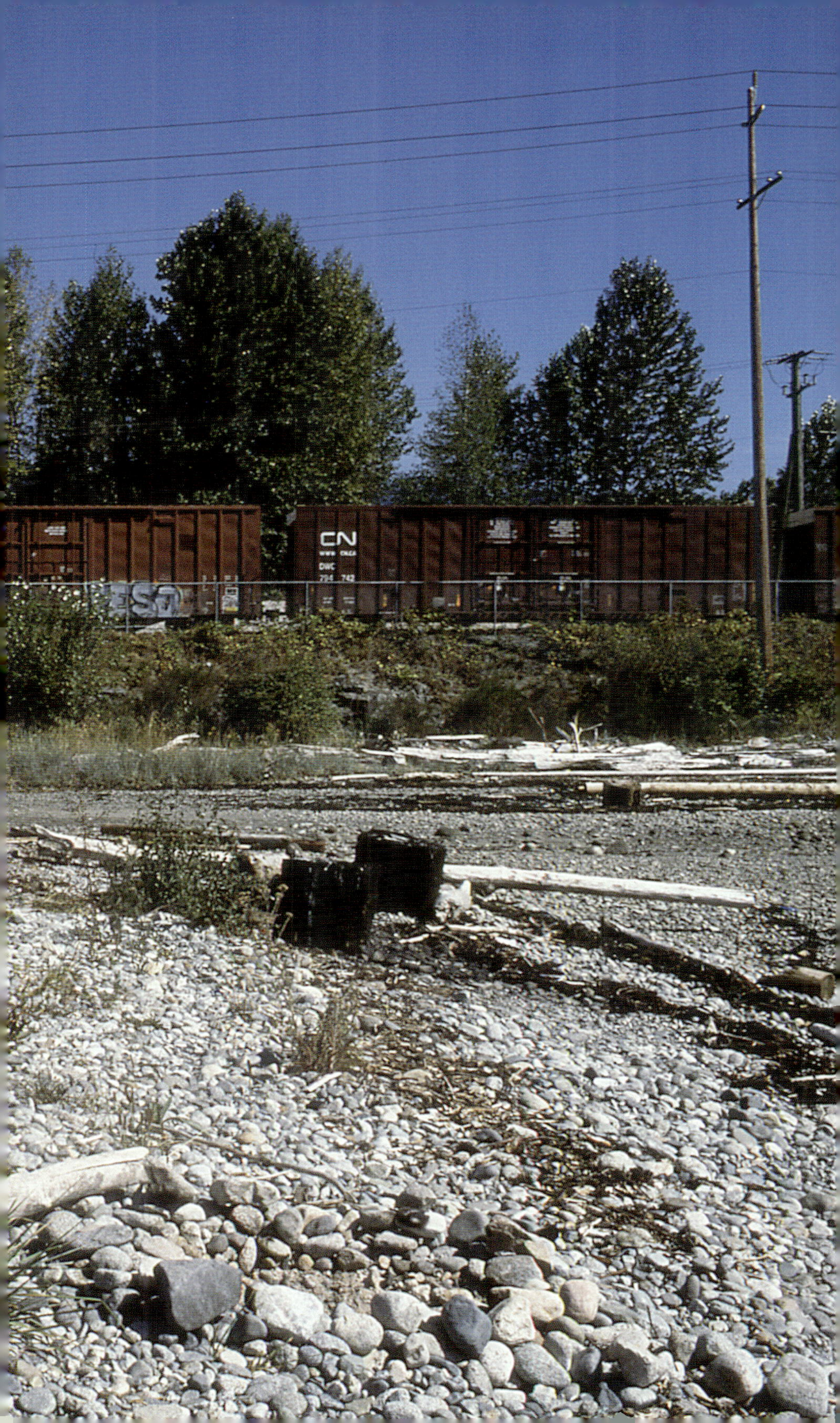
CN

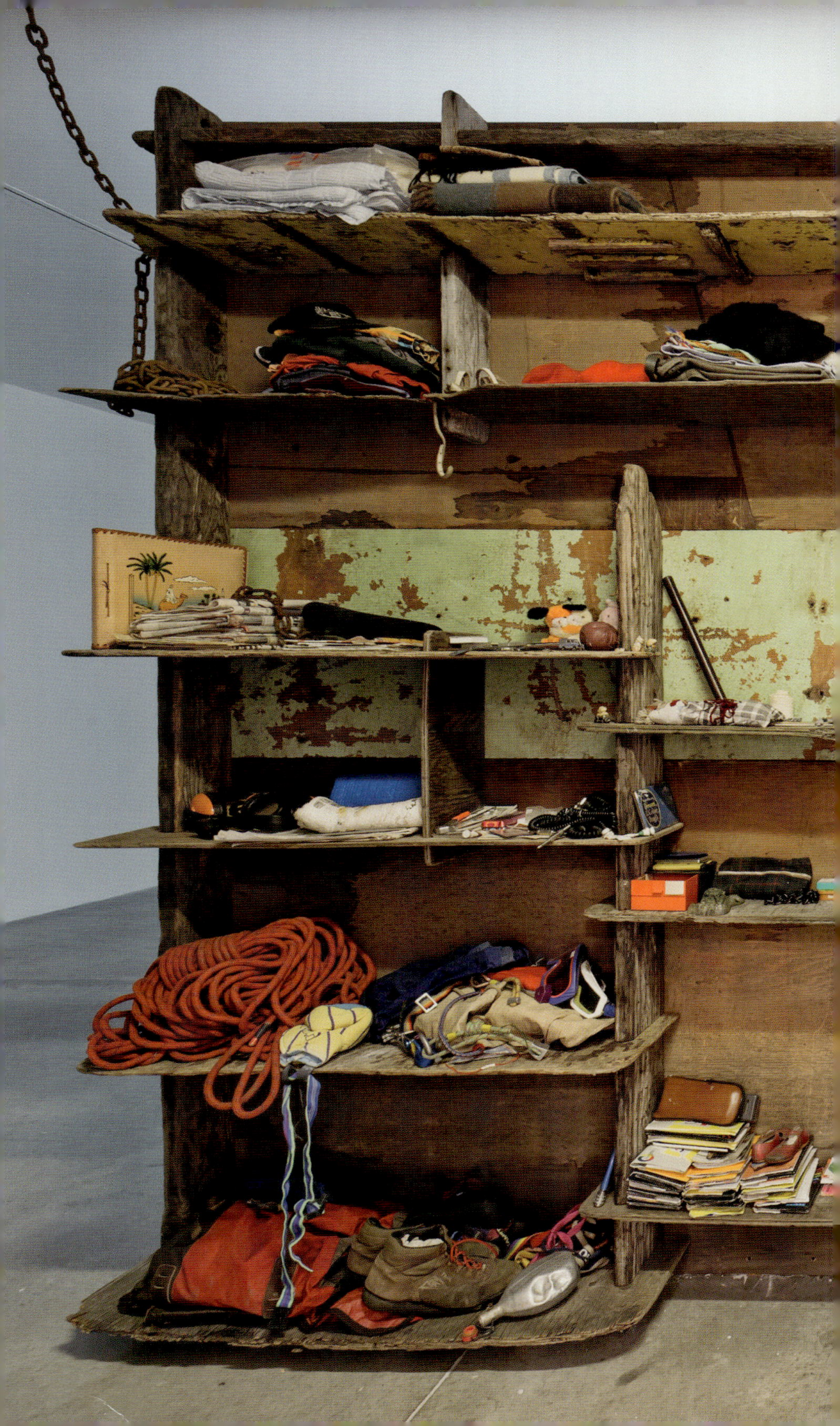

“Tom’s cairn is now on a public waterway of a popular summer outing ground. A boy’s camp is not far distant and it may be that the younger generation who go there yearly to learn the craft of the woodsman will see it and ponder the words engraved in brass ‘To the memory of Tom Thomson, artist-woodsman and guide who was drowned on Canoe Lake, July 8th, 1917; who lived humbly and passionately with the wild. It made him the brother to all untamed things in nature. It drew him apart and revealed itself wonderfully to him. It sent him out from the woods only to show these revelations though his art; and it took him to itself at last.’”

Afterword

Nigel Prince and Gaëtane Verna

Mike Nelson is best-known for his labyrinthine architectural installations that unfold as narrative structures, where the viewer moves through rooms like a reader turns pages in a novel. These immersive environments are often seemingly abandoned, devoid of figures, yet imagining the unseen occupants of these intricate spaces is central to the viewer's experience. Typical of his practice overall, the complexity of these fictional constructs gathers around us layer upon layer. While the works he creates are redolent of all myriad of neglected or half-forgotten places, their intrigue not only makes us feel an atmosphere but also stimulates our intellect. Hinted stories underpinned by meticulous detail draw us into a matrix of cultural, social and political considerations, differing arenas of thought. Nelson demands that our imaginations roam across territories and associations that are never obvious.

While his references are broad, often touching on particular moments in science-fiction and literature, much of Nelson's work can be linked through an archetypal figure of the lone wanderer. And so we arrive at the exhibitions and commissions comprising Nelson's first public exhibitions in Canada, brought together in this associated publication. Given this geographic and cultural context he seized the opportunity to revisit ideas and forms first seen in *The Amnesiacs*, a serial project begun in 1996, which references a narrative involving an imaginary cast of characters—a group of 'outsiders' to the mainstream who uncannily resemble a disembodied late twentieth-century biker gang, albeit without bikes. These quintessential outlaws of myth and literature, as depicted in the popular imagination of North America, are paralleled in the works produced with another favourite genre; that of the hunter or fur trader, exploring both groups' economic underpinning of these romantic façades, and the resulting conflicts involved in the expansion of territory.

In *Gang of Seven*, 2013, it is as if a beachcomber has gathered material from the ocean, imagined by Nelson as a gigantic intelligent entity, much like that of Polish science fiction writer Stanisław Lem's planet "Solaris", sifting the debris as a means to uncover truths about contemporary culture and our place within it. Roving characters, *The Amnesiacs*, have come together as interpreters, deciphering the collected material by creating assemblages akin to some form of disjointed memory or flashback, that when brought together may effect communication or reveal hidden meaning, the potential for a new and unified system of understanding. Nelson originally developed these thoughts after the unexpected loss of his friend and collaborator Erlend Williamson. In 1996 he fell to his death whilst climbing in the Scottish Highlands, at the time that Nelson was working on his first incarnation of what would become *The Amnesiacs*. Williamson, an artist and mountaineer whose family ancestry was of Orcadian descent, contributed again, his spirit very much around us as ideas unfolded. Parts of his own narrative and the very materials that surrounded him—those that remain present in his absence—were woven into the fabric of the 35mm slide projection and sculptural piece *Eighty Circles through Canada (the last possessions of an Orcadian mountain man),* 2013. A more fitting celebration and commemoration, poignantly entwining both private and imagined stories, known yet unseen, could not be imagined.

Made for presentation in Toronto, *Double negative (The Genie),* 2014, is based on a series of seemingly coincidental occurrences that took place while Nelson was travelling down the edge of Western China in 1998. The trip took place two years after the unexpected death of his friend and collaborator Erlend Williamson. During his travels, Nelson had sighted the ace of spades seven times within as many days. In *Double negative (The Genie)* every day of Nelson's card sighting is represented by one of the seven photocopiers. Each machine is accompanied by text from the artist's travel journal, black and white photocopied imagery of the ace of spades card and copied photographs that Nelson took during his travels. While on his trip, Nelson took black and white photos, many of which were self-portraits he developed some time after returning home to London. Unknowingly, he had double exposed the film, layering his shots on top of images from the installation of his first exhibition at Matt's Gallery, London in 1995. Williamson is in the background of the images, assisting Nelson on the installation of this show.

There was an opportunity for Nelson to return to this story in 2001 when he was invited to produce a bookwork that would structure and present his journey using the personal collection of aces of spades that he accumulated following his trip, a short text that provided an account of his sightings and the double-exposed images. The book never came to fruition and the publishing house disbanded without ever printing or returning the artist's material. All that remained in Nelson's possession were photocopies of the original cards and negatives of the black and white film. As a result, the artist was left with a growing disbelief in the sightings. Now, almost fifteen years later, Nelson publicly revisits his trip by manifesting his experience through the remaining evidence to produce *Double negative (The Genie).*

As in the work of Nelson, similarly a cast of characters is responsible for enabling these commissions and their consequent exhibitions to come into being, their contributions very much real. To the hosts of individuals detailed elsewhere in this publication who supported the projects in Vancouver morally and financially, we give sincere and heartfelt thanks, for without them the ambition of the proposed works and installations would not have been possible. In Toronto, we could not of been able to present such a powerful exhibition as *Amnesiac Hide* without the unwavering support of Lead Donors Nancy McCain and Bill Morneau, Jay Smith and Laura Rapp as well as Support Donors Sue Kidd and Susie Kololian, Michelle Koerner and Kevin Doyle, Liza Mauer and Andrew Sheiner, Margaret C McNee, Nadir and Shabin Mohamed, Elisa Nuyten and David Dime, Michael J Prokopow and Eric Collins, Eleanor and Francis Shen.

Charlene Quantz-Wold at The Banff Centre, Alberta also willingly came on board to help realise *Eighty Circles through Canada (the last possessions of an Orcadian mountain man)*, in part the result of road trips made throughout Western Canada. During the gestation and planning Frances Scott as part of the team supporting Mike Nelson at home was invaluable for her coordination and as a source of information. So too Nelson's representative galleries have been unstinting in their support and we acknowledge Lisa Spellman and Kathryn Erdman at 303 Gallery, New York; Franco Noero and Pierpaolo Falone at Galleria Franco Noero, Torino; Tim Neuger, Burkhard Riemschneider and Maia Gianakos of neugerriemschneider, Berlin and Robin Klassnik at Matt's Gallery, London for their help and advice.

Black Dog Publishing could not have been more receptive to our approach and in particular we single out Duncan McCorquodale for his attention to detail in allowing this publication to come to life through his sensitivity in conversation and planning.

Staff respectively at both the Contemporary Art Gallery and The Power Plant should be recognised for the fastidious manner in which they approached both projects, ably supporting Nelson to bring his ideas to fruition. In Vancouver Kieren and Claudine Beattie were a beautiful and crucial assistance to Nelson and the installation team headed by Phil Dion, a coincidence of time and place that was very much to our mutual advantage. In Toronto our installation team brought their expertise in order to realise this ambitious exhibition. They were led by our Head of Registration, Installation, and Facilities Paul Zingrone who managed all aspects of the installation with patience and humour. Garth Johnson, our Head Gallery Technician deftly dealt with numerous aspects of making the exhibition a reality. Our Curatorial Assistant Valerie Velardo provided invaluable support throughout the curatorial process. We are grateful to our respective curators, Jenifer Papararo and Julia Paoli. Together, their devotion to work in collaboration with the artist cemented our institutional partnership, enabling the demands and scope of such a project to be fully and confidently realised. That they provide such insightful texts within this publication further demonstrates the care and knowledge they have brought to every stage along the way.

With Mike Nelson, a common sense approach belies a keen intelligence and active, wide-ranging, inquisitive mind. His energy and precision when collecting then working with flotsam and jetsam from around the shores of British Columbia and in Ontario were truly inspiring. The conversation and his company on this journey could not have been bettered. For challenging us in the way we might work with artists and to do it with such modesty and good humour has been very much appreciated. To Mike we express our profound admiration and gratitude.

Nigel Prince
Executive Director, Contemporary Art Gallery, Vancouver

Gaëtane Verna
Director, The Power Plant, Toronto

Biographical Notes

Mike Nelson's work has centred on the transformation of narrative structure to spatial structure, and on the objects placed within them, immersing the viewer and agitating their perception of these environments. The narratives employed by the artist are not teleological, but multi-layered, and often fractured to the extent that they could be described as a semblance of 'atmospheres', put together to give a sense of meaning. The more discrete sculptural works are informed by this practice, often relying on their ambiguity to fade in and out of focus, as a sculpture or thing of meaning, and back to the very objects or material from which they are made. By working in this way the more overtly political aspects of the early works have become less didactic, allowing for an ambiguity of meaning, both in the way that they are experienced and understood. This has led to the possibility of the viewer being coerced into a state where the understanding of the varied structures of their existence, both conscious and sub-conscious, are made tangible.

Born in Loughborough, UK in 1967, Mike Nelson lives and works in London. His solo exhibitions and projects include: *Amnesiac Hide*, The Power Plant, Toronto, 2014; *Mike Nelson*, Contemporary Art Gallery, Vancouver, 2013; *More things (To the memory of Honoré de Balzac)*, Matt's Gallery, London, 2013; *M6*, Eastside Projects, Birmingham, UK, 2013; *space that saw (platform for a performance in two parts)*, neugerriemschneider, Berlin, 2012; *408 tons of imperfect geometry*, Malmö Konsthall, Malmö, Sweden, 2012; *I, IMPOSTOR*, British Pavilion, 54th Biennale di Venezia, 2011; *Quiver of Arrows*, 303 Gallery, New York, 2010; *A Psychic Vacuum*, Creative Time, New York, 2007; *AMNESIAC SHRINE* or *Double coop displacement*, Matt's Gallery, London, 2006; *Triple Bluff Canyon*, Modern Art Oxford, 2004; *Nothing is True. Everything is Permitted*. ICA, London, 2001; *The Deliverance and The Patience*, a PEER Commission for the Venice Biennale, 2001 and *The Coral Reef*, Matt's Gallery, London, 2000. His group shows include: *September 11*, MoMA PS1, New York, 2011; Singapore Biennale, 2011; *Altermodern*, Tate Britain, 2009; *Psycho Buildings*, Hayward Gallery, London, 2008; *Eclipse: Art in a Dark Age*, Moderna Museet, Stockholm Sweden, 2008; *Reality Check*, Statens Museum for Kunst, Copenhagen, Denmark, 2008; *Turner Prize*, Tate Liverpool, 2007; *Frieze Projects*, Frieze Art Fair, London, 2006; and *Turner Prize*, Tate Britain, London, 2001. He is represented by 303 Gallery, New York; Galleria Franco Noero, Turin; Matt's Gallery, London; and neugerriemschneider, Berlin.

Born in the UK in 1951, Dick Hebdige is a cultural critic and theorist who has published extensively on youth sub-cultures, art and design, consumer and media culture, and contemporary music. Hebdige currently holds the position of Professor in Film and Media Studies and Art Studio at the University of California, Santa Barbara, where his work focuses on the role of autobiography and fiction in cultural studies, critical writing and contemporary art. Prior to his current position Hebdige served as the Dean of the School of Critical Studies of the Writing Program at California Institute of the Arts, Valencia, California and, from 1984 to 1992, Reader in Communications in the Department of Media and Communications at Goldsmiths College, University of London, England. His publications include: *Hiding in the Light: On Images and Things*, 1989; *Cut 'n' Mix: Culture, Identity and Caribbean Music*, 1987; *Subculture: The Meaning of Style*, 1979. His essays include: "After Benning. After Math: 12, 13 and Counting" in *Two Cabins by JB,* ed Julie Ault, 2011; "Lucifer Setting: Art, Engineering and the Dawn of the Stadium Rock Light Show" in *Bullet Proof... I Wish I Was. The Lighting & Stage Design of Andi Watson,* ed Thom York, 2011; "Flat Boy vs. Skinny: Takashi Murakami and the Battle for 'Japan'" in *©Murakami,* ed Paul Schimmel, 2007; "Un-Imagining Utopia" in *Sound Unbound: Sampling Digital Music and Culture*, ed Paul D Miller aka DJ Spooky The Subliminal Kid, 2008; "Redeeming Witness: In the Tracks of the Homeless Vehicle Project" in *Cultural Studies,* 7,2, 1993.

Jaki Irvine currently works in Dublin and Mexico City. Through the use of single and multi-channel installations, she foregrounds the complex ways we imagine ourselves and the world around us. In 1995 Irvine was included in the seminal exhibition of Young British Artists, *General Release*, at the Venice Biennale, and she represented Ireland at the 1997 Biennale. She has also participated in numerous group shows throughout Europe, Australia and Japan including *NoWhere*, Louisiana Museum of Modern Art, Denmark; 1996; *White Noise*, Bern Kunsthalle, 1998; *Intelligence*, Tate Britain, 2000; and *Shifting Ground: 50 Years of Irish Art* at the Irish Museum of Modern Art (IMMA), 2000. Her solo exhibitions include Project Arts Centre, 1996; Kerlin Gallery, 2011, 2004; the Douglas Hyde Gallery, 1999, 2005, Dublin; Frith Street Gallery, 1997,1999, 2011; the Staatliche Kunsthalle in Baden-Baden, Germany, 1998; Delfina Project Space, 2001, London and Henry Moore Institute, Leeds, 2004. In 2005 she exhibited *The Silver Bridge* in IMMA, Dublin and Smart Project Space, Amsterdam. In 2008, Irvine produced *In a World Like This*, in collaboration with Chisenhale Gallery, London and The Model Arts and Niland Gallery, Sligo, Ireland. In 2011 *Before The Page is Turned* was presented at the Kerlin Gallery, Dublin. Her most recent solo exhibition *This Thing Echoes* was presented early 2014 at Frith Street Gallery, London. Her novel *Days of Surrender* was published by Copy Press in 2013. Irvine is represented in the collections of IMMA, the Irish Arts Council, Tate Modern, FRAC and in numerous other collections, both public and private.

Julia Paoli is a curator and writer based in Toronto, where she is currently Assistant Curator at The Power Plant Contemporary Art Gallery. Her practice is focused on researching and developing projects with artists that meld models of influence and actively consider the complexities of genealogy and history. Recent exhibitions include: *Julia Dault: Color Me Badd*, 2014; *Mike Nelson: Amnesiac Hide*, 2013; and *Jimmy Robert: Draw the Line*, 2013. She has recently edited a critical anthology on the work of Jimmy Robert. Paoli's other curatorial projects include: *Dispersion, Trinity Square Video*, Toronto, 2012; *Social Choreography*, Gallery TPW, Toronto, 2012; *The Rest is Real: Video Works by Aleesa Cohene*, Vtape, Toronto, 2012; *What's Past is Prologue*, Center for Curatorial Studies, Bard College, 2011; and a presentation of A.K. Burns and A.L. Steiner's Community Action Center, Toronto, 2011. She received Vtape's curatorial residency award and was featured in Dia: Beacon's Gallery Talks in 2013. Paoli holds a Hon BA from the University of Western Ontario and received her MA from the Center for Curatorial Studies, Bard College in 2011.

Jenifer Papararo was the Curator at the Contemporary Art Gallery in Vancouver since 2004 recently accepting a directorial role at Plug In Institute for Contemporary Art in Winnipeg. During her tenure at the CAG she has worked with a range of leading artists, curating Nairy Baghramian's first solo exhibition in North America, 2012, and Monika Sosnowska's first exhibition in Canada, 2013. She worked with Mike Nelson to co-commission two new works for CAG, one co-produced by The Power Plant and the other with The Banff Centre. In 2012 she co-edited with Kitty Scott a book on Frances Stark's pivotal work *My Best Thing*, featuring an essay by Mark Godfrey and published by CAG, Walter Phillips Gallery and Koenig Books, London. In 2010 she curated *Triumphant Carrot: The Persistence of Still Life*, which featured the work of 27 artists, including Hans-Peter Feldmann, Peter Fischli and David Weiss, Ceal Floyer, Rodney Graham, Liz Magor, Sam Taylor-Wood and Jeff Wall; and *Following A Line*, featuring work by Pablo Bronstein, Peter Gazendam, Susanne Kriemann, Kyla Mallett, Alex Morrison, Paul Sietsema and Frances Stark. From 2002 to 2004 she was Director of Programming at Mercer Union, Toronto. There she curated Mark Leckey's *Soundsystem*, which included an extensive programme of events. She is a founding member of the curatorial and artist collective Instant Coffee, whose work has been exhibited at the Vancouver Art Gallery; the Toronto Sculpture Garden; the Yerba Buena Center for the Arts, San Francisco; Subvision, Hamburg; Astronomical Futures, Copenhagen; Encuentro Internacional, Medellín; Sparwasser HQ, Berlin; the Americas Society, New York; and the 2nd Tirana International Contemporary Art Biennial, Albania.

List of Works

cover
Gang of Seven, 2013
Installation detail, CAG, Vancouver, Canada, 2013
Photograph: Scott Massey

pp 7, 88
Eighty Circles through Canada (the last possessions of an Orcadian mountain man), 2013
Installation view, CAG, Vancouver, Canada, 2013
Photograph: Scott Massey

pp 8–15, 84–87, 90–93, 154–160
Eighty Circles through Canada (the last possessions of an Orcadian mountain man), 2013
Detail of 35mm slide projection
Photograph: Mike Nelson

pp 46–47, 49, 50, 52–53, 54, 57, 62, 63, 65–66
Gang of Seven, 2013
Installation detail, CAG, Vancouver, Canada, 2013
Photograph: Scott Massey

p 51
Gang of Seven, 2013
Installation view, The Power Plant, Toronto, Canada, 2014
Photograph: Toni Hafkenscheid

pp 56 (top), 58–59, 60, 61, 64
Gang of Seven, 2013
Installation detail, The Power Plant, Toronto, Canada, 2014
Photograph: Toni Hafkenscheid

p 56 (bottom)
Gang of Seven, 2013
Installation view, CAG, Vancouver, Canada, 2013
Photograph: Scott Massey

pp 70, 89, 162
Eighty Circles through Canada (the last possessions of an Orcadian mountain man), 2013
Installation view, The Power Plant, Toronto, Canada, 2014
Photograph: Toni Hafkenscheid

p 73
Untitled (intimate sculpture for a public space), 2013
Installation detail, CAG, Vancouver, Canada, 2013
Photograph: Scott Massey

pp 100, 105, 106, 107, 111
Double negative (The Genie), 2014
Installation detail, The Power Plant, Toronto, Canada, 2014
Photograph: Toni Hafkenscheid

pp 102–103, 108–109
Double negative (The Genie), 2014
Installation view, The Power Plant, Toronto, Canada, 2014
Photograph: Toni Hafkenscheid

pp 112–117
Quiver of Arrows, 2010
Installation view, The Power Plant, Toronto, Canada, 2014
Photograph: Toni Hafkenscheid

pp 118–119, 130–131
Quiver of Arrows, 2010
Installation detail, 303 Gallery, New York, USA, 2010
Photograph: John Berens

pp 120–129
Quiver of Arrows, 2010
Installation detail, 303 Gallery, New York, USA, 2010
Photograph: Mike Nelson

pp 133–135
Lionheart, 1997
Installation view, Galerie Im Kunstlerhaus, Bremen, Germany, 1997
Photograph: Mike Nelson

p 136
Master of Reality, 1997
Installation view, Berwick Gymnasium Gallery, Berwick-upon-Tweed, Northumberland, UK, 1997
Photograph: Mike Nelson

pp 137, 144
Master of Reality, 1997
Installation view, Berwick Gymnasium Gallery, Berwick-upon-Tweed, Northumberland, UK, 1997
Photograph: Simon Starling

p 138–139, 141
Master of Reality, 1997
Installation detail, Berwick Gymnasium Gallery, Berwick-upon-Tweed, Northumberland, UK, 1997
Photograph: Mike Nelson

pp 142–143
Master of Reality, 1997
Installation detail, Berwick Gymnasium Gallery, Berwick-upon-Tweed, Northumberland, UK, 1997
Photograph: Simon Starling

pp 145, 151, 152–153
The Amnesiacs, 1997
Installation detail, Galleri Campbells Occasionally, Copenhagen, Denmark, 1997
Photograph: Mike Nelson

pp 146, 148–149
Untitled, 1996
Garnet Hill, Glasgow, Scotland, 1996
Photograph: Mike Nelson

*All works by Mike Nelson

Colophon and Acknowledgements

Texts by Dick Hebdige, Jaki Irvine, Julia Paoli and Jenifer Papararo
Edited by Jenifer Papararo
Designed by Albino Tavares at Black Dog Publishing

Images are courtesy of the artist and 303 Gallery, New York; Galleria Franco Noero, Turin; Matt's Gallery, London; and neugerriemschneider, Berlin.

British Library Cataloguing-in-Publication Data. A CIP record for this book is available from the British Library.

ISBN 978 1 908966 45 2

Black Dog Publishing is an environmentally responsible company. *Amnesiac Hide: Mike Nelson* is printed on sustainably sourced paper.

Distribution:
Black Dog Publishing, 10A Acton Street, London, UK, WC1X 9NG
+ 44 (0) 207 713 5097; info@blackdogonline.com

Contemporary Art Gallery, 555 Nelson Street, Vancouver, BC, Canada, V6R 6R5
+ 1 604 681 2700; info@contemporaryartgallery.ca

The Power Plant, Harbourfront Centre, 231 Queens Quay West, Toronto, ON, Canada M5J 2G8
+1 416 973 4949; info@thepowerplant.org

This book is published on the occasion of solo exhibitions by Mike Nelson at the Contemporary Art Gallery, Vancouver, curated by Jenifer Papararo and The Power Plant, Toronto, curated by Julia Paoli, including three new commissions *Gang of Seven*, 2013 co-produced by the Contemporary Art Gallery and The Power Plant; *Eighty Circles through Canada (the last possessions of an Orcadian mountain man)*, 2013 co-produced by the Contemporary Art Gallery and Walter Phillips Gallery, Banff; and *Double negative (The Genie)*, 2014 produced by The Power Plant.

Mike Nelson, Contemporary Art Gallery, 13 September to 3 November 2013, with the generous support of Rick Erickson and Donna Partridge and Jane Irwin and Ross Hill and special thanks to the Erlend Williamson Art Foundation, Orkney, Scotland.

Mike Nelson: Amnesiac Hide, The Power Plant, 1 February to 19 May 2014, with the generous support of Lead Donors: Nancy McCain and Bill Morneau and Jay Smith and Laura Rapp; Support Donors: Sue Kidd and Susie Kololian, Michelle Koerner and Kevin Doyle, Liza Mauer and Andrew Sheiner, Margaret C McNee, Nadir and Shabin Mohamed, Elisa Nuyten and David Dime, and Eleanor and Francis Shen.

All works were courtesy of the artist and 303 Gallery, New York; Galleria Franco Noero, Turin; Matt's Gallery, London; and neugerriemschneider, Berlin.

Mike Nelson would like to thank:
Kieren and Claudine Beattie, Wendy Chang, Rick Erickson, Carey Fouks, Dick Hebdige, Jaki Irvine, Ross Hill, Jane Irwin, Garth Johnson, Andy Law, Rachel Lowe, Sarah Munro, Sheldon Sean Moyer, Isabel and Nancy Nelson, Melanie O'Brian, Julia Paoli, Jenifer Papararo, Ania Rachmat, Bob Rennie, Frances Scott, Mari Spirito, Christy Thompson, Valerie Velardo, Clarrie Wallis, Mark Wayman, Nicole Westman, Phil Dion and Derek Brunen at the Contemporary Art Gallery, and Paul Zingrone.

Jaki Irvine, "Lionheart, Master of Reality (Featuring The Amnesiacs)", (1997) reprinted in *Extinction Beckons*, Matts Gallery, London, 2000.

Text in "A Rendezvous" taken from: Thompson, Hunter S, Hell's Angels, Penguin: London, 1967; Lavigne, Yves, Hell's Angels: "Three Can Keep a Secret If Two Are Dead", Carol Publishing Group, 1989; Billington, Ray Allen, The Far Western Frontier 1830–1860, Hamish Hamilton: London, 1956.

Text on p 163 taken from: FB Housser, *A Canadian Art Movement: The Story of the Group of Seven*, The Macmillian Company of Canada: Toronto, 1926, p 125.

Back cover text courtesy Dick Hebdige.

reuse recycle reduce

art design fashion
history photography
theory and things

black dog publishing
london uk

www.blackdogonline.com

The Contemporary Art Gallery is generously supported by the Canada Council for the Arts, the City of Vancouver and the Province of BC through the BC Arts Council and the BC Gaming Policy and Enforcement Branch. We are also grateful for the support of Vancouver Foundation and our members, donors, and volunteers; we especially acknowledge the multi-year support of BMO Financial Group.

The Power Plant is generously supported by the Canada Council for the Arts, the Ontario Arts Council and the Toronto Arts Council. Our gratitude goes to BMO Financial Group for their support of the ALL YEAR, ALL FREE initiative.

Canada Council for the Arts
Conseil des Arts du Canada

BRITISH COLUMBIA ARTS COUNCIL
An agency of the Province of British Columbia

ONTARIO ARTS COUNCIL
CONSEIL DES ARTS DE L'ONTARIO

CITY OF VANCOUVER

TORONTO ARTS COUNCIL

BRITISH COLUMBIA
The Best Place on Earth

BMO Financial Group

This book would not be possible without the generous financial support of 303 Gallery, New York; Galleria Franco Noero, Turin; and neugerriemschneider, Berlin

Galleria Franco Noero

NEUGERRIEMSCHNEIDER BERLIN

303 GALLERY

With special thanks to the Erlend Williamson Art Foundation, Scotland

THE POWER PLANT

CAG